BAHAMIAN SOCIETY AFTER EMANCIPATION

BAHAMIAN SOCIETY AFTER EMANCIPATION

Gail Saunders

Ian Randle Publishers
Kingston

Markus Wiener Publishers
Princeton

Revised edition published 2003 by
Ian Randle Publishers
11 Cunningham Avenue
Box 686
Kingston 6
www.ianrandlepublishers.com

First published in 1990
First published by Ian Randle Publishers in 1994

© Gail Saunders 2003

National Library of Jamaica Cataloguing-in-Publication Data

Saunders, Gail
    Bahamian society after emancipation / Gail Saunders. — 3rd ed.
       p. : ill. ; cm
    Includes Index
    ISBN 976-637-084-2

    1. Slavery — Emancipation - Bahamas   2. Slavery - Bahamas
    3. Bahamas - History
    I. Title
    326.097296   dc21

First published in the United States, 2003, by
Markus Wiener Publishers
231 Nassau Street
Princeton, NJ, 08542
Library of Congress Cataloging-in-Publication Data

Saunders, Gail.
    Bahamian society after emancipation / Gail Saunders.— Rev. ed.
       p. cm.
    Includes bibliographical references and index.
    ISBN 1-55876-313-9 (pbk. : alk. paper)
    1. Bahamas—Social conditions. I. Title.
    HN197.S38 2003
    306'.097296—dc21
                       2003007448

All rights reserved – no part of this publication may be reproduced, stored in a retrieval system, or transmitted in any form, or by any means electronic, photocopying, recording or otherwise without the prior permission of the author or publisher.

Set in Souvenir 9pt
Book and cover design by Allison Brown
Printed and bound in the United States of America

Contents

	List of Illustrations	vi
	Foreword	ix
	Preface and Acknowledgements	xi
	Introduction	xii
1	The Role of the Coloured Middle Class in Nassau, 1890-1942	1
2	Women in the Bahamian Society in the Late Nineteenth and Early Twentieth Centuries	18
3	A Historical Sketch of Family Life in the Bahamas	43
4	Isolation Within an Isolated Archipelago: The Out Island Communities in the Bahamas During the Late Nineteenth and Early Twentieth Century	57
5	Emancipation and 'Over-the-Hill'	75
6	Aspects of Traditional African-Bahamian Culture in the Late Nineteenth and Early Twentieth Century	82
7	The Blockade Running Era in the Bahamas: Blessing or Curse?	95
8	Prohibition: A Mixed Blessing for the Bahamas	102
9	The Changing Face of Nassau: The Impact of Tourism on Bahamian Society in the 1920s and 1930s	118
10	The 1937 Riot in Inagua	138
11	The 1942 Riot in Nassau: A Demand For Change?	151
12	The 1956 Resolution: Breaking Down the Barriers of Racial Discrimination in The Bahamas	171
13	The 1958 General Strike in Nassau: A Landmark in Bahamian Society	189
14	Race Relations and National Identity in the Formation of the Bahamian Society: A Historical Perspective	213
	Index	222

List of Illustrations

1. William Benjamin North (1873-1936) 4
2. Sir Etienne Dupuch
   (Courtesy of the Department of Archives, Nassau) 7
3. Alfred F. Adderley
   (Courtesy of the Department of Archives, Nassau) 8
4. Advertisement. W.B. North. 9
5. Thaddeus A. Toote
   (Courtesy of the Department of Archives, Nassau) 10
6. A Market Scene. Nassau in the early Twentieth Century
   (Courtesy of the Mary Moseley Collection and the Anglican Church of the Bahamas) 25
7. Sponge Clippers in the early Twentieth Century Bahamas
   (Courtesy of the Department of Archives, Bahamas) 26
8. Map of the Bahamas 58
9. 'Characteristic Homes of Sponge Fishermen' in the Nineteenth and early Twentieth Century Bahamas
   (Courtesy of G.B. Shattuck, ed., The Bahama Islands, 1905) 63
10. Grant's Town
    (Courtesy of the Department of Archives, Bahamas) 76
11. Nassau in 1862, showing a blockade-runner in the left foreground
    (From a drawing in the Illustrated London News) 96
12. Unloading cotton from blockade-runners at Nassau
    (Courtesy of the Department of Archives, Bahamas) 97
13. Barrels of liquor on Bay Street in downtown Nassau 1920s and early 1930s during Prohibition
    (Photograph by Stanley Toogood. Courtesy of the Department of Archives and Linda Huber) 103
14. Paradise Bathing Beach, Nassau, Bahamas 1920s and 1930s
    (Photograph by 'Doc' Sands. Courtesy of the Department of Archives and the C. Thackray Charitable Trust) 119
15. The British Colonial Tennis Courts in the early 1900s.
    (Courtesy of the Department of Archives) 120
16. Golf Links of Nassau, Bahamas early Twentieth century
    (Photograph by 'Doc' Sands. Courtesy of the Department of Archives and the C. Thackray Charitable Trust) 121

17. The Landing Place, Nassau, Bahamas, 1930s
    *(From a postcard. Courtesy of the Department of Archives and
    the C. Thackray Charitable Trust)*   123

18. Native Market, Prince George Dock, Nassau
    *(From a postcard. Photograph by Freddie Maura. Mid twentieth
    century. Courtesy of the Department of Archives and the C. Thackray
    Charitable Trust)*   127

19. A vendor from Grant's Town, early 1900s
    (Courtesy of the Department of Archives)   214

20. From a postcard entitled: 'Two Natives', Nassau, Bahamas
    *(Courtesy of the Department of Archives and the C. Thackray
    Charitable Trust)*   215

Foreword

Dr Gail Saunders, the Director of Archives for the Bahamas, has established herself over the last two decades as a leading authority on the social history of her native country in the post-slavery period. I first made contact with her scholarly work when I examined her doctoral thesis in 1985, and I have been impressed and gratified by her steady production of books, articles and papers on Bahamian history since that time.

In this useful volume, Dr Saunders brings together 14 of these essays, all dealing with the period between the 1830s and the present. It is an expanded version of the book published thirteen years ago under the same title. I think that these essays fulfil two major purposes. First, they will greatly advance our knowledge of Bahamian history, providing an in-depth study of specific episodes like the riots in 1937 and 1942 in Inagua and Nassau respectively, or particular communities like Over-The-Hill and the Out Islands, or important developments in social and economic life as in the case of the Nassau coloured middle class and its role, the Prohibition and blockade running eras, the evolution of family patterns and the role and position of women. A feature of the current expanded version is that it brings its chronological scope up to the late colonial period. There are new essays on Prohibition's effects on the Bahamas, and on the impact of the growing tourist industry on the face of Nassau. And following on logically from the earlier studies of the riots/strikes in Inagua (1937) and Nassau (1942) are two pieces on important developments in the 1950s: the controversy over ending racial discrimination (1956) and the major strike in Nassau (1958). All students of Bahamian history will find new and interesting information and analyses in these essays.

Second – and this is of particular interest to me as a student of Caribbean social history – these essays will help us to locate the Bahamas within a regional historical context. Though in a strict geographical sense the archipelago is not situated within the Caribbean Sea, Dr Saunders' work makes it abundantly clear that the Bahamian islands are indeed, historically, part of the Caribbean. Thus, her studies of the unrest in Nassau and Inagua in 1937 and 1942 must be read in the context of the Caribbean-wide protests of this era; the Nassau coloured middle class between 1890 and 1942 behaved and thought much like its counterparts elsewhere in the region; Bahamian family patterns developed in much the same way as in similar West Indian communities, though with significant differences; and Over-The-Hill looks very much like other communities of ex-slaves and their descendants from Jamaica down to Trinidad. Dr Saunders' essay on women in Bahamian social and economic life between the 1880s and 1930s suggests close parallels with the situation in Jamaica and Trinidad (where similar research has been undertaken) and no doubt elsewhere too. And the traditional African-Bahamian folkways described in chapter six fall easily within the general contours of African-Caribbean popular culture of the period.

The essay on the social history of the Out Islands seems to highlight unique aspects of the Bahamian past, but these small and isolated communities may be compared with other Caribbean islands such as Anguilla or the Grenadines, which were also largely outside the mainstream of Caribbean history. On the other hand, no other Caribbean society experienced such profound effects from the experiences of blockade running during the US Civil War and illegal transhipment of liquor to the United States of America during the Prohibition era (chapters seven and eight), again highlighting unique features in the country's history. Only Barbados, perhaps, experienced the kind of thorough-going apartheid which the colonial Bahamas knew, and so the campaign against racial discrimination in the mid-1950s was not precisely replicated elsewhere in the British Caribbean (not even in Barbados). The final essay discusses the Bahamian 'model' of colonial race relations generally, showing that it had more in common with the United States than the Caribbean patterns. These studies – along with other contributions from Dr Saunders herself and from other scholars, most notably the important two-volume work by Craton and Saunders, *Islanders in the Stream: A History of the Bahamian People* – will help us to integrate Bahamian history into the wider regional story.

I welcome this expanded volume of essays on Bahamian society after emancipation. It will enrich the steadily growing body of scholarly literature on Bahamian history, to which Dr Saunders has contributed so much, both as archivist and historian.

Bridget Brereton
Professor of History
The University of the West Indies
St Augustine, Trinidad and Tobago

Preface and Acknowledgements

Over the last few years I have written and spoken on a variety of historical themes on the Bahamas. Some topics have been directly related to the research I undertook for my doctoral thesis 'The Social History of the Bahamas, 1890-1953', and others have been based on my ongoing research. Since my articles and papers are widely scattered, some in journals which are not easily accessible, and some not published at all, I decided to publish a small collection in one volume, primarily for use by teachers and students in the Bahamas.

I should like to thank the editors of the *Journal of Caribbean History*, *Ethnic and Racial Studies*, *New West Indian Guide*, the *Journal of the Bahamas Historical Society*, and the Over-The-Hill Group for allowing me to republish these articles. I am grateful to Bridget Brereton and Howard Johnson for their support and advice and also to Michael Craton, my doctoral supervisor, with whom I collaborated on a major work in two volumes, *Islanders in the Stream: A History of The Bahamian People*.

Thanks are owed to the staff of the Department of Archives for their consistent support. A special thanks goes to Patrice Williams, Paulene Bastian Smith, Ivy Curry, Shane Roker, Edith Sturrup and David Wood for the photographs.

I am grateful to Mabel Smith and Lorraine Lightbourn for cheerful assistance. My sincere thanks to Bridget Brereton for writing the foreword. I owe a debt of gratitude to David Guest and Wanda Volpe of Beaman Porter, Inc. for help with the first edition of this volume which was privately published. Thanks also to Ian Randle for his interest in and for agreeing to publish this expanded third edition. Sincere thanks to Don and Kathy Gerace and the Bahamian Field Station for their support.

As always, my family, especially my father, Basil North, brother, Terry North and sister-in-law, Bunny, who have always supported me.

To my husband, Winston, thank you again for your love, support and encouragement.

Introduction

As Howard Johnson demonstrates in his book *The Bahamas From Slavery to Servitude*, the Bahamas until recently was generally excluded from the historiography of the West Indies.[1] Fortunately, his work among others including Michael Craton and this author, is changing this trend. Recently there has been a growing interest in the research and writing of Bahamian history. Michael Craton and this author recently published *Islanders in The Stream: A History of The Bahamian People* [2], a social history which attempts to tell the full history of the people who inhabited the Bahamas. That publication recognizes the similarities and differences, as does this one, and attempts to integrate Bahamian history into the general West Indian context.

A marginal non-plantation colony which never grew sugar commercially, the Bahamas did not succeed in replacing cotton after its failure in the early 1800s with a plantation staple. The lack of a staple and the scarcity of cash in circulation led to the development of the oppressive share and truck systems.[3] Nassau's economy, like Bermuda's, was essentially mercantile. Benefiting from various outside influences which created a 'boom' and 'bust' character in the economy, the urban elite found it more profitable to import foodstuffs from the United States and to a lesser extent Great Britain. It reaped profits from import duties which were levied on every class of import including basic foodstuffs.[4]

The articles making up this volume were originally written as independent essays. However, they are thematically linked as they focus on social aspects of the society.

The Bahamian society like that of the Caribbean was generally divided by class and race. The three-tier system which developed during slavery, survived with some changes in the post-emancipation era. As Bridget Brereton demonstrates, the most significant changes were the 'gradual increase in the size of the middle stratum and the improvement of the better educated members of that stratum.'[5]

Chapter One examines the behaviour and social life of the small coloured middle class in Nassau during the late nineteenth and early twentieth centuries, and describes how it changed over a period of time. Similar to its Caribbean counterparts, it was a divisive rather than unifying force and no doubt perpetuated colour prejudice.

Chapter Two focuses on the role of women both in the town of Nassau and in the more isolated Out Islands. As in the case of the British Caribbean generally, the place of Bahamian women in the society and economy was determined by their race, colour and class. There was little contact between women of two racial groups except in the servant/mistress relationship. Economic opportunities were limited for women generally. Although technological advances and World War I brought more women into the workplace, the role of women did not change dramatically until the Prohibition years. Bahamian women lagged behind most of the British Caribbean in organizing themselves politically. This trend was a reflection of the Bahamian society which remained largely unpoliticized until the 1950s.

A historical sketch of family life in the Bahamas, which is the subject of Chapter Three, demonstrates similarities to West Indian patterns but also alludes to some differences. The structure of the slave family in the Bahamas, where the nuclear unit dominated, was similar to that in British West Indian colonies. Post-emancipation years experienced a decline in the nuclear family, but as in the British Caribbean generally, monogamy was the norm for all classes. However, as David Lowenthal demonstrated, 'each (class) approaches it by a different route and to a different degree.'[6]

During the early part of the twentieth century, the family unit, strongly influenced by the church, was usually the nuclear type. This was especially so in white and bi-racial communities where illegitimacy was rare. Even in black communities where illegitimacy was more common, it was not the norm, and was generally lower than many other British Caribbean colonies. The rate of illegitimacy increased after World War I as did many social problems including unemployment, crime, juvenile delinquency and prostitution. Increasing migration from the rural Out Island settlements into Nassau and the effects of Prohibition contributed to these trends. By the late twentieth century, there was further erosion of the traditional western nuclear type family.

The dispersed nature of the Bahamian archipelago and its physical and economic separation from the British West Indies made for isolation. Poverty was the norm especially in the more remote Out Islands and most persons lived at the same social and economic level, with intense racial feeling and deep-set prejudice keeping the races apart. Chapter Four describes the isolated Out Islands communities which survived despite harsh social and economic conditions similar to those prevailing then in other West Indian islands. Isolation delayed change, but also helped to preserve Out Islands cultural customs and traditions.

Chapter Five takes a similar approach in examining a community of ex-slaves and liberated Africans in an urban area. This essay focuses on the social treatment of the Over-The-Hill community by whites, its political impotence and its economic dependency on the mercantile elite of Nassau. Despite discriminatory treatment by the powerful elite, Over-The-Hill people succeeded in creating positive institutions like the Friendly Societies. They also kept alive a number of African customs, including ways of cooking and the Asue which enabled them to save and accumulate cash. Life in Over-The-Hill was isolated and separated from that of white Nassau. It was indeed a 'world within a world'.

The Sixth Chapter gives details about the life and culture within the black community in the late nineteenth and early twentieth centuries. It examines traditions, belief systems and how the black majority spent its leisure time, demonstrating how traditional popular culture remained strong in black rural settlements in New Providence and on the Out Islands.

Chapter Seven examines the social effects of the blockade of the Southern states during the American Civil War on Bahamian society. Many authors have portrayed Bahamians as lazy, immoral and opportunistic. This account shows that a large number of Bahamians, including those in the lower stratum of society, benefited at least temporarily from the blockade. In the long term however the 'boom' largely benefited the mercantile elite which tightened its control over the Bahamian labourers by the use of sharecropping, labour tenancy and the truck system. When the blockade era ended, the majority of Bahamians, who then lived in the Out Islands, resorted to farming and fishing. In Nassau, the blockade running era helped to harden social divisions which were based mainly on race.

Chapters Eight and Nine underscore the effects of Prohibition and tourism on Bahamian society. Rum running and tourism brought important social and economic changes. Materially, some Bahamians were better off but as tourism expanded, agriculture and fishing which had sustained the rural settlements were neglected. Increased migration to Nassau, the capital, eventually led to the decline of Out Island communities. With the growth of tourism came deep-rooted social problems and marked discrimination which had a pervasive effect on Bahamian society.

Chapters Ten and Eleven deal with the 1937 and 1942 riots in Inagua and Nassau respectively. These protests against socioeconomic and political injustices in Bahamian society must be examined within the context of the Caribbean-wide labour protests of the era.[7]

While the 1937 riot in Inagua highlighted oppressive economic conditions, dissatisfaction and neglect, its impact was limited as Inagua was a very small, sparsely populated isolated island with poor communications. It was not until many Out Islanders including Inaguanians with heightened expectations, had migrated in sufficient numbers to Nassau that the more serious riot in 1942, in a tense, racially charged atmosphere, erupted. It followed in the wake of the Caribbean disturbances of the 1930s and led to the appointment of a local Commission of Inquiry. However, it did not lead to immediate political, economic or social transformations as in many other West Indian colonies.

Chapters Twelve and Thirteen focus on two significant events – the adoption of part one of the Resolution against Racial Discrimination in Public Places and the 1958 Strike in Nassau. Both demonstrated the growing dissatisfaction of the black population against racial discrimination and the white elite's stranglehold over the political and economic machinery. While the 1956 Resolution revealed the deep-seated segregationist policies, the adoption of the first part of the Resolution failed to solve the problem. The 1958 Strike, led by the Labour Movement, resulted in significant electoral reforms and satisfied labour grievances, but failed to bring structural changes in the constitution. However, the 1958 Strike transformed the Colonial Office's complacent policy towards the Bahamas.

The last chapter which explores race and national identity summarizes race relations in the Bahamas from the early years of settlement until Bahamian independence. It concludes that racism which continued in post-emancipation years was fanned in modern times by the development of tourism whose primary beneficiaries were the Bahamian 'haves', who were mostly white.

These essays firmly place the Bahamas within the West Indian context. Despite the absence of sugar, and its commercial rather than agricultural economy, the Bahamas' social development bears great similarities with the countries of the Caribbean. Bahamians experienced extreme poverty and oppressive socioeconomic conditions, and acute racial and social divisions developed in the post-emancipation era. One of the most significant changes in the late nineteenth and early twentieth century Caribbean, as Bridget Brereton[8] has shown was the growth of the middle stratum which made race relations and class stratification more complex. While the intermediate middle class in the Caribbean generally made a significant contribution to economic and social development, in the Bahamas, its contribution was less significant.

The Bahamas' relatively high percentage of whites, its proximity to the Southern United States with its severe segregation practices, and close cultural ties between white and black Bahamians with the United States, made for more antagonistic race relations than in the other British West Indies islands.[9] Black leadership, both socially and politically, took a longer time to emerge in the Bahamas than in the British Caribbean in general.

Notes

1. Howard Johnson, *The Bahamas From Slavery to Servitude 1783-1933* (Gainesville: University Press of Florida, 1996).
2. Michael Craton and Gail Saunders, *Islanders in The Stream: A History of The Bahamian People*, 2 vols. (Athens, Georgia: Georgia University Press, 1992-1998)
3. Johnson, vi.
4. Gordon Lewis, *The Growth of the Modern West Indies* (New York and London: 1969), 308-11.
5. Bridget Brereton, 'Society and Culture in the Caribbean: the British and French West Indies 1870-1980' in *The Modern Caribbean*, ed. by Franklin Knight and Colin Palmer (Chapel Hill and London: 1989), 90.
6. David Lowenthal, *West Indian Societies* (London: Oxford University Press, 1972), 105.
7. Brereton, 87.
8. Brereton, 90.
9. Colin Hughes, *Race and Politics in The Bahamas* (St Lucia, Queensland: University of Queensland Press, 1981), 224.

1

The Role of the Coloured Middle Class in Nassau, 1890-1942

In the Bahamas, as was the case in many nineteenth century West Indian societies, a coloured middle class emerged after emancipation. Even before the end of slavery in numerous Caribbean territories, and especially in Jamaica, there was a distinct group of free coloureds who lived mainly in the towns.[1] Although no detailed work has been done on free coloureds in the Bahamas or of the immediate post-emancipation Bahamian society, it can be gleaned from newspapers and travelogues that by 1890, Nassau, the commercial and political capital of the Bahamas, located on New Providence Island, had a small coloured middle class. The intermediate coloured class in Nassau had an ambiguous position, in the strictly stratified society in Nassau,[2] between the white elite at the top, and the black labouring class at the bottom. It comprised freed coloureds who had emerged out of slavery, those who were products of European and African ancestry born in a free society and the upwardly mobile liberated Africans. As in most West Indian colonies, miscegenation had ensured that 'the true African strain had suffered admixture'. By the turn of the nineteenth century the coloured community of Nassau comprised a widely graduated scale of hue and appearance and a highly complex parentage.[3] The coloureds were not a homogenous group, and as Etienne Dupuch noted, 'they ranged from black or off-black at the bottom, to "light brown" and "high-yaller" and near white at the top'.[4]

Metropolitan and local whites who believed that Africans and their descendants were racially inferior imposed their opinions on the entire society, in such a way that non-whites developed an inferiority complex.[5] Proximity to the United States with its deteriorating race relations did not help matters. A person known to have negro blood was socially a Negro in America while in the Bahamas, as in the West Indies generally, many light-skinned coloureds, because it was to their advantage, 'passed' for white and were accepted by the elite. Various writers, including Irish Magistrate Powles commented on the ambiguous colour line in Nassau:

> Although there is plenty of pure unspotted white blood scattered through the Bahamas, a good deal of that of the upper crust of Nassau society

is decidedly mixed ... Though the skins of most of them are fair enough to pass for pure white anywhere in Europe, their African blood would at once be detected by any Southerner or West Indian.[6]

A person might not be pure white, but his associates would always be 'light' or 'lighter'. Indeed, someone who was 'passing' would not 'associate with anyone a shade darker than themselves'. A man who was admittedly coloured could not even talk to a lady of a 'so-called' white family.[7] Nassau's society was segregated in almost every respect with colour separating the races in housing, education, occupation and social intercourse. Even certain mail boats, like the *Dart* which plied between Nassau and Harbour Island, had sections for whites only, and no coloureds were allowed to enter the *Dart*'s cabin.[8] The racial situation was perhaps not as harsh as in the southern States of America with its inflexible colour line, but on the other hand it did not conform to the West Indian norm. As Northcroft observed, 'It lacks the exclusiveness of the former and the equality of the latter'.[9] At the same time, the role of the coloured middle class in the Bahamas did not differ dramatically from that in some West Indian colonies, especially in Jamaica. As in that colony, the Bahamian middle class rather than being a force that brought society together, acted more as a 'divisive element more apt to perpetuate than to eliminate colour prejudice'.[10] While those classified as coloured were generally ignored by the white elite, they themselves looked down on the black labouring class. Class lines were not as clearly demarcated in the widely scattered Out Island settlements where the majority of the population lived. Out Islanders lived either in black, white or bi-racial communities. Those living in all-white settlements strictly separated themselves from blacks, being mostly endogamous. In bi-racial settlements whites segregated themselves socially and residentially from blacks. Out Islanders were extremely poor in material terms, most living at the same economic and social level. Yet despite their poverty, intense racial feeling and deepest prejudice kept the two races apart.[11] Where considerable miscegenation had occurred in the Out Islands, for example in Eleuthera and Long Island, social stratification was based not on race alone, but also on social attitudes and associations. It was easier in some Out Islands than in Nassau, for a 'bright' or light-skinned person with black ancestry to be considered white,[12] especially if he held a position such as a priest, teacher or commissioner in the settlement. Undoubtedly race difference, rather than class, was the most important in Bahamian society.

Despite the acute racial feelings, coloureds in Nassau could gain some respectability even among the white community. This was most readily achieved by imitating whites as much as possible. Aspiring coloureds also attempted to obtain a good education, secure good jobs, own land, enter politics and attend the right churches.[13] Perhaps Peter J. Wilson's theory in *Crab Antics* for the black community of Providencia can be applied to the more elite of the Nassau coloureds. They not only had 'reputation', a characteristic held by the majority of the coloured population, but they also gained some 'respectability' which separated them from the rest of the black community.[14]

While attempting to acquire white values, the coloured middle class created social distance between itself and the black labouring class although some had relatives among that group and even attended the same churches and their children the same schools. Coloureds hired blacks as domestics, gardeners, and to do other menial tasks employing them usually for a lifetime. They trusted their children under the care of black maids and often loved their black retainers as part of the family.[15] The two classes with differing views on type of occupation, education, morality, marriage and religion, did not socialize. Often coloureds, among whom snobbery was rife, formed themselves into intimate cliques.[16] Coloureds did not completely deny their African heritage; they enjoyed watching and even participated in the African-inspired 'Fire-Dance', and their children often learned 'Ring Play' at school from their black class mates. Coloured children also delighted in hearing 'old stories' from their black maids.[17] Although underprivileged blacks were the originators and main participants of the Junkanoo festival, coloured and even some whites joined in the parade spontaneously.[18] Later in the 1930s, when the festival was seen as a tourist attraction by the white elite, the coloured middle class became more actively involved in it and it began to take on greater respectability.

In economic terms, as was common in the British West Indies, the coloured middle class despised manual labour related to agriculture and the plantation. Unlike the Out Islands where agriculture and sponge fishing were the mainstays, Nassau's economy was essentially mercantile. New Providence's fine harbour and its proximity to the United States, had led to close economic ties between the two. The 'boom' and 'bust' characteristics of the Bahamas' economy influenced by outside events[19] especially in the United States, largely benefitted Nassau and its white mercantile community. Finding it cheaper and more profitable to import foodstuffs from the United States, and to a lesser extent from Great Britain, than to subsidize the local economy, it benefitted from import duties which were levied on nearly every class of import including basic foodstuffs. Thus the bulk of the revenue of the colony was derived from indirect taxation which nominally boosted the economy.[20]

Not only did the white mercantile elite dominate the economy in the town, it also controlled the large and 'impoverished labour force' in the Out Islands through the truck[21] and share systems. While there was hardly any circulation of cash in the Out Islands, in Nassau the operation of the import and export agencies and the large dry goods stores brought more money into circulation. The majority of the coloured middle class generally had no business experience and worked for wages or fees, as artisans, tradesmen and in the lower ranks of the civil service.

By the turn of the century, however, numerous coloured men had accumulated some capital and were land owners and proprietors of their own businesses. They were active in the liquor trade, importing and retailing, and the restaurant and grocery businesses. William B. North, mulatto son of English merchant James A. North, for example, at the turn of the century, owned a liquor business on Balliou Hill Road and was also a grocery retailer. He was also involved in the sponge industry as an outfitter.[22] His friend, Harry S. Black, owned and managed Black's Candy Kitchen on Bay Street.

William Benjamin North (1873-1936), *the son of James Albert North, was born in Nassau. He owned a liquor business, was a retailer of groceries and was also engaged in the sponge business as an outfitter.*

An outstanding example of a darker coloured man who excelled in business was William P. Adderley, son of Joseph R. Adderley and grandson of Alliday Adderley of Yoruba descent. Born in Grant's Town, he followed in the footsteps of his grandfather, who by the 1860s through extensive agricultural enterprise had become a man of substance.[23] By the latter part of the nineteenth century, William Parliament Adderly who began as a contractor, had moved on to become a grower, buyer, and exporter of fruits and vegetables. By the turn of the century he was the proprietor of a grocery and dry goods shop called 'The Big Store' located at the south-western corner of George and King Streets in close proximity to Bay Street.[24]

Some coloureds, including mulatto C.O. Anderson who was appointed Postmaster General in 1913, succeeded in rising to high positions in the Civil Service mainly through obtaining a secondary education. This was, however, rare.[25] Most coloureds were deprived of a secondary education, which up to the first quarter of the twentieth century was still largely private and the preserve of the upper class, who felt that it was undesirable to educate the children of working class blacks and coloureds. On the one hand the elite thought them incapable of learning and on the other feared that education might make them too 'uppity'.[26] Since the government did not provide secondary education, the majority of coloured children either had only a primary education or remained outside of the private school system.

A few coloured children from well-respected and well-off families, however, did manage to get a fairly good education either through the Boys Central School, the premier government elementary school which offered a sound basic education and produced a number of white and coloured teachers, or through private tuition.[27] Occasionally, coloured boys attended the Anglican Nassau Grammar School and the girls, St Hilda's Anglican High School. The latter only allowed in very few coloured girls. May Anderson, daughter of the Postmaster General, was the first coloured to attend in the early 1900s. Rowena Eldon, an orphan, was the second, her education being supported by the Aaron Dixon Fund.[28] The Anglican schools had a more liberal policy of admission for coloured children than Queen's College, which was originally founded to educate the sons and daughters of the white Wesleyan and Presbyterian founders.[29] By the early 1900s, however, some coloured children, usually fair-skinned, but not always from 'respectable' and well-to-do families had gained admission to the school. Rev. R.P. Dyer later observed that although the whites' 'desire earnestly that their children be educated separately from the children of the other race', that there 'have always been a certain number of coloured children in the school'.[30] If colour did not debar coloureds from having a secondary education, high fees usually did. Not many coloured families could afford to send their children to private schools.[31] Those who did obtain a secondary education felt privileged to be 'accepted' by whites. Their opportunities were increased but their children served to create a greater cleavage between them and other coloured children.

The coloured middle class generally lacked a strong political tradition. Although coloured men sat in the House of Assembly at least since 1834,[32] and voiced independent opinions, their numbers were never significant enough to form a coherent bloc against the white mercantile elite which dominated the House. Individuals, however, made their presence felt. For example, James C. Smith, a light-skinned coloured 'gentleman', held in high esteem by the community, while representing the West District, worked tirelessly to upgrade conditions of the poor, black and oppressed. He established a newspaper, the *Freeman,* in 1887 which was critical of the many injustices of the day, including the truck system and poor educational facilities.[33]

In 1889, six coloureds, four more than sat in the previous Assembly, were returned to the twenty-nine strong House.[34] However, it seemed that colour was not an issue. Governor Shea commented that the increased number of coloureds elected was of 'little significance as the question of race or colour was scarcely heard of ...'[35] Moreover, the election of coloureds to the legislature was not seen as a threat to the white elite. Shea observed that the 'presence of the coloured men in the House of Assembly will not be the cause of any inconvenience'.[36]

White members, who were mainly merchants, maintained their majority and directed policies to suit their own interests by informal as well as by legislative means. The white minority kept control of the legislature not only through a restricted franchise which was steadily widened, but also by means of corrupt elections. It also maintained and increased its power by means of an outmoded constitutional system. Magistrate Powles complained:

> This mockery of representation is the greatest farce in the world. The coloured people have the suffrage, subject to a small property qualification, but have no idea how to use it ... The elections are by open voting, and bribery, corruption and intimidation are carried on in the most unblushing manner under the very noses of the officers presiding over the polling booths. Nobody takes any notice, and as the coloured people have not yet learnt the art of political organization, they are powerless to defend themselves. The result is that the House of Assembly is little less than a family gathering of Nassau whites, nearly all of whom are related to each other, either by blood or marriage. Laws are passed simply for the benefit of the family, whilst the coloured people are ground down and oppressed in a manner that is a disgrace to the British flag.[37]

The role of the intermediary coloured middle class did not change dramatically during the early years of the twentieth century. Garveyism and World War I had little immediate impact on the social structure of Bahamian society. There was however an increasing consciousness among coloureds of the racist policies of the day and also of the importance of educational attainment as a means of upward mobility. Garvey's appeal was generally limited among the coloured middle class in the Caribbean and in the Bahamas. Undoubtedly some coloureds, especially those who participated in World War I, had heard of the Pan-African Movement. Although not much materialized from the Garvey movement in the Bahamas, his ideas were nevertheless known and important. For example, Reverend Richard Higgs, a Bahamian emigrant of twenty-three years in Florida, was violently assaulted by whites and forced to return to Nassau for advocating social equality in a sermon that he preached in 'Coloured Town', Miami.[38]

It appears that a number of black and coloured Bahamians were ardent admirers of Garvey, and there might have been, as Tony Martin states, a United Improvement Association branch established in the Bahamas.[39] A group of Garvey supporters, with A. F. Adderley as their lawyer, in the early 1920s proposed a Union Mercantile Association, independent of whites. Claiming that blacks were badly treated on scheduled boats, it planned to run a boat for them between Nassau and Miami.[40] The idea was obviously influenced by Garvey's Black Star Steamship line with which Joshua Cockburn, a Bahamian ship captain, then living in New York, was associated.[41] It was also significant that a group of black Bahamians headed by Claudius R. Walker founded the Bahamas Rejuvenation League in New York in 1921 in order to improve education for Bahamians. A member of the League was Frederick A. Toote, brother of T. A. Toote, who had emigrated to the United States where he obtained a college education. He was the energetic president of the Philadelphia division of the UNIA in the 1920s.⁴²

World War I and Garveyism heightened the racial consciousness of the coloured middle class and provided a catalyst in bringing together many Bahamians who ordinarily were separated by class and distance. Additionally, Bahamian soldiers met West Indians, both white and black, some of whom were commissioned officers who thought that social and political changes were needed in the Caribbean.⁴³ Coloured Bahamians also experienced kindness from whites, especially in France, and formed friendships with European girls.⁴⁴ In the colour-conscious Bahamas this would have been impossible.

Sir Etienne Dupuch
(Courtesy of the Department of Archives, Nassau)

Perhaps the most lasting impression on black and coloured Bahamian soldiers was their exposure to the blatant discrimination encountered in the army. Although painfully aware of the prejudice which existed in the Bahamas, soldiers like Etienne Dupuch were nevertheless shocked and humiliated by the treatment they received. As loyal British soldiers fighting for 'King and Country' and for freedom, they constantly met signs stating 'Out of bounds to native troops'.⁴⁵ Dupuch, like hundreds of other coloured and black West Indians, returned home with a different outlook on the world. Dupuch admitted:

> I was a changed person when I returned to my island home at the age of 20 after seeing the peoples of Europe wallowing in a cesspit of human degradation. I was a very bitter man and swore that never again would I lift a finger, certainly not risk my life, in defence of King and Country, or of anything removed from my limited sphere of activities.⁴⁶

With new knowledge and a broader outlook, Etienne Dupuch and other coloureds and blacks took a greater interest in the affairs of the country. However, economic considerations, the struggle to make ends meet, and the power of the white elite tempered radicalism. No Cipriani, as in Trinidad, emerged to take up the banner of the black labouring class. Neither were there post-war riots or unrest as in other territories in the West Indies.

Dupuch, himself, soon took over as editor of his family newspaper, the *Tribune*, which brought racial issues to the fore⁴⁷ but only to a limited clientele. Dupuch's criticism of the status quo had to be limited by necessity if he wished his paper to survive. Entering the House of Assembly in 1928, his efforts to initiate major social and political changes were stymied by the lack of a strong, united coloured faction. The introduction of the secret ballot and an end to discrimination, two issues which he strongly supported, would be a long time in coming.

At the end of World War I, the colour situation had not changed appreciably since the 1890s. The slowly growing racial consciousness was helped by the continued emigration of Bahamians to the southern United States. Additionally, the arrival of several professional, coloured and black West Indians in Nassau, and the return of some black Bahamians who had been educated abroad, created some racial pride.

Since the mid nineteenth century, depressed conditions in the Bahamas had caused emigration of Bahamians, especially Out Islanders, to Florida and other parts of the United States. This trend continued in the late nineteenth century and early twentieth century.[48] Additionally, at the end of World War I about 3000 Bahamians were recruited as labourers at Charleston, South Carolina, to construct port and terminal facilities which would provide for the provisioning and maintenance of the American army in France.[49] As a Methodist Minister commented, 'The colour question horrid and hateful enough in the Bahamas, is far worse in the Southern States ...'[50] Bahamians who settled in Miami and Key West were forced by discriminatory practices to establish churches of their own and were pushed into ghettos such as Coloured Town in Miami.[51] Many, who experienced the growing bigotry, intolerance and violence fanned by the rebirth of the Ku Klux Klan after 1915, returned to the Bahamas with different attitudes towards colour.[52]

Alfred F. Adderley
(Courtesy of the Department of Archives, Nassau)

The coloured middle class gained self-respect with the arrival and settlement in Nassau of several coloured and black professional West Indians including physicians, C. H. Knight, William Pitt, and a lawyer, Walter E. S. Callender. They were joined later by others including medical doctors, E. S. Worrell and Roland Cumberbatch. These immigrants swelled the ranks of the very small group of Bahamian coloured and black professionals, including two outstanding men, both lawyers, Thaddeus A. Toote and Alfred F. Adderley. Both were sons of successful merchants and politicians who had taken advantage of the educational opportunities available to their sons both at home and abroad. Thaddeus A. Toote and A.F. Adderley, educated at the Inns of Court and at Cambridge University in England, soon became respected in their professions and as politicians by whites and blacks alike. In addition to their educational attainments, their political power and professional expertise, their marriage to respectable coloured women made them acceptable members of the coloured middle class. As their reputations grew, the social distance between them and the black labouring class widened. Even within their own class they were held in awe, but did serve as models and an inspiration to aspiring coloureds and blacks. While gaining the respect of the white professionals, it was unthinkable that there would be any social intercourse between the two races.

During the early years of the twentieth century the coloured middle class expanded, accepting into its ranks black professionals, merchants, civil servants and successful artisans. No one at that time, neither black nor white, was wealthy. It was Prohibition rather than the First World War that made a difference to the social structure in the Bahamas. Before the 1920s, an entrenched mercantile elite had little real capital. Their colour more than their wealth separated them from non-whites. Bootlegging profits, augmented by those from the land boom, brought quick money into Nassau, creating a new monied class which was mostly white.[53]

Some coloureds and blacks in Nassau benefitted from Prohibition and expanded or established businesses on or near Bay Street. W.B. North's liquor business had, by the 1920s, moved from Balliou Hill Road to the Market Range just off Bay Street. His relatives by marriage the De'Gregory brothers, expanded and improved their meat business by installing refrigeration. W.P Adderley's 'The Big Store' still flourished. Joseph Whitfield and Edward (Durham) Isaacs operated restaurants on the corners of Deveaux and Bay Streets and Bay and Market Streets respectively. Christopher C. Smith not only bought 'Johnson House' on the corner of Bay and Union Streets, he also operated a large grocery business in conjunction with the new Magnolia Apartments nearby.[54]

Advertisement. W.B. North.

The coloured businessmen could not however compete with the *nouveau riche* white class which soon consolidated its wealth in large successful businesses and its power by seeking seats in the legislature. The new monied white class primarily benefitted from the growth of tourism and increased American investment which followed Prohibition. By the mid-1930s, coloured and black businessmen, pitted against the powerful wealthy white establishments, were gradually being pushed off Bay Street. Those coloured businesses which managed to survive the Depression years underwent little expansion.

Coloureds and blacks, including an increasing number of migrants from the Out Islands, established businesses in the Over-the-Hill district, the black section of Nassau, a trend that entrenched the socioeconomic split. As Colin Hughes asserted, structural colour, a concept described by M.G. Smith,[55] was most important in the Bahamas. Among the variables listed by Smith, 'wealth has had a pre-eminent place in the Bahamas'. Wealth attracted power and authority, and therefore in the Bahamas racial differences were linked to economic relationships.[56] Money 'whitened'. An illustrative case was Roland Symonette, a poor light-skinned coloured seaman from Current Settlement, Eleuthera. Having actively participated in bootlegging,[57] he rose to a position of wealth and power in the mid 1920s, consolidating his position in several legitimate enterprises, and by his election to the House of Assembly in 1925. Legend has it that when he was refused entry into the white elitist Royal Nassau Sailing Club, he established the Nassau Yacht Club which

Thaddeus A. Toote
(Courtesy of the Department of Archives, Nassau)

also was to discriminate against coloureds. In less than a generation, he and his family were accepted by the white community.[58]

The white community, by the 1930s, included an emergent middle class comprising mainly of Out Islanders from Harbour Island and Abaco. Often related or known to the white elite, because of their colour, they stood a better chance than the coloured middle class of finding employment as shop assistants and clerks in Bay Street establishments. Rowena Eldon was one of the first among the few coloureds to work in a clerical position for a Bay Street establishment.

With the advent of American investors such as Frank Munson, came the Jim Crow attitudes. Because of the growing importance of the tourist industry and the dependence on American investment, the white elite, who needed few lessons in racism, did little to stop the increasingly blatant discrimination against non-whites in public places and educational establishments. In Nassau, discrimination was practiced in certain places such as hotels, cinemas, barber shops, some schools like Queen's College, the Royal Bank of Canada and J.P Sands' shop. Girl Guide and Boy Scout troops were also segregated. In nearby Miami, Bahamians were nevertheless shocked to see actual signs indicating race on public facilities such as lavatories, doors and water fountains. As Nassau's reputation grew internationally during the 1930s, the influence and wealth of the white mercantile clique increased, while that of the coloured and black middle class diminished relatively.[59] The discriminatory policies which permeated the entire society pushed coloureds nearer to blacks, to what Hoetink called the Deep South variant.[60] Some coloureds however discriminated against members of their own class if they were too dark. Black's Candy Kitchen, for example, catered to all races but only allowed the fair-skinned and whites in the sit-down back section of its establishment. Blacks and darker coloureds were served in the front section.[61]

Few coloureds and blacks by the mid 1920s had been exposed to higher education. The establishment of the Government High School in 1925, brought about after some public pressure especially from the enlightened coloured and black politicians such as T.A. Toote, A.F. Adderley and R.M. Bailey, was therefore a major achievement. The school, intended to accommodate the growing coloured middle class and the more upwardly mobile blacks excluded by discriminatory policies from private secondary schools, soon became a prestigious black institution with very few whites attending. In less than two decades the school had created a coloured and black elite group which, excluded from the white establishments, increasingly turned to the professions, especially law. Other graduates of the Government High School were absorbed as teachers in the public school system and as clerks in the Civil Service.[62] It was significant that a coloured Government High School graduate, Anatol Reeves (who later married Dr Kenneth Rodgers, a member of the tightly-knit coloured middle class) along with

Cecil Bethel, a Codrington College graduate, were appointed as Assistant Teachers at the Government High School in 1941.[63] Despite the heightened consciousness through exposure to secondary education and to outside influences, the coloured and black middle classes failed to effect political or social change. The unification of a group of coloured and black politicians and a few enlightened whites over several issues including the secret ballot in March 1925, soon evaporated.

Increased migration into Nassau in the 1920s and during the Depression years of impoverished Out Islanders barred from the United States by stricter immigration laws, put extra strains on the fragile infrastructure of the capital. The flocking of Out Islanders to Nassau also created new social problems including unemployment. However, despite the increasing poverty and restlessness among the migrant and black labouring population, the Bahamas did not experience the riots and strikes which reverberated throughout most of the British Caribbean. The unrest in the Bahamas was more isolated and not serious enough to cause alarm. Whereas in Jamaica, coloured middle class leaders such as Norman Manley and Bustamante were becoming known as spokesmen for the black labouring class, no such coloured leaders emerged in the Bahamas. Neither did the coloured and black middle class leaders espouse the fledgling trade union movement or form political parties – institutions so vital to the success of coloured West Indian leadership.

More vocal than the coloured and black middle class in its support of the underdog in the society was a group of enlightened whites or near-whites including Henry M. Taylor, Cyril Stevenson, Jack Stanley Lowe and Holly Brown, most of whom had Out Island roots. Lowe and Brown founded the *Herald* newspaper in May 1937 and it soon became, more than Dupuch's *Tribune*, the 'champion of the working man'[64]. Outspoken in its criticism of high public officials, the *Herald* particularly identified with the labouring class, something that the coloured and black middle class was reluctant to do.

Another critic of the Establishment was Milo B. Butler, a fiery black Out Islander with little education. By the late 1930s he had established a business, but was described as a merchant of 'small means and little standing'.[65] After losing his deposit and the seat for the West, which had been traditionally won by a black person, to Canadian millionaire Harry Oakes, Butler, with some support from the black labouring class, complained and announced his intention to lodge a protest against the glaring bribery which took place during the election. He later organized a demonstration on Emancipation Day, 1938, consisting of seven or eight hundred people who carried banners in support of the secret ballot. This political incident revealed the increasing unrest in a substantial section of New Providence's population. The coloured and black middle class failed to channel it into a national movement.

Four years later in June 1942 when the first mass uprising erupted over a wage dispute,[66] the coloured and black middle class did not attempt to use it to its political advantage although black anger was obviously directed against the white ruling elite. Stunned and appalled at the behaviour of the rioters, coloured and black leaders did little to articulate demands, other than pleading for wage increases. In fact they acted as mediators between the rioters and the government.

White, coloured and black leaders including Adderley, Dupuch, Walker, Cambridge and Butler realized the blatant injustices and hardships under which the labouring classes lived, but they lacked the political will or machinery to effect change and seemed willing to negotiate for a gradual peaceful solution. The coloured and black middle class could not condone violence or risk ruining its increasingly comfortable lifestyle. Class-wise, it still found it difficult to identify with the black labouring class. By the 1930s, the wives of the coloured elite including Ethel Adderley and Clarita Toote, having leisure time at their disposal, formed committees to help the poor and aid hurricane victims. Coloureds also headed and patronized several sporting clubs, including the Nassau Cricket Club and the Gym Tennis Club.[67] The social distance between the two classes was considerable; Governor Murphy commenting in the mid 1940s believed that A.F. Adderley, a highly respected lawyer and politician, had 'reached that stage in the evolution of a gentleman of colour at which his own community ceased to regard him as truly representing their outlook'.[68] Etienne Dupuch observed much later that Adderley's '... approach to politics was conservative and while I believe he had a genuine desire to help in the advancement of black people, he knew that he was culturally head and shoulders above the great majority of them'.[69]

A.F. Adderley, although of outstanding intellect and ability, typified the conservatism held by others of his class. The expanded intermediary coloured and black middle class in 1942 was better educated and more aware of the injustices in the society but was politically impotent. Although it was excluded from white circles which controlled the economy, at the same time its members were not expected to participate in agricultural and menial jobs. A few became professionals, while an increasing number of coloureds entered the teaching profession and lower ranks of the Civil Service. By the early 1940s, some coloureds and blacks were beginning to benefit financially from the growth of tourism and foreign investment.

Most coloureds suffered discrimination in a society deeply divided by colour and class. The definition of a coloured person in the Bahamas in the 1940s was still ambiguous, varying according to a person's family, wealth and its attitude. A wealthy person who had a 'tinture' of coloured blood would be accepted as white if he associated with the 'right' people.[70] Fair-skinned coloureds were accepted at some segregated restaurants and movie houses. The proximity to the caste-conscious Southern United States and the development of tourism exacerbated racist attitudes in the Bahamas. Exposure to so many whites tended to emphasize the already deeply entrenched feelings of inferiority among the coloured and black middle class. The latter, which absorbed white values, tried to overcome its racial identity by imitating whites. A hierarchy was thus created within the non-white community where not only colour but physical attributes such as hair quality and facial structure mattered. The settlement in Nassau of white and near-white Out Islanders with their intransigent attitudes towards colour, also intensified racial divisions. Nassau's relatively large white population and its commercially based economy made for a social structure more resembling that of the Atlantic 'outpost' of Bermuda than that of the British West Indies.

While favouring change, the coloured and black middle class adopted gradual, not revolutionary methods. Most coloured leaders, including Dupuch and Adderley, were conservative and by the 1940s had much affection for the British Empire. Despite the humiliating treatment it suffered because of the racist policies of the white elite, the coloured and black class lacked the political will to challenge the power of the white Bay Street clique. Later, in 1953, when the first political party was established, its conservatism hindered it from identifying with the party. History would show that the early success of the Progressive Liberal Party did not hinge on the lukewarm support of the coloured and black middle class.

Notes

1. Edward Brathwaite, *The Development of Creole Society in Jamaica 1770-1820* (Oxford:1971), 167-75. See also Mavis C. Campbell, *The Dynamics of Change in a Slave Society: A Sociopolitical History of the Free Coloureds of Jamaica, 1800-1865* (Rutherford, N.J.:1976); and Gad J. Heuman, *Between Black and White, Race, Politics, and the Free Coloureds in Jamaica, 1792-1865* (Westport, Connecticut: 1981).
2. See Lloyd Braithwaite, 'Stratification in Trinidad', in *Slaves, Free Men, Citizens, West Indian Perspectives*, edited by Lambros Comitas and David Lowenthal (Garden City, New York: 1973): 212-239. See also David Lowenthal, *West Indian Societies* (Oxford University Press:1972), 91-100.
3. G. J. H. Northcroft, 'Sketches of Summerland, Giving Some Account of Nassau and the Bahama Islands' (Nassau: *The Nassau Guardian*, 1912), 62.
4. Etienne Dupuch, *The Tribune Story* (London: 1967), 37.
5. Christine Bolt, *Victorian Attitudes to Race* (London and Toronto:1971), 134-37.
6. L.D. Powles, *The Land of the Pink Pearl* (London: 1988), 120-121.
7. Ibid., 122.
8. Ibid., 211. See also James H. Stark, *History of and Guide to the Bahamas* (Boston: 1891), 139.
9. Northcroft, *Sketches of Summerland*, 61.

10. Sidney Olivier, *White Capital and Coloured Labour* (London: 1910), 38-9. Cited in Lowenthal, *West Indian Societies*, 72.
11. D. Gail Saunders, 'The Social History of the Bahamas, 1890-1953' (Ph.D thesis, University of Waterloo: 1985), 139.
12. Marc Tull, 'Colour Pride in Tarpum Bay. A Bahamian Community Reacts to Equality', in *Anthropological Perspectives on Eleuthera Island 1973-1974* (Corning, New York: College Center of the Finger Lakes, 1974): 71.
13. See Saunders, 'Social History', 89-91.
14. Peter J. Wilson, *Crab Antics: The Social Anthropology of English Speaking Negro Societies of the Caribbean* (New Haven and London: 1973), 95-8, 222-34.
15. Interview with E. Basil North, Nassau, January 1, 1986.
16. Interview with Dr Terry North, London, August 5, 1983.
17. Interview with E. Basil North.
18. E. Clement Bethel, 'Music in The Bahamas, Its Roots, Development and Personality' (MA thesis, University of California, Los Angeles: 1978), 217. The Junkanoo festival, which is celebrated twice every year on Boxing Day and New Year's day, can be traced back to the slavery period not only in the Bahamas but in several West Indian territories including Jamaica, Belize and St. Vincent. See Bethel, ibid., pp. 186-207.
19. These included the coming of the Loyalists after the American Revolutionary War, and the blockade running era during the American Civil War. See Gordon Lewis, *The Growth of The Modern West Indies*, 311.
20. Ibid., 313.
21. Practice of paying workmen in goods instead of money, or in money on the understanding that they will buy provisions etc. in truck shop from their employers. See Howard Johnson, *The Bahamas in Slavery and Freedom* (Ian Randle Publishers: 1991), 55-109.
22. Saunders, 'Social History', 85-6.
23. Benson McDermott, A. F. Adderley, 'Giant Strides Across the Bahamian Stage', *Bahamas Handbook and Businessman's Annual* (Nassau: 1980), 18.
24. Ibid., 21. See also *Almanack, 1901* (Nassau: Nassau Guardian), Advertisements at end of book.
25. *Bahamas Blue Books*, 1901-02, 1913-40.
26. Bridget Brereton, *Race Relations in Colonial Trinidad, 1870-1900* (Cambridge University Press: 1979), 77. See also Christine Bolt, *Victorian Attitudes to Race* (London and Toronto: 1971), 106.
27. See Saunders, 'Social History', 80.
28. Interview with Rowena Eldon, Nassau, December 8, 1983. Aaron Dixon, a Scotsman who had lived in the Bahamas, willed his property for the benefit of the poor and for the education of fatherless children. *Almanack 1894* (Nassau: Nassau Guardian), 1894, 26.
29. Saunders, 'Social History', 81.
30. R.P. Dyer to the Methodist Missionary Society, London, February 1937. The Bahamas District Weslyan Methodist Missionary Society (WMMS) papers, Box 715.
31. *Board of Education Annual Report 1892*, PRO/EDU/5-18, p. 2. Cited Colbert Williams, *The Methodist Contribution to Education in The*

Bahamas, Gloucester, England, (Waterloo:1968) 1982, 112.
32. Michael Craton, *A History of the Bahamas*, England, (Waterloo:1968) p. 128. See also Colin A. Hughes, *Race and Politics in the Bahamas* (St. Lucia, Queensland: 1981), 10.
33. Powles, *Land of the Pink Pearl*, 101-05. The *Freeman*, after Government Administrator refused to recognize it, ceased publication just over two years after its establishment. *Blue Books*, 1889-1890.
34. All six coloured men elected to the House of Assembly in 1889 were involved in private businesses or in the Civil Service. Leon E. Dupuch, elected for the district was a printer; James C. Smith, representing the Western District, was the Postmaster General; G.A. McGregor, also for the West, was a Resident Justice; William C. Adderley, a merchant, was elected for the City and J.W.H. Deveaux, a farmer, was the Representative for Cat Island. *Blue Books*, 1887 and 1889. See also *Almanack* 1894 (Nassau: Nassau Guardian, 1894), 108-09.
35. Shea to Knutsford, July 2, 1889. C023/231/256-257.
36. Ibid.
37. Powles, *Land of the Pink Pearl*, 41.
38. Minute Paper. Colonial Secretary's Files. Confidential, No. 13. July 13, 1921.
39. Tony Martin, *The Pan-African Connection: From Slavery to Garvey and Beyond* (Cambridge, Mass: 1983), 59.
40. Minute Paper, Colonial Secretary's Files. Confidential. No. 21, May 29, 1920. As far as can be ascertained the plan never materialized.
41. Robert A. Hill, (ed.) *The Marcus Garvey and Universal Negro Improvement Association Papers*, Vol. 1 (Berkeley:1983), 515.
42. Minute Paper. Colonial Secretary's Files, No. 145, January 21, 1921. See also Robert Hill, (ed.) *The Marcus Garvey and Universal Negro Improvement Association Papers*, Vol. II, 371.
43. Etienne Dupuch, *A Salute to Friend and Foe* (Nassau: 1982), 63-4, 68.
44. Ibid., 33.
45. Dupuch, *Tribune Story*, 27.
46. Dupuch, *A Salute to Friend and Foe*, 100.
47. Saunders, 'Social History', 212. See also the *Tribune*, February 24, 1911.
48. Saunders, 'Social History', 183-85.
49. Allardyce to Long, August 24, 1918, C023/283/124-126.
50. Eardley to Andrews, Nassau, March 16, 1917. Wesleyan Methodist Missionary Society Papers.
51. Ibid. See also Ibid., February 19, 1918, WMMS.
52. Interview with Audrey V. Isaacs North, June 20, 1984.
53. Gordon Lewis, *The Growth of The Modern West Indies*, 319.
54. Saunders, 'Social History', 277-78, 358-59, 375.
55. M.G. Smith, *Framework for Caribbean Studies* (Mona, Jamaica, 1955), 65.
56. Colin Hughes, *Race and Politics*, 22.
57. Grant to Churchill, August 31, 1922, Conf. CO23/291/215 and Hughes to Geddes, June 26, 1922, C023/292 Misc.
58. Saunders, 'Social History', 275-77.
59. Saunders, 'Social History', 280-81; 288-89.

60. H. Hoetink, *The Two Variants in Caribbean Race Relations* (Oxford: 1967), 46-7.
61. Interview with E. Basil North, July 31, 1984.
62. Clifford to Shuckburg, February 25, 1933, C023/477.
63. Bahamas Civil Service List, 1944 (Nassau: 1944), 23.
64. Interview with Holly Brown, September 10, 1984.
65. Dundas to MacDonald, July 11, 1938. Conf. C023/653.
66. D. Gail Saunders, The 1942 Riot in Nassau, Bahamas. A Demand for Change? *The Journal of Caribbean History*, 20: 2. 117-46.
67. *Tribune,* September 30, October 1, 2 and 4, 1935. See also *The Gym Tennis Club Souvenir Programme, Historical Day, 22 August 1981* (Nassau: 1981). See also chapter 11 in this book.
68. Personal Letter, Murphy to Hall, November 28, 1945, CO. 23/799/28
69. Benson McDermott, A.F. Adderley, 41.
70. Denyer to Noble, April 10, 1947, Governor's Harbour, Eleuthera, WMMS.

2

Women in the Bahamian Society in the Late Nineteenth and Early Twentieth Centuries

Historical research on Caribbean women began fairly recently. Notable pioneering work has been done by Lucille Mathurin on the experience of women in Caribbean slave societies while Edward Kamau Brathwaite, Barbara Bush, Barry Higman, Michael Craton, Marietta Morrissey and Hilary Beckles have also made important contributions.[1] Much more research, however, needs to be done on the immediate post-emancipation period and the first half of the twentieth century to expand the work of Brodber, Reddock, Massiah, French, Ford-Smith and Silvestrini among others.[2]

Little has been written about Bahamian women. General histories hardly mention them although more recent accounts of Bahamian social history give some detail on women.[3] Several biographical articles and talks on the general historical development of women have appeared, mainly in the newspapers[4], but there has been no systematic and detailed examination of women in Bahamian history. Historical studies have largely excluded 'women's concerns and experiences' because of the definitions of history. As Brereton states:

> At the risk of over-simplification, history was conventionally defined as the ideas and action of male members of the ruling class of past societies. It was about government, state-building, war, formal institutions, founding official religions, mastering the environment – all activities in which the male elite believed women's roles were insignificant, or at best supportive only.[5]

This chapter examines the part women played in Bahamian society and their role in the economy during the late nineteenth century and explores the changes which occurred during the first quarter of the twentieth century. Traditional sources utilized include Colonial Office and local official papers, censuses, almanacks, travellers' accounts and relevant secondary writings. Oral history also proved to be useful. By studying the normal documentary evidence from the view of feminism more material became apparent than previously realized.

As in the case of the British Caribbean generally, the place of Bahamian women in the society and economy was determined by their race, colour and class. Rosina Wiltshire Brodber has stated that 'the dominance of race, colour and class in Caribbean colonial societies, historically made the issue of gender peripheral to an understanding of power, dominance and change.'[6]

The elite comprised the British official class including the governor and senior officials in the church and government and the Nassau whites and their wives. Males were mainly merchants, senior civil servants and lawyers who were usually members of the legislature and also controlled the economy. Some whites worked as clerks in shops and in the lower ranks of the civil service, their colour bringing them together as a class. Unlike the plantocracy in the larger British Caribbean colonies, the mercantile elite was generally poor and perhaps not an elite in the classical sense.

In analyzing Bahamian women's role in the society and economy, it is necessary to distinguish those of Nassau, the mini-metropolis, and those who lived in the more rural Out Island settlements.

Extremely proud of its British traditions, the white elite of Nassau, as did its counterparts in the British West Indies generally, emulated the upper and middle classes of England. Its society revolved around the 'official' life of the 'miniature metropolis', various recreational clubs and the Church.[7] For elite women, led by the governor's wife, sister or daughter, who was recognized as the leader of the colony's society, social life was a series of private visits, the occasional dinner party, picnics, dances and participation in tennis parties.[8]

Elite women enjoyed attending social functions such as the opening and closing of the legislature. Coloured and black women were among the spectators. Whites entertained occasionally by hosting dinner parties with the help of black servants, many of whom became trusted family retainers and remained in the same family for a lifetime. Another pastime for elite women was making private visits and stopping for tea. Not many people of the upper class read or had travelled very much. Travel writer, J. H. Stark, commented in a similar vein as D. Hart did on the ladies of Trinidad,[9] in describing the manners and hospitality of the Bahamian elite particularly the women:

> A simplicity almost Arcadian characterizes their manners, especially these women. Many who have led very circumscribed lives, who have never been away from the island possess an ease and grace which would do credit to the most polished society.[10]

Conversation, however, was usually very limited and humourless. It consisted mainly of small talk, covering such topics as dress, the 'wicked' coloured servants and the inferiority of the coloured race in general. The upper class also delighted in scandal.[11]

Dancing seems to have been a favourite pastime of the upper class. Lady Shea, wife of the governor, hosted a small dance at the end November

1890 for Neville and Austin Chamberlain who were visiting Nassau. Neville Chamberlain, 'remarked that the ranks and fashion, the beauty and talent of Nassau were displayed before our astonished eyes'.[12]

Sports were very important in the lives of the upper class especially the men. Women, however, played tennis and a few of them golf. They frequently attended tennis parties at private courts owned by white Nassauvians and some belonged to the premier club, the exclusively white Nassau Lawn Tennis Club which sponsored occasional tournaments.[13] Other pastimes enjoyed by both white men and women were bicycling, carriage rides, sea-sports and picnics.

Elite women who belonged to the 'small and narrow' upper class society upheld the racist attitudes of the day. They imposed their opinion on the society that Africans and their descendants were racially inferior. They therefore had no social contact with coloured middle class women or blacks except in the mistress and servant relationship. Most coloureds knew and accepted their place and socialized within their own small circle.

Recreational activities for the coloured middle class were limited, especially for the women. Housework and child rearing occupied most of their time. More talented families amused themselves at home on the harmonium or piano. Informal visits were made to friends and there was the occasional dance in the lodge hall or schoolroom. Some coloured men and women were members of a lodge, while the majority of labouring blacks, although involved in some lodges, belonged predominantly to friendly societies. By the turn of the century, membership in the friendly societies had decreased, while that in the lodges, which had allegiance to a parent society outside the colony, usually England or the United States, grew rapidly. Apparently it was more prestigious to belong to a lodge than a friendly society and Dr Eneas hinted at the social segregation which manifested itself in different lodges and church orders.[14]

One lodge, Star of Hope No. 3 Daughters of Samaria, consisted entirely of women and was also a temperance society which gave females leadership roles. Ruth E. Sturrup, for example, held the office of Past Presiding Grand Daughter of the District Grand Lodge in 1910 and had been a member of that lodge for seventeen years. Mrs Sturrup stated that a pledge had to be signed on joining the lodge and temperance society and that women were more disposed to signing the pledge and kept it better than men.[15]

Coloured men and women occasionally attended dramatic presentations which were put on by the church. They, along with people of all classes, were attracted to band concerts in the park (now Rawson Square). It was only rarely that coloureds gave a private party or dance since not many could afford to host such an event.

Coloured and black women did not generally participate in sporting activities because they had little leisure time and there were no facilities open to them. It was not until the Gym Tennis Club was established by Nurse Florence Wood in the late 1920s, that coloured and black women began to play tennis.[16] Women with better-off husbands were occasionally taken on carriage rides 'out-west' stopping at Prospect Ridge or Cable Beach for coconuts and for a picnic. Bicycling, as for the elite, became a popular recreation in Nassau in the late nineteenth century for both coloured men and women. A more sedentary pastime was sitting on the 'piazza' or porch, watching the world go by, and catching up with the latest gossip from passersby.[17]

While the coloured woman was anxious to distance herself from her African roots, black women in their recreational activities kept many traditional practices alive. Music derived from the antebellum slave songs of the United States and from the early Wesleyan and Baptist hymnals was important in the lives of the labouring black population. Women participated fully in wakes, usually held on the night when a friend or relative was thought to be dying[18] and gathered at sunset and on other occasions such as the eve of Emancipation Day and Christmas to sing all night. Women also participated in the telling of traditional folktales and dancing, another popular form of entertainment. Dances for black women and men included ring dances, the jumping dance and the fire dance, which were usually to the accompaniment of the goatskin drum. The Christian church's efforts to suppress these dances which it saw as disreputable failed. Where there was a strong African element, such as Bain Town and the liberated African settlements of Fox Hill, Adelaide and Gambier, the holding of ring dances was quite frequent.[19]

Emancipation Day, as in most ex-slave colonies, was celebrated throughout the Bahamas on August 1 in various ways. Powles observed that every August some of the Africans who still retained tribal distinctions elected a queen whose will was law on certain matters, while Northcroft noticed that processions, dances and entertainments of various sorts were held and sometimes the proceedings were kept up for nearly a week.[20]

Women were also a part of the celebrations held on Fox Hill Day which was celebrated one week after Emancipation Day. Relatives and friends of Fox Hillians, especially those from Bain Town, moved to Fox Hill to stay a week before the great day. Women participated in the programmes which included church services, recitations, music and some drama, the plaiting of the May pole, ring play and singing. They also prepared a variety of foods including the traditional African dishes such as accara, moi-moi, agedi and foo-foo.

Black women also participated in the Guy Fawkes night celebration when his effigy was 'carried in procession with bands of music and torches, and solemnly hung on a gallows prepared for that purpose'.[21] They were mainly spectators in the John Canoe parade.

Women of all classes, as did men, participated enthusiastically in church activities. Elite women usually belonged to the Anglican, Methodist and Presbyterian Churches which afforded them prestige and status, and also supplied their sons and daughters with a decent, segregated secondary education not offered by the Board of Government Schools. Church membership led to their involvement in the ladies' visiting and sewing societies and charitable societies which were established to 'lessen ignorance, want and suffering in Nassau and the Out Islands'.[22] These activities also entrenched their sense of leadership. Elite women were involved in the Diocesan Temperance Society headed by the Bishop of Nassau and also the St Andrew's Temperance Society.

A few coloured women were also members of the temperance movement; Mrs Annie Dillet for example, supervised the juvenile templars of the Independent Order of Good Templars and was treasurer of the Women's Temperance Union. Coloured middle class women belonged generally to the Anglican or Methodist Churches which offered respectability and in exceptional cases provided education for their children. Church also gave women the opportunity to 'get out' and to dress up in their Sunday best.[23] Coloureds were particularly attracted to the Anglican Church, especially St Mary's, St Agnes and St Matthews, with their High Church ritualism and because they offered a myriad of activities and some responsibility. Women participated in guild activities and also helped at the annual bazaars.

While the elite and coloured middle class put emphasis on formalized institutional structures and systems of belief, the black labouring population combined 'traditional, evangelical and fundamentalist forms of Christianity with revivalism and spiritualism'. Their God was more 'accessible to direct persuasion' and they believed 'both in salvation by faith and in a spiritual world, where the dead possessed supernatural powers and mediated among the living'.[24] Although some held membership in the Anglican and Methodist Churches, more and more were attracted to folk sects such as the African Episcopal Methodist 'Shouter Chapel' and the Native Baptist Church. These demanded active congregational participation and were renowned for fiery emotional sermons and lively hymn-singing, 'traditionally accompanied by hand-clapping and the phenomenon of spirit possession'. Women took an active part in the services and often experienced spirit possession, 'the supreme religious experience for the person of African origins'.[25]

Anglican and Methodist Churches offered a high school education for those of their white members who could afford modest fees. Children were rarely sent abroad. White girls and boys were privately tutored or attended 'Dame Schools' and some girls attended St Hilda's Anglican High School, which was established in 1886 to provide a good education for children of the upper classes, together with the Church of England teaching on the Bible and Prayer Book. Elite girls also attended the slightly less prestigious and co-educational Wesleyan Queen's College, established as the Nassau Collegiate School in 1871 to 'give ... a superior Commercial and Classical education...' to the sons and daughters of the white Wesleyan and Presbyterian founders.[26] Also catering to upper class girls was St Francis Xavier's Academy, a fee-paying private school established in 1890 by the Roman Catholic Sisters of Charity of Mount St Vincent-on-Hudson, New York.

All three institutions were segregated by colour. Very light-skinned children from well-to-do 'respectable' coloured families might be admitted, but no dark-skinned coloured child was acceptable. Early in the 1900s, a black well-respected West Indian physician, Dr William Pitt, who had some of the leading white families as his patients, applied for the admission of his two daughters to Queen's College. The Trustees, embarrassed, reluctantly admitted them. Etienne Dupuch records, however, 'the children took care of the situation. They made it so uncomfortable for the girls that the doctor had to send them away to school.'[27]

Most coloured and black children, debarred by racist policies and prohibitive fees, attended government primary schools which were underfinanced, short of supplies and lacking in trained teachers. Secondary education, not as yet provided by government, and still largely the preserve of the upper class, was very limited for coloured and black girls. Boys stood a better chance of receiving a secondary education at the Anglican Nassau Grammar School than girls did at St Hilda's or Queen's College, which drew a stricter colour line. Some coloured girls received a sound elementary education at Bishop Eastern, an Anglican institution.

General attitudes of the metropolitan and colonial upper classes prevalent at the time militated against the secondary education of non-whites. On the one hand, the elite thought them incapable of learning, and on the other hand they feared that education would make them too 'uppity'. They therefore were disinclined to vote the necessary expenditure. Additionally some coloured parents saw no wisdom in providing their daughters, who would become housewives and mothers, with a secondary education.[28]

The church influenced attitudes on morality. As in the British West Indies generally, monogamy was the ideal for all classes, but as Lowenthal demonstrated, 'each (class) approaches it by a different route and to a different degree'.[29] Formal marriage was the norm for the upper class Nassau and Out Island whites and the coloured middle class which emulated the mating patterns of the elite. For the black urban working class and some Out Island blacks, marriage did not necessarily precede the birth of children, and common law marriages were not unusual.

Most women married very young, usually between fifteen and twenty-one,[30] to someone within the community. Intermarriage within the Nassau circle of whites was common as in the white and bi-racial Out Island communities. Coloureds and blacks on the other hand, although expected to marry within their class, could not marry a close relative.[31] Marriage, which followed a formal courtship, gave both men and women a new status in the community. Women of all classes were expected to bear a large number of children who were regarded as an economic asset. They were also helpmates and companions to their mothers with whom they often established close relationships.

Most women accepted the double standard which existed for men. Provided they cared for their families, it was not uncommon, or overly frowned upon for white, coloured or black men to have 'sweethearts' or mistresses by whom they had several children. For women, especially in the white and coloured middle class, an affair outside the marriage was scandalous, and illegitimacy carried a searing social stigma. If a girl of the elite or coloured middle class got pregnant and did not marry the father of the child, she was ostracized – a terrible fate in a small community. Her parents, if they could afford it, sent her to the United States or Britain where she remained, either forever, or at least until the scandal subsided. If she had the baby at home, she was permanently banished from society by her peers.[32]

Illegitimacy was rare in all white and bi-racial Out Island settlements. In black Out Island communities, it was more common but not the norm. However, not much shame was felt among urban (Nassau) blacks about illegitimacy and the 'outside child'. Men and women living in consensual unions and raising children were accepted by their community. The matrifocal family was also accepted. Dr Eneas stated of Bain Town, a black suburb of Nassau:

> The women were the stronger factors in most of these families, and the cementing agent that held them together. They knew how to handle their men and did it most effectively. The "father image" was noticeably lacking in my neighbourhood.[33]

In Bain Town and in Over-the-Hill Nassau there was a kinship system that extended beyond the usual nuclear family. 'Every woman was an aunt' and 'full of authority, and each had the right to set the correct behaviour of every child in the neighbourhood'.[34]

Evidence is scanty but it seems that women often suffered violence at the hands of men. Few cases of rape or indecent assault were reported, but women were often beaten. Dr Eneas recorded the story of Aun' Cooley, a Bain Town woman who received a beating from her husband nearly every afternoon when he returned from work to find she had not cooked dinner. The neighbours who believed in the age old rule 'never get between man and wife', refused to intervene.

Controversial Irish Magistrate L. D. Powles caused an uproar when he sentenced a white man, James Lightbourn, to one month's imprisonment without the option of a fine, for assaulting a black girl.[35] Apparently it was common practice for whites to hire a black or coloured girl, pick a quarrel with her and at the end of the month turn her out without paying her wages.

The Bahamas was a marginal non-plantation colony, where sugar never succeeded as a commercial crop. After the failure of cotton in the early 1800s, there was no plantation staple. A variety of crops was grown in the Out Islands and some like pineapple, sisal, citrus and tomato became export crops. These one by one failed or drastically declined and agriculture was never put on a sound scientific basis. Additionally, because of the lack of a staple and the scarcity of cash in circulation, the oppressive share and truck systems developed.[36]

A Market Scene, Nassau in the Early Twentieth Century
(Courtesy of the Mary Moseley Collection and the Anglican Church of the Bahamas)

Economic opportunities were very limited for women generally in the late nineteenth and early twentieth centuries. Most urban elite and coloured women, after marriage, became housewives. The endemic poverty in the Bahamas made it acceptable for white upper class women to make their own clothes and to assist in household chores, although some had servants. Well-off coloured women also supervised their domestics. Most, however, did their own household chores and spent much time rearing children while some elite women earned their own living by teaching at home or at St Hilda's or Queen's College. Others operated bakeries, became shopkeepers of dry goods, manufactured and sold fancy shell work and ran boarding houses. This was unusual in the British Caribbean context where elite usually implied a non-earning wife. Perhaps, Bahamian elite women, because of real poverty, found it expedient to supplement the small incomes of their husbands.

Coloured middle class women, who had more limited opportunities, sold bread and cakes baked at their homes. Others became seamstresses, operating genrerally out of their homes.[37]

Black women worked as labourers, including sponge clipping, cutting quarry stones and weeding, domestics, farmers and petty shopkeepers. They worked very hard for very low wages.[38] They were ambitious for their sons, some of whom rose to middle class status through the accumulation of capital or less often through education. Many black women made their living through

Sponge Clippers in the Early Twentieth Century Bahamas
(Courtesy of the Department of Archives, Bahamas)

marketing which traditionally played a significant part in their lives and those of their slave and African forbears.[39] Most grew vegetables in their own garden plots, or 'yards', which when harvested, would either be sold from door to door, or at small roughly made stalls in the streets, often in front of their homes[40] or in the Nassau market. According to Dr Eneas, nearly all these market women were of Yoruba descent and resided in Bain Town, Grant's Town and Fox Hill.[41]

Women of the latter settlement, which was at least three miles from town, often walked into Nassau balancing a large wooden tray or basket of fruit and vegetables on their heads, calling out their wares as they walked. In the more distant settlements of Adelaide and Gambier, women and men usually brought their produce to town on a donkey cart.

The Nassau market, in existence since the early 1800s and located on Bay Street, opposite Market Street which led into Grant's Town, was the central node of Nassau local commerce. Each day, Over-the-Hill women took small quantities of produce to market. The market women had their own system of measurement. Vegetables and fruit were laid out in heaps at 'so much a lot', and nothing was sold by specific quantities. Rents charged by the government for the use of stalls were prohibitive for some of the vendors, many of whom began their business careers with as little as 25 cents. They later accumulated cash through their sales and the Asue, an informal system of saving money.[42] Some women (and men) vendors also frequented the Royal Victoria Hotel's portico, a well-known tourist attraction where they sold in addition to fruit and vegetables, shells, shell work, baskets, sponges and lace called 'Spanish work'.

Women living in Out Island settlements had more limited opportunities than those in Nassau. Poverty, isolation, poor communications and sheer neglect by the Nassau mercantile elite, caused great hardships on the Out Islands. Living at the same economic and social level, the majority of the adult population engaged in subsistence peasant farming, laboured as tenants under the share system, or signed up as fishermen on the truck system.

Women were involved in farming at all levels from cleaning the fields to harvesting the crops. In fact women and children usually took produce on their heads from the fields to settlements as far as six miles apart. At home they shucked and thrashed corn and shelled peas. Dried corn was ground in a mill and separated into three major products: grits (or hominy), the flour used for making bread and johnny cakes, and husks (or chaff) which was fed to chickens, hogs or thrown away.

Out Island women also worked in pineapple canning factories in Eleuthera and Abaco in the late nineteenth century and engaged in salt production especially in communities such as Inagua, Ragged Island and Rum Cay where salt was the predominant industry. In the late nineteenth century salt production was operated under the credit and truck system.

Social life for Out Islanders was limited especially for women. It revolved mainly around the church and membership in friendly societies. Women worked almost constantly both at home and in the field. Because of racial prejudice and rank discrimination, there was little social interaction between white and black women. However, the lack of doctors in most Out Island settlements meant that white women employed midwives, most of whom were black. Whatever colour, midwives had a special place in the community and were held in high esteem.

The role of women did not change dramatically during the early years of the twentieth century. Technological advance and the coming of World War I brought more women into the workplace but increased migration from the Out Islands into Nassau, and Prohibition was to have a more profound effect on women and on the society in general.

New developments worldwide in the areas of electricity, communication and transportation in the late nineteenth century, led to important improvements in the colony of the Bahamas. The upgrading of cable communication, the introduction of the telephone and electrical systems, the typewriter and medical improvements facilitated expansion of the civil service. The inauguration of the telephone in 1906 and its installation the following year in downtown Nassau only marginally affected the lives of Bahamians, mainly the urban elite. It particularly impacted on the lives of several elite women who were hired as telephone operators.[43]

This was unusual, but because of the central system and the sensitivity of the transactions – most calls were between members of the white Nassau community – elite women were employed. Similarly, the introduction of electricity to the city of Nassau in 1909 mainly affected the Nassau elite and better-off coloureds or the middle class. For those who could afford it, electricity made for lighter house work. For example, women and girls no longer had to clean sooty lamp shades. Food preservation became easier as ice and ice boxes were available.[44]

The typewriter, which came on the market in 1874 transformed business, bringing about the introduction of commercial schools. Its impact was worldwide as most of the stenographers and typists were women. In Nassau, a few elite and middle class women were taught typing and shorthand.

Small advances in health and sanitation services in the early twentieth century had a positive effect on women. By the Medical Department Act of 1911, the Board of Health widened and strengthened its powers. Besides defining standards for doctors, the legislation also stipulated the minimum qualifications for the matron (held by a British woman until 1962 when Hilda Bowen was appointed), nurses and midwives. Before receiving a licence, midwives had to be examined on their skills by the resident surgeon. This was important, as midwives, although generally well respected, were completely untrained, and were indispensable where doctors were not available. Unsatisfactory conditions however were to persist well into the twentieth century. In 1925, a medical officer complained:

> There are on the Island (Cat Island) a number of women who call themselves midwives and attend expectant mothers – women devoid of obstetrical training. Some were an absolute danger to women in labour.[45]

A year later the Registration of Midwives Act was passed but this did not solve the problem immediately. Untrained and unregistered midwives, through necessity, continued to deliver babies in the isolated Out Island communities. Those with training were discouraged by poor conditions and low wages. Governor Clifford who in 1936 attempted to remedy the situation, explained that it was:

> Impossible to get midwives or nurses to remain on Out Islands as residents are too poor to pay for services rendered. At present residents

pay in kind only, and as a result the midwife or nurse has no actual cash with which to purchase their own necessities.[46]

The economy in late nineteenth century Bahamas was affected by the depression of the previous decade common to the rest of the British West Indies during the crisis in sugar production. Chronic poverty and worsening economic conditions, partly because of the decline in salt production, caused an exodus, which began as early as the late 1860s, of Bahamians to Florida, particularly Miami, Key West and other parts of the Southern United States. During this period, many men worked as labourers on steamships plying between the West Indies and Central and South America.[47] Most of the emigrants to America were men between the ages of 15 and 64. Although much of the emigration was temporary, a fairly large number of Bahamians, including some women, made a permanent home in Florida, especially Coconut Grove, Miami. The majority of women, however, stayed at home, alone with their children. Migration upset family life and the demographic balance, especially on the Out Islands. By 1921 females in the overall population of 53,031 outnumbered males by 5,451. Married females exceeded married males by 928.[48]

World War I also took Bahamian men overseas.[49] The vacuum created by their absence gave women more responsibilities and brought more of them out of the home into the workplace. In Nassau, which was also developing its tourist industry, an increasing number of women especially black women worked in the domestic field as cooks, laundresses, and cleaners. The growth of the Bahamian servant population between 1911 and 1943, as in Jamaica, was due mainly to the rural-urban migration and an expanding middle class. An untrained maid in 1925 earned between fourteen shillings and twenty shillings a week. A cook with experience could earn about a pound a week.

Elite women had the opportunity in post-war years to learn shorthand and typing from Mrs Percy Lightbourn who was trained abroad. This qualified them to work in private offices and as clerks in the civil service and at the Royal Bank of Canada. Enid Boyce stated that she did not remember women working in offices during the war. She began in 1922 at the age of 18 or 19 to work in the office of Duncombe and Butler at the very low salary of a pound a week. She admitted 'a woman in the office was a very strange thing'.[50] An increasing number of elite women joined the workforce outside the home. A number of them, such as Ella Tucker Sands owned and operated dry goods shops and many were employed as shop assistants, caterers, fancy shell workers, librarians[51] and teachers in private schools, and one as a publisher. Miss Mary Moseley, a woman of exceptional energy, was by the 1920s a seasoned editor and proprietress of the *Nassau Guardian,* a family newspaper. She had taken over its management at the age of 26 on the death of her father in 1904 and the ownership shortly afterwards. Besides practicing journalism, Miss Moseley also served during the war in England where she formed the ladies committee of the West Indian Contingent. She was honoured by the King for her work on behalf of the men in the armed forces from the West Indies.[52] Miss Moseley also served on the board of trustees of the Nassau Public Library and was an avid collector of material on the history of the Bahamas. She published *The Bahamas Handbook* in 1926.

Coloured middle class women had less opportunities of finding satisfactory occupations outside the home. The rigid colour line and excessive racial discrimination barred most from office jobs in private businesses and within the civil service. While there was also colour discrimination in Trinidad, many light-skinned women were employed as clerks in larger shops and also as stenographers in the 1920s and 1930s.[53] In Nassau, the relatively larger white population, expanded by migration from Harbour Island, Abaco and Long Island, meant that more whites were available and were preferred by the Bay Street proprietors, especially as many were catering to an increasing number of white American tourists.

Moreover, Prohibition in the United States (1919-1933) profoundly affected Bahamian society and widened the gap between classes. It created a new *nouveau riche* (mainly white) which would eventually be accepted by the traditional elite. The new wealth also forged a division between whites. By the 1920s a white middle class had emerged. Its members, including women, were sought as shop and office clerks by white proprietors and lawyers. Wealth separated Nassau whites but their colour and small numbers united them as a social group. Known to one another, although they did not socialize, they assisted each other by finding positions in businesses and in the civil service.[54]

Among the few light-skinned coloured women who found work in the civil service were Mary (May) Anderson and Naomi Dupuch, who were employed at the Post Office as assistant clerks in 1920,[55] positions probably recommended by Mary Anderson's father, C.O. Anderson, who was appointed Postmaster in 1918. A few coloured women were employed in offices and downtown shops. Rowena Hill Eldon, after spending six years at St Hilda's School, later worked for an insurance company and afterwards in a wholesale business owned by T. H. G. Lofthouse, a wealthy white merchant. She was one of the first coloured women to work in a Bay Street store in Nassau.[56] Black and coloured lawyers including A. F. Adderley, T. A. Toote and W. E. S. Callender and coloured proprietors like Harry S. Black usually hired light-skinned coloured secretaries and clerks.[57]

The majority of coloured and some black women who found paid employment became nurses, dressmakers, music teachers, public school teachers and stenographers. The governor was impressed with Bahamian women; he commented in 1918 that 'with few exceptions the local youth is past praying for. The young women have a much larger sense of responsibility'.[58]

Prohibition also significantly affected the economic life of Bahamians. Financially the colony benefitted from the increased revenues brought by the unprecedented rise in exports and the heavy duties imposed by the Bahamas Customs Act of 1919 on imported alcoholic beverages. The Bahamas' newly acquired wealth was expended mainly in financing large public works projects in Nassau, financing hotels and generally making the island of New Providence attractive to tourists.[59]

New jobs were created especially for the white elite and middle class whites. Commercial prosperity and high wages lured whites into shopkeeping and other business enterprises. An increasing number of elite women were employed in the civil service in positions considered prestigious and formerly held by men. Cynthia Duncombe and Sybil Burnside, for example, were appointed as clerks in the Governor's Office and Colonial Secretary's Office, respectively. Some women were promoted into executive positions. Isabel Butler had been appointed as a clerk in 1906 and risen to the position of Assistant Registrar in 1927. Ellen Menendez Johnson, first appointed to a clerical position in 1914, became Assistant Postmaster in 1926.[60] It is interesting to note that the heads of departments were men and the majority of Butler's and Johnson's subordinates were women. It was an unwritten rule that as far as possible women should not have authority over men.

Although a small number of light-skinned coloured middle class women entered the service from positions in certain government departments such as the Governor's office and the secretariat, they could not aspire to posts beyond the clerical grades. Most of the coloured women who were in the service worked at the Post and Telegraph Office and in the Registry of Records.

The immediate impact of Prohibition was the provision of jobs for black women. Besides being employed to roll barrels of liquor from the wharves to warehouses, they were also hired by liquor merchants to repack and sew the imported liquor into burlap sacks. These sacks, each containing six bottles, were easily disposed of and handled.[61] As bootlegging profits declined, black women returned to domestic work, petty shopkeeping and selling in the market.

Prohibition while mainly benefitting the mercantile elite also impacted on coloureds and blacks who benefitted from the brief prosperity with quite a number having businesses in or near Bay Street. In addition to being concerned about their sudden wealth, they were becoming more aware of the benefits of higher education and the advancement it offered. Educated men such as lawyers Alfred F. Adderley and Thaddeus A. Toote served as role models and as inspiration for the middle class and aspiring blacks. Most coloureds and blacks who received higher education during the 1920s were men. However, a few coloured middle class girls such as Yvonne North, Carmita DeGregory and Alice Hill, studied nursing in New York. Yvonne North, a graduate of Queen's College High School studied at Lincoln Hospital (a black institution) in New York, returned to Nassau and entered private practice. She was one of the early officers of the Nurses Association.[62] Alice Hill was educated at Anglican Bishop Eastern School and trained as a nurse at Bukley Training School (a predominantly white institution) for nurses in the early 1920s. She pursued the New York State Board Examination in 1926 and practiced as an operating room supervisor for eight years. After working private duty at various other New York hospitals for four years, she returned home in 1934 where she worked mainly as a private nurse before becoming the first welfare nurse in the 1940s.[63]

Public nursing was not particularly attractive in the 1920s. The accommodation provided was unsatisfactory, conditions in the hospital abysmal, and the hours long. In 1927 the nursing staff comprised a British matron, four European sisters and between ten and twenty Bahamian women, most of whom had been locally trained. Local nurses lived at the Bahamas general hospital and trained on an apprenticeship system over a three year period. Most nurses who had trained abroad because of conditions in the hospital, preferred to work privately, attending patients in their homes.[64]

A serious problem which hindered women's development as professionals was the lack of secondary education. It was not until 1925 that the first government secondary school, the Government High School, was established. The idea of the white dominated Board of Education was that the school should be used to train teachers for government primary schools. Government High's policy was to admit children of all classes and colours whose parents could afford the fee of ten pounds a year.[65] The institution quickly became a prestigious black school accommodating the children of the growing coloured and black middle class and the upwardly mobile blacks.

Government High, however, was out of reach for most coloured and black parents. In addition to fees, some parents saw little justification in providing secondary education for their children, particularly the girls. Many parents believed that secondary education would 'create a class of persons' who could not 'be absorbed into the community'.[66] Attitudes were changing however, and by 1935, the Government High School had established a fine academic reputation and with an average of thirty-seven children between 1927 and 1935, boasted twenty-three Senior Cambridge School Certificates and forty-eight Junior Cambridge Certificates.[67]

Several females were included among the graduates of Government High in the 1930s. Among them were Miriam Cash and Anatol Reeves, both of whom obtained their Cambridge Senior Certificates with distinction and were exempted from the London Matriculation. Predictably, they entered teaching. While Miriam Cash continued her career as a teacher at the Western Senior School and later at the Board of Education, Anatol Reeves was sent by her parents to Spellman College in Alabama. After graduation, Anatol Reeves returned to Nassau in the early 1940s and was posted as a teacher at the

Government High School – the first Bahamian woman to hold such a position at the school.[68]

While expansion and new developments in education were taking place in New Providence, the Out Islands were neglected. Poverty, compounded by natural disasters, increased the migration from the Out Islands into Nassau. This trend continued especially after the passage of the 1924 United States Immigration Act. Between 1921 and 1932, the population of New Providence increased by 6,781 or by 52.3 per cent.[69] Whereas less than a quarter of the total population lived in New Providence in 1921, a decade later, the population had risen to a third.

Internal migration and the effects of bootlegging in Nassau caused severe social problems which affected women. Juvenile delinquency increased and offenders in the early 1920s included girls as well as boys. Women began to drink in public and people began noticing among groups of rowdy young people, girls roaming the streets at night. By the 1930s, with the promotion of tourism, and the establishment of local night clubs and the development of local entertainment, social drinking among women was accepted.[70]

Prostitution although not new, became more visible in post-war years. Female migrants often arrived alone and found themselves in a difficult financial situation. In order to make ends meet, or to supplement their earnings, they sometimes turned to prostitution. In 1914 the government was forced to pass an act to punish persons involved in prostitution.[71] Despite this act, prostitution remained prevalent in Nassau. Apparently, any night 'women of the lowest classes' could be found on Bay Street in the vicinity of the principal wharves, openly soliciting, or at the dance halls, where liquor was sold and 'vulgarity prevailed'. The dance halls were particularly notorious:

> .... They appeared to be Meccas for the worse type of prostitute and the happy hunting ground for characters of ill repute. The women go there for the purpose of soliciting and the men for the purpose of picking up a woman.[72]

Illegitimacy was also increasing with many children appearing in the Magistrate Court from single parent homes. In 1922 the rate of illegitimacy for the whole colony was about 30 per cent, relatively low compared to some other British Caribbean colonies such as Jamaica, where it was about 75 per cent for the same period. However, in the Over-the-Hill area (the predominantly black section of Nassau), the illegitimacy rate was nearly 72 per cent.[73] Many single mothers had numerous children and because of poverty could not care for them properly. Fathers of outside children were not compelled by law to contribute to their maintenance and women therefore were forced to work. While so engaged, their children often wandered the streets and frequently got into trouble.

Opportunities had widened for urban women by the 1930s although employment outside the home was limited. Most women were still housewives;

life for Out Island women had not changed significantly. Increasing economic constraints in the capital, and the development of tourism which provided additional jobs in the public and private sectors, forced more women into the workplace. Nassau was becoming a seasonal resort and winter home for wealthy North Americans and Europeans. These annual visitors hired domestics, particularly women, many of whom trained at the Dundas Civic Centre, opened in 1931 by Governor Charles Dundas, to train blacks as cooks, general household maids and as menial workers in the hotels.[74]

Additionally, black women benefitted from the development of the fledgling straw industry. During the late 1920s, early 1930s, the formative years of the tourist industry, a few straw vendors began to congregate in the 'Park', (Rawson Square) in Central Nassau. Among the early vendors were Estelle, Melissa and Manette Davis, Eunice Demeritte and Rebecca Jarvis from Fox Hill who made articles from sisal.[75] During the 1930s and 1940s, the straw craft industry expanded as vendors from the fruit and vegetable market, led by Albertha Brown, Rebecca Rahming and Eva Adderley began to sell articles made of straw palm. Out Islanders and Over-the-Hill women supplied the plait which was sewn together to make baskets, hats and mats which were sold to tourists.[76] Some straw work was exported. Early dealers in Nassau were Myrtis Thompson, Albertha Brown and Florence Pyfrom. Mrs Pyfrom, a white American, was married to a white Eleutherian, and was an agent for an American hat company. By the mid-1940s, she employed about two hundred black Bahamians in her straw 'factory'.[77]

The majority of Bahamians lacked a tradition of popular organized protest. Favouring a commercially oriented economy based in Nassau, the white mercantile elite neglected the poverty-stricken Out Islands and dominated the House of Assembly, which under the archaic representative system wielded great power including the control of the purse strings. The white minority controlled the legislature by favouring propertied interests, excluding half the population (that is the women) and through a corrupt voting system. Voting by secret ballot was only temporarily introduced in New Providence in 1939.[78] While coloured and black politicians were aware of the injustices, they were too conservative and weak to change the status quo. They also lacked political parties and an effective trade union movement. Moreover, real poverty caused the migration of thousands of Bahamians to Florida between 1911 and 1921 when the overall population of the Bahamas declined by five per cent.[79] Increasing prosperity brought by Prohibition profits and the development of tourism in the 1930s and 1940s delayed any real political change.

The early women's movements in the West Indies took a variety of forms. Women in the Spanish Caribbean perhaps had the most developed organizations and programmes. In the British Caribbean, Women's Self-Help Societies and Home Industries Organizations were the forerunners of 'women organizing in their own interest'.[80] Evidence is scanty for the early women's movement in the Bahamas. However, an oral history source has revealed that there was a Self-Help shop in downtown Nassau which provided an outlet for upper class women to sell their preserves, candies and handwork. Women who sent articles remained anonymous.[81] This indicated that the shop hoped to 'provide income-earning possibilities for gentlewoman who had fallen on reduced circumstances'.[82] A Bahamas Home Industries Association, an offshoot of the Imperial Order of the Daughters of the Empire (IODE) headed by elite ladies existed in the early 1920s and met at Government House. Annie Finlay served as secretary.[83]

As in the British West Indies generally, upper class and coloured and black middle class women focused on charitable organizations and social work. It gave them 'the opportunity for public activity'[84] and also satisfied their sense of *noblesse oblige*. White elite women established the Red Cross Society in 1915 and a decade later organized the Infant Welfare Centre primarily to serve the coloured and black population. Clinics were opened in three areas with the aim of controlling the high mortality rate. Besides treating children, the centres issued supplies of dried milk to mothers who were also given talks and pamphlets on 'mother craft'.[85]

Similarly, Lady Cordeaux, wife of the then Governor, founded the Oleander Club which aimed to train black labouring class women in housewifery skills including cooking, sewing, smocking, crochet and knitting. Among those assisting in the club were members of the coloured middle class such as Ethel Adderley, wife of Alfred F. Adderley, Rita Toote, wife of lawyer and politician Thaddeus Toote, Rowena Eldon, and Mamie Worrell, a coloured American teacher who operated a guest house for black tourists in the thirties.[86]

Coloured middle class leaders who spearheaded charitable works in the thirties were Clarita Toote, and Ethel Adderley. They formed a Ladies Committee which organized relief work in collecting money and clothing for the hurricane victims of Bimini and Grand Bahama in 1935. This charitable work led to the formation of the Christmas Cheer Committee which treated the needy at the end of every year.[87]

There is little evidence of any organized black and coloured social workers organization similar to those formed in Trinidad and Tobago by Audrey Jeffers. There was a Civic League Working Women's Club which was established 'for the improvement of young girls'.[88] It sponsored exhibitions of 'native products' and talks by prominent blacks.

However, several black women, particularly Frances 'Mother' Butler and Lettie Tinker, both of whom had travelled and were exposed to other cultures, were associated with clubs which catered to the social needs of women. They were aware of the new social and cultural consciousness among coloureds and blacks. Mother Butler, on returning to Nassau after living in Miami for some years, founded the Mothers' Club, the chief purpose of which was to collect used clothing and furniture for distribution to the poor, aged and needy

– most of whom had suffered in the 1929 hurricane. As the years passed, the Mothers' Club became a predominantly black and Over-the-Hill institution. A special committee was set up to promote a Christmas treat for the aged. In 1940, the Mothers' Club built its own headquarters in Gaol Alley, off East Street.[89]

Lettie Tinker, wife of Daniel Tinker, a contractor, was employed as the housekeeper of Dr and Mrs Parsons. She travelled with the Parsons to England, Gibraltar and Palestine and lived in England for a number of years. On returning to Nassau, she identified herself with the Oleander Club, joined the Working Women's Club and also founded the Elks Juveniles, a member of Excelsior Temple of Elks.[90]

The early women's organizations did not fight for increased political rights. There is little evidence that the United States and British feminist movements during the late nineteenth and early twentieth centuries influenced Bahamian women as it did Cuban, Puerto Rican and some British Caribbean women. In the Bahamas, women took a mainly passive role in the fledgling trade union movement which began in Nassau in 1936. No Audrey Jeffers as in Trinidad, or Amy Bailey and Mary Morris Knibb as in Jamaica, emerged to spearhead the struggle through social and labour organizations for increased political rights and participation for women during the 1920s and 1930s. However, it is possible that women participated in the 1938 political demonstration led by Milo Butler in support of the secret ballot and were certainly among the rioting crowd during the Nassau riot of 1942.[91]

It seems that some coloured and black women were acutely aware of racial discrimination and social injustices in Bahamian society. Culturally, this was highlighted by Meta Davis Cumberbatch, a black middle class Trinidadian who had studied at the Royal College of Music in London and moved to Nassau with her husband in 1927. During the early and mid 1930s Meta Cumberbatch gave piano recitals in London and Nassau and combined classical work with West Indian folk songs. She created a new feeling of black pride and fostered through her piano teaching a new cultural awareness among coloureds and blacks.[92]

There is little evidence of black women sympathizers of Garveyism and the Pan African Movement or of participation in the United Negro Improvement Association, a branch of which was established in Nassau in the 1920s.[93] Apparently there were over a thousand members of the UNIA in Nassau in 1921. However, it appears that the more aggressive elements of the population had migrated and belonged to the Miami branch of the UNIA which encouraged female participation and leadership.[94]

Bahamians, and women in particular, remained unpoliticized until the early 1950s. Women generally accepted the status quo and it was not until the mid-1950s that the Women's Suffrage Movement was founded. It allied itself with the Progressive Liberal Party, the Bahamas' first political party, established in 1953 to fight for the rights of Bahamians. While Jamaicans and Trinidadians won universal suffrage in 1944 and 1946 respectively, it was not until 1961 that Bahamian women were granted the vote. They voted for the first time in the 1962 general elections.[95]

This study demonstrates that an analysis of the role of Bahamian women is essential to the understanding of Bahamian society. While showing that many of the experiences of women differed from that of men, it reinforces the dominance of race, colour and class in shaping Bahamian society. The same forces which divided the society also separated women of different classes. In the Bahamian context, however, racism was more pervasive and severe. As Colin Hughes has noted, '... it is clear that in 1900 Bahamians formed a single society deeply divided into two antagonistic groups by racial differences. So it was too in 1950...'[96]

Women's roles were influenced by general trends in social development. Poverty, which characterized the Bahamian society until the 1920s, differentiated the white elite there from the plantocracy in the British Caribbean. It also impacted on females as it drew elite women out of the home into the workplace much earlier than in most British West Indian colonies. Similarly, the neglect of education by the reactionary Nassau elite also barred most coloureds, black middle class and Out Island women from obtaining a secondary education. Because of discriminatory policies, fewer opportunities were available to coloureds, blacks and Out Islanders, especially women.

Similarly, heightened racial consciousness in the years following World War I and during the 1920s affected Bahamians, many of whom were admirers of Garvey. However, no strong leadership emerged from among the weak coloured and black middle class to mobilize the movement.

Prohibition in the United States profoundly affected Bahamian society. The profits it generated increased the wealth, power and influence mainly of the mercantile elite and created a new monied class which was mostly white. A few coloured and black middle class families benefitted from bootlegging profits to provide higher education for their sons and daughters. More important, however, was the emphasis placed on wealth and commercial enterprise. Most whites, both male and female, preferred shopkeeping and clerking in banks to higher education. After the 1920s, social distinctions between whites widened. Class was now distinguishable by wealth as well as by colour.

Racism, however, fanned by an increasing number of American visitors and American investment, grew worse during the 1930s. While new positions in offices and business houses in downtown Nassau were becoming available to whites, including women, coloureds and blacks, especially women, were debarred from the more prestigious jobs because of their colour, despite the fact that some had obtained a secondary education. Gender issues were overshadowed by racism.

The failure of women to organize was a reflection of the racially divided society that remained virtually unpoliticized until the 1950s. The upheavals during the 1930s in the British Caribbean which paved the way for political change had little impact on the Bahamas. Women (and most men) lacked the will and the necessary educational background and outside exposure to lead a labour or political movement. An elite woman such as Mary Moseley, who had received a sound secondary education and had travelled to Britain during the First World War, might have been capable of leading a feminist movement. However, typical of her type, she was too conservative and too bound by her class to offer such leadership.

It was not until the effects of World War II were felt and after large numbers of Out Islanders had migrated to Nassau, that the Bahamas Islands were to experience serious unrest and the forces of change began to mobilize. Black and coloured women soon joined the struggle for the right to vote and for majority rule.

Notes

1. See especially Lucille Mathurin Mair, 'A Historical Study of Women in Jamaica 1655-1844' (Unpublished PhD dissertation, University of the West Indies, Jamaica 1974); 'The Arrivals of Black Women', *Jamaica Journal*, 9: 2-3 (1975): 2-7; *The Rebel Woman in the British West Indies During Slavery* (Kingston, Jamaica: 1975); 'Reluctant Matriarchs', *Savacou 13* (1977): 1-6; Edward Kamau Brathwaite, 'Submerged Mothers'. *Jamaica Journal*, 9: 2-3 (1975): 48-9; *Nanny, Sam Sharpe and the Struggle for People's Liberation* (Kingston, Jamaica: 1977); 'Women of the Caribbean During Slavery. Elsa Goveia Memorial Lecture', University of the West Indies, Barbados, 1984; Barbara Bush, *Slave Women in Caribbean Society, 1650-1838* (London, Kingston, Bloomington: 1990); Barry Higman, 'African and Creole Slave Family Patterns in Trinidad', *Journal of Family History* 3 (Summer 1978): 163-80; 'Domestic Service in Jamaica Since 1750'. In *Trade, Government and Society in Caribbean History, 1700-1920*, edited by Barry Higman (Kingston: 1983) 117-138; *Slave Populations of The British Caribbean, 1807-1834* (Baltimore: 1984); Michael Craton, *Searching For the Invisible Man: Slaves and Plantation Life in Jamaica* (Cambridge, MA: 1978); Marietta Morrissey, *Slave Women in the New World: Gender Stratification in the Caribbean*, (Kansas: 1989); Hilary Beckles, *Natural Rebels: A Social History of Enslaved Black Women in Barbados* (London: 1989).
2. Erna Brodber, 'Afro-Jamaican Women at the Turn of the Century', *Social and Economic Studies*, 35 (Sept. 1986) : 23-50. Ibid, 'Perceptions of Caribbean Women' (Cave Hill: 1982); Rhoda E. Reddock, 'Women, Labour and Struggle in 20th Century Trinidad and Tobago: 1898-1960' (Unpublished PhD thesis, Institute of Social Studies, The Hague, 1984);

Joycelin Massiah, 'Employed Women in Barbados: A Demographic Profile 1946-1970' (Cave Hill:1984); Joan French and Honor Ford-Smith, 'Woman and Organization in Jamaica 1900-1944' (The Hague: 1985); Blanca Silvestrini, 'Women and Resistance: Her Story in Contemporary Caribbean History' (Mona: 1990) Elsa Goveia Memorial Lecture, Mona, 1989.

3. See especially Cleveland W. Eneas, *Bain Town* (Nassau: 1976) and Saunders, 'Social History' (Unpublished PhD thesis, University of Waterloo, Canada, 1985).

4. See Gail Saunders, 'Talk to Woman '80 Exhibition on Mother Butler and Meta Davis Cumberbatch', *Tribune*, June 10, 1980; *Ibid*, Thelma Gibson, *Tribune*, June 17, 1980; *Ibid*, Nurse Alice Hill Jones, *Tribune*, July 1980; see also a series of articles in the *Nassau Guardian* prepared by DAWN (Developing Alternatives for Women Now) on women who were involved in or could recall events leading to the enfranchisement of Bahamian females in 1962. The articles appeared in the *Nassau Guardian* on Sept. 28, Nov. 5, Nov. 19, Dec. 17 and 21, 1987 and Jan. 13 and 28, 1988. See also, Kim Outten 'A Chronological History of Women's Suffrage in The Bahamas', in the series Aspects of Bahamian History, Department of Archives in the *Nassau Guardian* Nov. 23, 1987.

5. Bridget Brereton, 'General Problems and Issues in Studying the History of Women', in *Gender in Caribbean Development*, ed. by Patricia Mohammed and Catherine Shepherd (Mona: 1988), 123.

6. Rosina Wiltshire-Brodber, 'Gender, Race and Class in the Caribbean', in *Gender in Caribbean Development*, 142.

7. G.J.H. Northcroft, *Sketches of Summerland Giving Some Account of Nassau and the Bahama Islands* (Nassau:1912), 55.

8. Saunders, 'Social History', 67-69. See also Northcroft, 54 and L.D. Powles, *The Land of The Pink Pearl* (London: 1888), 127 and 310.

9. See Bridget Brereton, *Race Relations in Colonial Trinidad 1870-1900* (Cambridge: 1979), 59.

10. J.H. Stark, *History of and Guide to the Bahamas* (New York: 1891), 177.

11. L.D. Powles, *The Land of The Pink Pearl*, 129-30.

12. Neville Chamberlain's Diary, 1890-98, Fri. Nov. 28, 1890, NC 3/2/1. See Saunders, 'Social History', 33-5.

13. Saunders, 'Social History', 69.

14. Cleveland Eneas, *Bain Town* (Nassau: 1976), 17.

15. Appendix to Votes of the House of Assembly, 1911, Nassau, 191 I., 164-65.

16. The Gym Tennis Club Souvenir Programme, Historical Day, Aug. 22, 1981 (Nassau: 1981), 9.6. Saunders, 'Social History', 347 and 536.

17. Saunders, 'Social History', 89. See also Shea to Ripon, April 29, 1893 C023/236/256-263.

18. Charles L. Edwards, *Bahama Songs and Stories* (1895. Reprint. New York: 1942), 17.

19. E. Clement Bethel, 'Music in The Bahamas: Its Roots, Development and Personality' (Unpublished MA thesis, University of California, Los Angeles, 1978), 125-6.

20. Powles, *Land of The Pink Pearl*, 147 and Northcroft, *Sketches of Summerland*, 66.

21. Powles, *Land of The Pink Pearl*, 147.
22. Northcroft, *Sketches of Summerland*, 88.
23. *Nassau Quarterly Mission Papers (NQMP)*, 2,1886, Sept. 1, 51.
24. David Lowenthal, *West Indian Societies* (Oxford: 1972), 115.
25. Bethel, 'Music in the Bahamas, its Roots', 55-56. See also Amelia Defries, *In a Forgotten Colony: Being Some Studies in Nassau and at Grand Bahama During 1916* (Nassau: 1917), 107-08.
26. Saunders, 'Social History', 81. See also *Bahamas Almanack, 1901*.
27. Etienne Dupuch, *Tribune Story* (London: 1967), 25.
28. Taped interview with Miriam Dean, Nassau, October 27, 1990.
29. Lowenthal, *West Indian Societies*, 105.
30. Girls under 21 needed the written consent of their father, mother (if the father was dead) or a guardian. An Act Relating to Marriages. 4 of 1908
31. Saunders, 'Social History', 92.
32. Ibid.
33. Eneas, *Bain Town*, 45.
34. Ibid., 41 and 45.
35. Powles, *Land of The Pink Pearl*, 108-109: and Powles to Sec. of State for the Colonies, July 29, 1886, CO23/229/625.
36. Howard Johnson, *The Bahamas in Slavery and Freedom* (Kingston: 1991), 55-68; 84-109.
37. *Almanack*, 1901.
38. Unskilled females were paid between nine pence and a shilling a day. Unskilled male workers were paid between one shilling and nine pence and 2 shillings a day. Saunders 'Social History', 115. See also Encl. in Haynes Smith to Chamberlain, Aug. 15, 1896, CO23/244/394.
39. Saunders, 'Social History', 98.
40. Northcroft, *Sketches of Summerland*, 67.
41. Eneas, *Bain Town*, 37.
42. Eneas, *Bain Town*, 17.
43. Saunders, 'Social History', 186.
44. Ibid., 187.
45. Bahamas Medical Reports 1925. File 37318 CO23/347.
46. Clifford to Ormsby-Gore Dec. 15, 1936 CO23/593.
47. Klaus de Albuquerque and Jerome L. McElroy, 'Bahamian Labour Migration 1901-1963', *New West Indian Guide*, 60: 3 and 4 (1986), 177-78.
48. *Report on The Census of The Bahama Islands*, taken on April 24, 1921 (Nassau: 1921).
49. Seven hundred Bahamian men served overseas during World War I. In 1918, after America's entry into the war about 3000 Bahamian men were recruited as labourers in Charleston, South Carolina for between 3 to 6 months by the Mason and Hangar Contracting Company, one of the largest firms of its kind in the United States. See Saunders, 'Social History', 214.
50. Taped interview with Mrs Enid A. Boyce, November 26, 1990.
51. Miss Harriet E.T. Sutton was appointed Librarian at the Nassau Public Library in 1924, *Blue Book 1924*.
52. Ruth Bowe, 'Mary Moseley 1878-1960', *Journal of the Bahamas Historical Society*, II: 1 (Oct. 1980), 20.

53. R. Reddock, *Women, Labour and Struggle*, 290-91.
54. Saunders, 'Social History', 275 and 354. It was estimated in the 1943 Census, the first taken since 1931, that 7,923 whites out of a total population of 68,846 lived in the Bahamas. Of that number 3950 or about half resided in New Providence. *Report on The Census of The Bahama Islands* 25 April, 1943, (Nassau: 1943).
55. *Bahamas Blue Books*, 1920-1921.
56. Saunders, 'Social History', 217.
57. Interview with E.B. North, March 2, 1991.
58. Allardyce to Grindle, Private, Oct. 5, 1918, C023/283/205.
59. Saunders, 'Social History', 253.
60. *Bahamas Blue Book*, 1927.
61. Interview with E. Basil North and Audrey North, July 31, 1984. See also Hughes to Geddes, June 26, 1922, C023/292.
62. Interview, *Ibid*.
63. Saunders, 'Talk to Woman '80 Exhibition', *Tribune*, July 8, 1980.
64. Report on The Public Health and on Medical Conditions in New Providence, Bahama Islands by Sir Wilfred W.O. Beveridge, 1927, London: Medical and Sanitary Reports 1924-1925. Encl. Cordeaux to Amery, March 31, 1926, C023/297.
65. Colbert Williams, *The Methodist Contribution to Education in The Bahamas* (Gloucester: 1982), 67.
66. Clifford to Conliffe-Lister, January 29, 1934, Conf., C023/504.
67. Saunders, 'Social History', 360.
68. Randol Fawkes, *The Faith That Moved The Mountain* (Nassau: 1979), 15-16.
69. See chapter 3 of this book. See also *Report on The Census of The Bahama Islands*, April 26, 1931 (Nassau: 1931).
70. Saunders, 'Social History', 330.
71. The Immoral Traffic Act. 4 Geo V., c. 13.
72. Report of the Commission on Venereal Diseases (Nassau: 1918), 23.
73. Report to Enquire into the Establishment of an Industrial School, Jan. 1923 (Nassau: 1923), 18. Encl. Cordeaux to Thomas, March 12, 1924 C023/295.
74. *Tribune*, June 13, 1931.
75. Kim Outten, 'A Brief Historical Review of Straw Work in The Bahamas', in Aspects Of Bahamian History, Department of Archives, *Nassau Guardian*, March 23, 1989.
76. Saunders, 'Social History', 388.
77. Kim Outten.
78. 3 Geo 6 c. 40. In order to vote, a man had to be over 21 and own land to the value of £2 8s in New Providence and not less than £1 4s on an Out Island.
79. See *Report on the Census of tne Bahama Islands* 1921.
80. Rhoda Reddock, 'Feminism and Feminist Thought: An Historical Overview', *Gender In Caribbean Development*, 55 and 66.
81. Taped interview with Mrs E.A. Boyce.
82. Reddock, 'Feminism and Feminist Thought', 66.
83. *Tribune*, Sept. 28, 1921.
84. Reddock, 'Feminism and Feminist Thought', 65.
85. Report on The Public Health by Sir Wilfred Beveridge, 1927, 37-8.

86. Taped interview with Mrs Ivy Mackey, December 6, 1990.
87. Saunders, 'Social History', 363. See also taped interview with Rowena Eldon, May 3, 1983.
88. *Tribune*, November 14, 1925.
89. Saunders, 'Talk to Woman '80 Exhibition on Mother Butler', *Tribune*, June 10, 1980.
90. *Tribune*, Nov. 14, 1925.
91. Saunders, 'The 1942 Riot in Nassau. A Demand for Change?', *The Journal of Caribbean History*, 20:2 (1985-6), 122.
92. Saunders, 'Social History', 363.
93. *Tribune*, Aug.1, 1925.
94. Robert A. Hill (ed.), The Marcus Garvey and Universal Negro Improvement Association Papers (Berkeley: 1984), Vol. III, 247.
95. Doris Johnson, *The Quiet Revolution in the Bahamas* (Nassau: 1972), 39 and 171.
96. Colin Hughes, *Race and Politics in The Bahamas* (St Lucia, Queensland: 1981), 30.

3

A Historical Sketch of Family Life in the Bahamas

The scarcity of pertinent literature and records especially for the earlier periods makes it difficult to present an in-depth history of family life in the Bahamas. This is compounded by the fact that family patterns varied among the different classes of the two main racial groups in the Bahamas. The family can be defined as a social group characterized by common residence, economic co-operation and reproduction. Persons in a family are often (but not necessarily) united by ties of marriage, blood or adoption, interact with one another in their respective social positions as mother and father, son and daughter, brother and sister, and create and maintain a common culture.[1]

The family group should not be confused with:
- (a) household – because there may be boarders who share a common residence in the household.
- (b) kindred – although related, kindred may be resident in several households.
- (c) marriages – because marriage is between a man and woman and the parent-child relationship might be absent from the marriage pair. Additionally, there need not be a legal marriage in the family group. A cohabiting pair of adults might head a family.[2]

Information from historical sources about the Lucayans ('Island People'), a sub-culture of the Arawak speaking Neo-Indians who had migrated from South America into the Greater Antilles, is limited. It is believed that the Lucayans were the aboriginal Bahamians and that they migrated into the Bahamas between 500 and 600 AD. It seems that Lucayans lived in family units and that villages comprised largely kin groups or clans. In the more sophisticated Taino culture of the Greater Antilles social divisions were strictly demarcated being divided into different classes – the aristocrats (nitainos), commoners (quajiros) slaves (naborias). Each village was headed by a headman or hereditary chief (cacique). In the Bahamas, there were no such strict social divisions, but there were caciques.[3]

The successor to the chief was not his son, but usually the eldest son of the eldest sister, or other sons of that sister. Failing that, the sons of other sisters took over as head of the village. If there were none, the brother inherited this position. The son of the cacique was the last choice.[4]

Among the male headed Lucayan society, monogamy was common as most of the ordinary people could not afford to support more than one wife. Some of the caciques had several wives. One chief named Behechio in the Greater Antilles was said to have had 30 wives.[5] It was forbidden for a man to marry a close relative, for example a sister or daughter of a sister or nephew.

There was a type of formalized wedding which was attended by those within the class of those being married. It was said that at a marriage of the common people, 'guests had a chance to try the bride first'. In the Greater Antilles (Hispaniola and Cuba especially) Peter Martyr observed that 'a marriageable woman who has granted her favours and prostituted herself to the greatest number is reputed to be the most generous and honourable of all'.[6]

Additionally, chiefs in the Greater Antilles, offered their wives to important visitors. For example, when Columbus was received by Guacanagari on his second voyage, the latter offered his wife and twelve naked girls to show his hospitality.[7]

Family life was reflected in daily village life, where everyone shared property in common. Farming was a joint activity of males, females and older children, while fishing and hunting were almost exclusively male activities. Men also made pottery and executed other crafts. Women were responsible for food preparation, cooking and other domestic chores, in addition to plaiting and weaving. They seemed to have taken a greater part in the bringing up of the children than the men.[8]

The Bahama Islands were depopulated of its Lucayan population after the arrival of Columbus in 1492. By 1513, there were few if any Lucayans living in the archipelago.

The English who settled in Eleuthera in 1648 seemed to have come in family units – the nuclear type with man/woman/children.[9] Families seemed to have been father-centered or patriarchal units knit primarily by the marriage bond. Little is known about the black slaves brought by the early settlers. From early slave regulations, it seemed that the dominant (both numerically and politically) white population encouraged their slaves to be instructed in the Christian religion. Some may naturally have lived in family units, or may have been encouraged by the clergy to do so.

The white Loyalists who settled in the Bahamas between 1783 and 1789, like the English settlers, came mainly in family units – the nuclear type – bound usually by a legalized marriage. Charles Farquharson, a Loyalist of Scottish descent lived on his plantation at Watlings Island (later San

Salvador) with his wife, two daughters, Christianna and Mary and one son, James.[10] It was not uncommon however for white married men to have casual relationships with slave women. Some even took slave women on as mistresses and recognized their mulatto children.[11] Miscegenation was most common in Eleuthera, New Providence, Crooked Island, Acklins Long Cay and Abaco. Nassau, the administrative and commercial centre, naturally had more whites in its population, and numerically had the highest number of mulattoes at the time of emancipation.

Miscegenation often occurred when a planter lived on his own either through death or abandonment by his wife. In most cases mulatto children were born of white fathers and black slave women. However, although rare, it was not unheard of for white women to have a child by a slave.[12]

It is possible that the American slaves brought over to the Bahamas by the Loyalists profoundly affected the Bahamian slave family. American historian, Herbert Gutman, attacked the traditionally held view that the black family, both before and after the Civil War, was disorganized, unstable and matriarchal. He contends that the normal American slave family was not matrifocal but was a stable nuclear unit, the two-parent household.[13] Barry Higman in his study of slave families from three different British West Indian colonies – Barbados, Jamaica and Trinidad – reconsidered the West Indian family along the lines similar to those of Gutman in the United States. Higman's conclusion, though guarded, was that the image of the 'slave family as matrifocal, unstable and promiscuous fits the Caribbean no better than North America'.[14] Likewise, Michael Craton, who compared slave populations on a sugar plantation in Worthy Park, Jamaica and the Rolle slaves on Exuma, argued that the Rolle data suggested an occurrence of the nuclear family at least twice as high as in populations studied by Higman.[15] This author analyzed the five Returns of Registration of Slaves (Bahamas) for 1822 to 1834, for the Farquharson Estate, Watlings Island and for evidence of family structure among slaves in the Bahamas. It seems from the data studied that family units did exist. The most common family household consisted of a man, his 'wife' and their children in a nuclear family setting. It is clear that the simple family household type accounted for the greater part of the slave population at the Farquharson Estate[16] and among the Bahamian slave population in general. Some slaves had mates on other plantations. On September 17, 1832, Farquharson recorded: 'sent out Diana to John Dickson to work and to be a wife for his Cuffey as it appears that she is already with child for Cuffey ....'[17]

Slave families probably ate, sang, danced, enjoyed story-telling, worshipped and celebrated Christmas together. A special dance would be held by the slaves at Christmas or the day after Christmas. Farquharson wrote on December 26, 1832, 'Some of our people gone abroad to see some of their friends and some at home amusing themselves in their own way threw (sic) the day, but all of them at home in the evening and had a grand dance and keep it up until near day light'.[18]

It must not be forgotten, however, that slave families were separated by sale, and that slaves especially women were sometimes brutalized and abused by their slave masters.

Not much is known about the immediate post-emancipation black family. From the studies made of slave families, between the first and last registration of slaves, there was a noticeable decline in the more 'nuclear' type of family. Both Higman and Craton argue that the decline was probably caused by a drop in the African population. In the first slave generation, the African population tended to form 'elementary nuclear families'. It was the second slave generation that began to establish extended families. Kinship networks expanded in subsequent generations and slaves increasingly practised exogamy. Higman also noticed from his study of the creole (that is, slaves born in America or the West Indies) slave family pattern in Trinidad, that a matrifocal tendency was noticed as the creole population grew. Higman asserted that the norm for creoles remained the extended family, although this was difficult to achieve outside the large plantations. Therefore, the nuclear family was predominant in most rural areas.[19] Craton agreed that Africans were more inclined toward family formation than creole slaves in the Bahamas.[20]

By the mid-nineteenth and early twentieth centuries, marriage influenced by the church was one of the main factors separating the different classes. The society was divided into the three-tier social/racial structure with the white elite at the top, the black labouring class at the bottom and the intermediate coloured class in the middle stratum. As in the British West Indies generally, monogamy was the ideal for all classes, but according to David Lowenthal, 'each (class) approaches it by a different route and to a different degree'.[21] Formal marriage was the norm for the upper class and coloured middle class which emulated the mating and family patterns of the elite.

Girls were expected to marry young, usually between the ages of 15 and 17, after a long and formal courtship. When a young man fell in love with a young lady, the couple courted for months but neither the girl nor her parents took it seriously until the suitor had written a proposal letter addressed to her parents. The letter, if accepted, meant that the couple were formally engaged and it was a binding agreement. Weddings, as in England and in most British colonies, customarily took place in church with the bride dressed in white, even if, as in some cases, (not all that rare) she was pregnant. She was usually accompanied by several bridesmaids in a ceremony that was followed by a reception generally held at the home of the bride, where sandwiches, cake, ice cream and soft drinks were served. Liquor was available for the men only, as women did not drink, at least not in public.[22]

After marriage, women were expected to have many children whom they cared for along with other housekeeping chores. Intermarriage within the Nassau circle of the white elite was common. The choice of partners was limited by the desire to keep the race pure, by the small number of white families, and the lack of suitable white immigrant families. Coloureds, on the other hand, although expected to marry within their class, could not marry close relatives.[23]

For coloured men, as for the elite, a double standard existed. Provided that they cared for their families, it was not uncommon, or overly frowned upon, for coloured men to have 'sweethearts' or mistresses, by whom they usually had several children. For middle class coloured women, an affair outside the marriage was scandalous. As for the white elite, illegitimacy carried searing social stigma.[24] An illustrative case was the scandal which shook Nassau in 1893. Mr Stephen A. Dillet, the respectable coloured First Mate of the Lighthouse Tender, discovered that his 25 year old daughter, Elizabeth, was pregnant by the Postmaster of the Bahamas, Mr James C. Smith, a fair-skinned, respectable and esteemed coloured man. Stephen Dillet insisted that an investigation be made, and this was duly held before the Governor and the Executive Council.[25] While Mr Smith was willing to settle the matter quietly like a gentleman, he was not prepared to marry Miss Dillet. In fact, when the scandal broke, he was courting a Yorkshire girl who was visiting Nassau at the time, and whom he married later in the same year.[26] Three years later, in December 1896, he was appointed Assistant Postmaster at Freetown, Sierra Leone. Miss Dillet, on the other hand, was taken from New York, where her father found her in a 'House of Refuge', to London and vowed not to return to Nassau as 'she refused to face the shame'.[27]

Among the black masses, such an uproar would not have occurred. To the coloured middle class, illegitimacy was immoral and irresponsible, but to the black labouring population of the West Indies and the Bahamas, 'illegitimacy and the mother-centered home' were not 'symptoms of social organization'. They were 'accepted features of folk life'.[28]

Monogamy was the norm for the black working class, but marriage did not necessarily precede the birth of children. Very often a woman might have the children first and afterwards enter into a 'common law marriage' without a formal ceremony. In the case of such a consensual union, the woman might own the house and the household probably included her children by a former partner. Marriage might follow, but not until late in life. Marriage gave the urban working class an 'established position in the community'.[29]

Very little stigma, however, was attached to separation and illegitimacy. Anglican priests wrote often of 'the looseness' of the marriage ties and one went so far as to say that 'husbands and wives separate far more easily than they marry'.[30] A married man might live with another man's wife and have a family of illegitimate children. Women might leave their husbands and emigrate to the southern United States and there 're-marry after the American fashion'.[31] The man left behind often found a woman to live with and bring up a third family. According to Bishop Shedden, bigamy was 'far from uncommon in the Bahamas'. He too blamed it on the emigration to Key West and other parts of Florida, where men often formed other relationships or took other spouses. 'Fidelity to marriage vows and the sense of marriage obligations', according to Shedden, were 'far from characteristic of the Bahamas'.[32] No shame was felt among the blacks about illegitimacy and the 'outside child'. Men and women living in consensual unions and raising children were accepted by their community. Usually the child would be given the surname of its father, but not always. Nor did all homes have men at their heads. The matrifocal family was common and, as Dr Eneas pointed out, in Bain Town, a black suburb of Nassau, women were the stronger factor in most of the families, and 'the cementing agent that held them together'. He added that the 'father image' was noticeably lacking in his neighbourhood. In Bain Town, besides, there was a kinship system that extended beyond the usual nuclear family. Every woman was an aunt, 'full of authority', and each had the right to discipline every child in the neighbourhood.[33] Compared to other parts of the West Indies, the percentage of illegitimate births was not high in the Bahamas.

The family unit was an important facet in the Out Island settlements which comprised three types – the all white settlements such as Spanish Wells, Cherokee Sound, Man-O-War Cay and Hope Town, the all black settlements, such as those on Long Cay, Rum Bay, Cat Island, Mayaguana and Andros, and at the bi-racial settlements such as Harbour Island and Green Turtle Cay. It seems from the available evidence that the most common household was the nuclear type. Adult children usually remained in their natal household until marriage. In all-white settlements, such as Man-O-War and Hope Town, it was customary for girls to marry very young, between fourteen and sixteen, but sometimes as early as thirteen. In bi-racial settlements, it seems that whites married a little older, usually in their late teens and early 20s. In the case of very young girls the groom was often considerably older than his bride. In all types of settlements, couples built their family home before marrying.[34]

The majority of whites were endogamous, marrying within the community to someone they had known all their lives.[35] It was not uncommon for the couple to be closely related. In fact first cousins often married in Hope Town, and second were considered to be 'distant family' in Green Turtle Cay. An Anglican priest remarked of the marriage patterns at Hope Town in 1897, 'They do not go for the most part beyond the settlement as such names as Russell, Roberts, Albury and Malone occur again and again'.[36] Close intermarriage was also common at Spanish Wells. Tenaciously retaining their racial integrity, the Spanish Wellians, though themselves limited in number, persistently intermarried with sometimes disastrous results.[37]

Blacks, who usually married later than whites, considered it taboo to marry a kinsman and therefore sought wives in another village. Blacks rarely married relatives, and even then, such a marriage was more likely among coloured Bahamians than among blacks.[38]

Courtship for whites and blacks on the Out Islands was formal and similar to the custom in Nassau. A man on an Out Island, if he liked a girl, would consult his parents for their views about his intended and the girl's parents requesting visiting rights. If the suitor was illiterate, he would employ a competent scribe to write his love letters. Proposals were expected to describe to 'his would-be-betrothed all the points in her moral character which he particularly admires'.[39] Initially, virginity was highly valued. After some months, the man would send an engagement letter and ring to the girl's family. A courtship could last as long as three years during which a greater degree of sexual intimacy was permitted.[40] The wedding, often hastened by a pregnancy, was held in a church and the reception at the home of the bride's parents who hosted the celebration.

Marriage gave both the man and woman a new status in the community. Large families were normal for both races in the late nineteenth and early twentieth centuries. Children were proof of virility in the men and fertility in the women; they were also regarded as an economic asset. The difficulty of providing enough food for a sizeable family was overcome by the fact that the children provided a larger workforce to the peasant lifestyle. They helped with domestic tasks and also assisted in the fields. They were companions to their mothers often establishing close relationships with them, and were believed to be an insurance for old age.[41]

Divorce, which was almost impossible to obtain, was virtually unknown in all Out Island settlements.[42] Marriage was considered to be permanent and final. In many instances, husbands left temporarily in order to find work, and even if they stayed away for several years, this was not considered a step towards divorce or a permit for promiscuity. If a couple separated by mutual agreement and lived apart, they were still considered by their community to be married.

'Outside' or illegitimate children, so common in the British West Indies, were rare in all-white and bi-racial communities in the Out Islands.[43] In black communities illegitimacy was more common, but not the norm. Otterbein commented in the late 1960s on the low rate of illegitimacy reported for Cooper's Town, Abaco, an all black community. An explanation for this is that the majority of people over eighteen were married.

Women with illegitimate children often had difficulty finding a husband and were considered 'second rate'.[44] If such a woman married, the 'outside child' might be raised by either her mother or another close female relative. Illegitimate children were not usually brought to a new union, at least in the only settlement extensively studied. Some families therefore were headed by women.

In other cases, the man moved in with the woman and her children by another mate and became responsible for the family. This consensual union or common-law marriage, although common in many areas of the Caribbean and the New World, was unusual in the Bahama Out Islands, and was likely to be practised only by those who could not marry or remarry. The two important mating patterns for the blacks were marriage and extra-residential unions. Very often, during the courtship, the fiancée became pregnant. Rather than co-habit with her consensually, the man waited until his house was finished before marrying, and the first child was consequently often born out of wedlock.[45]

A young man was expected to have premarital sex in black communities. Once married, he could have love affairs, and was expected to do so, often establishing an extra-residential union with a single, separated or widowed woman. This double standard of sexual morality, characteristic of Caribbean family systems,[46] insisted that the woman remained a virgin until she had intercourse with her fiancé, and after marriage to remain faithful to her husband. If she was unfaithful, and it was discovered, the husband often left her.

The formal commitment to monogamy, the predominance of marriage and the stigma attached to illegitimacy, were no doubt influenced by the church. The early advent of the Anglican, Methodist and, to a lesser extent, the Baptist churches in the Bahamian Out Islands was significant. Each tried to inculcate ideas of Protestant morality in its members. The church was very important in the lives of everyone in the three types of settlements.[47]

Several factors affected family life during the four decades between World War I and the middle of the 1960s. Emigration of Bahamians to the southern United States in search of more lucrative jobs, especially to Florida, increased during the First World War and took a toll on Bahamian family life. Likewise, emigration from the Out Islands into Nassau caused the dislocation of the family.

Despite a healthy birthrate, the Bahamas' population, especially on Cat Island and Nassau, between 1911 and 1921 decreased by 2913 or 5.27 per cent.[48] The sex ratio was severely affected. Females in the overall population of 53,031 in 1921 outnumbered males by 5451. Married females exceeded married males by 928. Many husbands were presumably absent from the colony. The proportion of widows in 1921 also was higher than usual, there being four widows to every widower. Women, who had traditionally been the backbone of the Bahamian family especially in the area of farming, took on even greater responsibilities and more diverse occupations. In Nassau, more women worked, especially black women in the domestic field. Some white elite and coloured middle class women joined the civil service as clerks or as wireless operators. Some white women owned dry goods shops while others were employed as shop assistants, caterers, fancy shell workers, publishers, librarians and private school teachers. Coloured women found occupations as nurses, dressmakers, stenographers, music teachers and public school teachers.[49] The Governor commented in 1918 that 'with few exceptions the local youth is past praying for. The young women have much higher sense of responsibility'.[50] In fact between 1914 and 1915, more girls were receiving a secondary education in private schools than boys. The majority of women still remained housewives, but by the end of the war it was no longer taboo for a woman to have a high school education and to work outside the home.

The 1920s saw a general decline in the traditional agricultural pursuits and in sponge fishing. Influenced by large revenues accumulated from bootlegging, and the investment brought by the land boom, the House of Assembly concentrated its efforts on developing tourist amenities in Nassau, while adopting an indifferent attitude to planning a constructive agricultural policy to assist the majority of the population still living on the Out Islands.

While expansion was taking place in New Providence and so many significant improvements were being made, the Out Islands remained almost forgotten. Poverty, compounded by natural disasters, increased, and migration from the Out Islands to Nassau continued especially after the passage of the 1924 US Immigration Act. Between 1921 and 1931 New Providence's population increased by 6,781 or 52.3 per cent.[51] Whereas less than a quarter of the total population lived in New Providence in 1921, ten years later the proportion had risen to a third. This trend put more pressure on the already unsatisfactory state of public amenities in Nassau.

Social problems in the capital therefore intensified during the decade, despite improvements there. The result of internal migration and the effects of bootlegging on the capital were unemployment and underemployment, crime, juvenile delinquency, increased social drinking and the growth of prostitution and illegitimacy.[52]

Family life was definitely affected by migration and Prohibition. As early as 1923 a commission was appointed to enquire into the establishment of an Industrial or Reformatory School. Its report and numerous newspaper accounts revealed that juvenile vagrancy and crime were common in Nassau. Drinking and the use of bad language were also on the increase. Between August 1921 and February 1923, 112 juvenile offenders, ranging from ages nine to fourteen, had been brought before the Magistrate's Court charged with larceny and breaches of the Vagrancy Act. About 20 of the boys were habitual offenders and gave the police constant trouble. There was a similar number of female offenders and troublemakers. A letter to the *Nassau Guardian* in September 1922 commented on the problem of drinking among teenagers and women. Vandalism was also increasing. While most of the young people, particularly the boys, were from Nassau, a great number, especially the girls, came from the Out Islands, with or without their families. In search of a fortune in the newly prosperous capital, some of the girls, aged between sixteen and eighteen, often rented a room in a disreputable area. Some shared with other girls, and in order to make ends meet, or to supplement their earnings, they turned to prostitution.[53]

Interrelated causes and effects were an increase in poverty, illegitimacy, the lack of parental control and the influence of bootlegging. Many children appearing in the Magistrate's Court were illegitimate, and came from single parent homes. The rate of illegitimacy in 1922 for the whole colony was about 30 per cent.[54] In comparison to some other Caribbean colonies, such as Jamaica, where it was about 75 per cent for the same period, the Bahamas' rate was not excessive. However, in the southern district of New Providence, that is Over-the-Hill, the illegitimacy rate was nearly 72 per cent.[55] The mother almost invariably had several children, and often was in 'such a destitute condition' that she could not care for them properly. Fathers of 'outside children' were not compelled by law to contribute towards their maintenance.

Numerous children, described as 'waifs and strays', were simply left by emigrating parents with relatives or friends in Nassau. They themselves were very poor, and were therefore unable to care properly for the children. Those Out Islanders who remained in Nassau did not always register their children in school, and they subsequently took to the streets. Truancy was common, both in Nassau and the Out Islands.

During the early years of the Depression, the majority of the Bahamas' population on the Out Islands suffered severe hardship and poverty. The failure of traditional industries and the unusual succession of hurricanes which hit the archipelago between 1929 and 1932 accelerated the flow from the Out Islands into the capital. Despite the prolonged prosperity brought by Prohibition, the rapid growth in Nassau's population led to increased social problems and the further disruption of the family.

The Overseas Project or Contract in the United States, although providing jobs and earning power for so many Bahamian labourers during the 1940s, 1950s and early 1960s, also affected family life. Many workers, especially men, spent six to nine month periods on the Contract in the United States and returned. Others, however, deserted their communities, settling permanently either in Nassau or the United States.[56] Some Out Island settlements were therefore left with a scarcity of men, usually in their most productive years. Women and children were left in charge of the farms, and some learned to cope with the heavy work of cutting the fields. Because of scarcity of manpower, however, farming except for subsistence, was often neglected. In the absence of their spouses, women gained more independence. These women became, at least temporarily, heads of their households, and were solely responsible for its smooth running, including the rearing of the family.

By the 1950s and early 1960s, there was a large number of Out Island immigrants, particularly single women living in New Providence. More women worked outside of the home resulting in the disruption of family life. Although marriage was still the norm, at least among the black urban labouring class, illegitimacy rates were increasing. The stigma of illegitimacy among the coloured and black middle class, although painful, did not cause the sensation that it had at the turn of the century. If a girl of that class became pregnant and did not marry, she was no longer ostracized or banished from society. Among the black urban labouring class there was little shame attached to children born out of wedlock. The 1953 census did not report illegitimate rates. It did indicate, however, that a large number of unions were of the 'common law' type. Ten years later (in 1963) census takers recorded that 35 per cent of all Bahamian births were illegitimate. The Out Island average among black communities was 32 per cent. Not typical of the Out Island black communities in this respect was Cooper's Town, Abaco, a maritime settlement at the northernmost end of Great Abaco Island. The predominance of marriage in 1964, and the infrequency of consensual or extra-residential mating in that settlement resulted in the extremely low illegitimacy rate of 5.8 per cent.[57] A similar pattern was also found among white settlements.

The matrifocal family which was generally increasing among the black labouring class in the British West Indies, was becoming more common in the Bahamas. In 1953 greater numbers of Bahamian children were dependent on their mothers. Some women maintained relationships with a variety of extra-residential lovers who participated in the 'sweetheart' relationship. Other women, after having a number of children while still very young, formed common law relationships, establishing a consensual union with one male. Often women also moved in with their parents or mothers, creating an extended family. The 'yard' system, so common on the Out islands, was often duplicated in Over-the-Hill, Nassau. Some mothers who lived alone, alternatively, sent their children to live with their parents or other relatives who had remained on the Out Islands. Generally, throughout the British Caribbean, the black labouring class had larger families than the coloured middle class. Despite the tendency of blacks to have larger and larger families which put pressure on traditional family ties, kinship networks remained important. This ensured that most children received physical, and to a large extent, emotional comfort. Whatever form it took, the family remained a very significant institution for all Bahamians.[58]

Although monogamy and the nuclear type family are still recognized as ideal, the trend has been away from this image. During the 1970s and 1980s, there was further erosion of the traditional western nuclear type family. The trend as Dr Tim McCartney showed has been towards a more matriarchal situation[59] and as Leila Green has demonstrated, statistics show the presence of the extended family.[60]

Between the early 1970s and mid 1980s, there has been a rise in illegitimacy. In 1971, there were 1521 illegitimate births representing 30 per cent of all live births. Ten years later in 1981 there were 3115 illegitimate births representing 59.3 per cent of all live births. In 1984, 62 per cent of all live births were illegitimate.[61]

Not only was there a steep rise in illegitimate births, but statistics show that divorce rates were also increasing. This was particularly so in the mid 1980s. In 1984, for example, there were 362 divorces, more than double those granted in 1983. This trend can perhaps be attributed to the Matrimonial Causes (Amendment) Act of 1982 that provides other grounds than adultery for filing for a divorce.

Therefore when we speak of the Bahamian family today, we mean:

(1) The structured nuclear – or western type family – a legally married couple and their children living together.

(2) The Common Law family – that is 'faithful concubinage' or 'non legal union'. The man and woman live together without being legally married.

(3) The single female (or unwed mother) family – that is a woman living alone with her children without a permanent partner.

(4) The 'three generation' (or extended family) – that is the unwed woman and her children living with her parents. The children are often brought up by the grandparents.[62]

It seems that the numbers of single unmarried female headed families are increasing.

Notes

1. *Encyclopedia Britannica*, Vol. 9 (Chicago: 1972), 54.
2. Ibid.
3. Sven Loven, *Origins of the Tainan Culture, West Indies* (Goteborg: 1935), 499.
4. Ibid., 503-4.
5. Ibid., 526.
6. Ibid., 527-28.
7. Ibid., 528.
8. Ibid., 532.

9. See Registrar General's Department, Book C, 166-178. See also, A.T. Bethell, *The Early Settlers* (Nassau: 1914), 64-71 and 77-9.
10. Gail Saunders, *Bahamian Loyalists and Their Slaves* (London: 1983), 27-32.
11. Mary K. Armbrister, (ed.), *Henrietta My Daughter* (Connecticut: 1970), x.
12. Gail Saunders, *Slavery in The Bahamas, 1648-1838* (Nassau: 1985), 107-09.
13. See Herbert G. Gutman, *The Black Family in Slavery and Freedom, 1750-1925* (Oxford and New York: 1976).
14. See Barry W. Higman, 'The Slave Family and Household in the British West Indies, 1800-1834', *Journal of Interdisciplinary History*, VI:2, (Autumn, 1975): 261-87.
15. See Michael Craton, 'Hobbesian or Panglossian. The Two Extremes of Slave Conditions in the British Caribbean, 1783-1834', *William and Mary Quarterly*, 3rd Series, XXXV, (April, 1978): 324-56.
16. Saunders, *Slavery in The Bahamas*, 112-13.
17. A. Deans Peggs (ed.), *A Relic of Slavery, Farquharson's Journal, 1831-1832*, (Nassau: 1957): 75.
18. *Ibid.*, 83.
19. Barry Higman, 'African and Creole Slave Family Patterns in Trinidad', paper delivered at the Tenth Conference of Caribbean Historians, March/April, 1978.
20. Michael Craton, 'Changing Patterns of Slave Families in the British West Indies', *Journal of Inter-disciplinary History*, X:1 (Summer 1979), 1-35.
21. David Lowenthal, *West Indian Societies* (Oxford: 1972), 105.
22. Gail Saunders, 'Social History of the Bahamas 1890-1953', (Unpublished PhD Thesis, University of Waterloo, 1985), 91-2.
23. *Ibid.*, 92.
24. Ibid.
25. Shea to Ripon, April 29, 1893, C023/236/256-63.
26. Powles to Buxton, July 31, 1893, C023/238/281-82.
27. Shea to Ripon, April 29, 1893 C023/236/263.
28. David Lowenthal, *West Indian Societies*, 113.
29. Ibid.
30. *Nassau Quarterly Mission Papers*, (NQMP) No. 2, Sept. 1, 1886, 56; also Vol. II, No. 10, Sept. 1888, 61; Vol. X, No. 39, Dec. 1895, 82-3.
31. *Ibid.*, 83.
32. Roscow Shedden, *Ups and Downs in a West Indian Diocese* (London: 1927), 162.
33. Cleveland W. Eneas, *Bain Town* (Nassau: 1976), 41.
34. See especially Keith Otterbein, *The Andros Islanders. A Study of Family Organization in the Bahamas* (Kansas: 1966); Alan G. La Flamme, 'Green Turtle Cay: A Bi-Racial Community in the Out Island Bahamas', (unpublished Ph.D. thesis, University of New York at Buffalo, 1972).
35. Haziel Albury, *Man-O-War. My Island Home* (New Jersey: 1977).
36. *NQMP*, Vol. XI, No. 44, March 1897, 112.

37. See C.A. Penrose, 'Sanitary Conditions in the Bahamas', in *The Bahama Islands*, ed. By E.B. Shattuck (New York: 1905).
38. La Flamme, 'Green Turtle Cay'.
39. *NQMP* Vol. X, No. 40, March 1896, 114.
40. Otterbein, *The Andros Islanders*, 44.
41. Haziel Albury, *Man-O-War*, 5.
42. Otterbein, *The Andros Islanders*, 71.
43. La Flamme, 'Green Turtle Cay', 106.
44. Otterbein, *The Andros Islanders*, 77.
45. *Ibid.*, 84.
46. M.G. Smith, *West Indian Family Structure* (Seattle: 1962).
47. Saunders, 'Social History', 133.
48. *Report on The Census of The Bahama Islands April 2, 1911* (Nassau: 1911).
49 Saunders, 'Social History' 217. Michael Craton and Gail Saunders, *Islanders in the Stream. A History of the Bahamian People* Vol. 2 (Athens: University of Georgia Press, 1998): 252-257.
50. Allardyce to Grindle, Private, Oct. 5, 1918, C023/283/205.
51. *Report on The Census of The Bahama Islands*, April 26, 1931 (Nassau: 1931).
52. Saunders, 'Social History', 269-80. Craton and Saunders, *Islanders in the Stream* Vol. 2 : 250-252.
53. Report to Enquire into the Establishment of An Industrial School, Jan. 1923 (Nassau: 1923).
54. Ibid.
55. Ibid.
56. See Saunders, 'Social History', 448.
57. Keith Otterbein, 'Cooper's Town, Bahamas: A Statistical Survey', *Social and Economic Studies*, 19: 2 (June 1970): 266.
58. Saunders, 'Social History', 539-40.
59. Timothy McCartney, *Bahamian Sexuality* (Nassau: 1976), 22.
60. Leila Greene, 'Social Services Director Says Divorce Rate Up', *Nassau Guardian*, July 18, 1986.
61. Bahamas Department of Vital Statistics Reports, 1984 (Nassau: 1984).
62. Timothy McCartney, *Neuroses in The Sun* (Nassau: 1971), 138-39.

4

Isolation Within an Isolated Archipelago:
The Out Island Communities in the Bahamas during the Late Nineteenth and Early Twentieth Century

Gordon Lewis described the Caribbean at the end of the nineteenth century as 'a forgotten derelict corner of the world'. Geographically, the Bahamas was isolated from the West Indies proper. As an 'Atlantic Outpost' and because of the absence of sugar, the Bahamas never saw itself as part of the West Indies and traditionally was not accepted as a member of the family.[1] The Bahamian archipelago was, in fact, the least important of an insignificant group of colonies. It was also one of the most isolated and poorest parts of the British Empire. Widely scattered, the islands stretch approximately 600 miles from Grand Bahama in the north to Inagua in the south. The entire archipelago covers an area of 5,400 square miles.

From early in its history, New Providence had become the most important island. Its fine, sheltered harbour made the town of Nassau the leading port and very soon it became the commercial, political and social capital of the Bahamas. Nassau was the most cosmopolitan and affluent town. Although generally poor, it benefitted by any 'bonanza' in the economy and was constantly visited by foreigners who wanted to do business or simply to relax. It also had British officials to assist in operating the civil service. Its mercantile-based economy and strictly stratified society distinguished it from the Out Islands, that is, those islands out of New Providence, which were dependent on agriculture.

The physical separation of the Out Islands from New Providence and from each other made for isolation. The novelist Samuel Selvon declared 'An Island is a World'[2] and David Lowenthal has contended that 'the network of social relations seldom survives the sea'. Separation by water led to the development of strong local sentiments. Very often, islands developed special characteristics, 'a unique self-image, and a particular view of one another'.[3] It was said that white inhabitants of the Bahamian cays could identify people from other white communities by their speech. They gave each other nicknames generally not known to outsiders. Hope Town people were 'Crabs' while those from Spanish Wells were 'Cigillians'.[4]

Islands were also characterized by their individuality. Duncan Town and Ragged Island, for instance, a small isolated cay over 200 miles from Nassau, and only 60 miles north of Cuba, although extremely poor, was self-sufficient. Most of its predominately black population of 348 persons,[5] worked in its two industries, salt and basket and mat-making. They worked together as a community 'for their mutual benefit, and in this way, they succeeded in

shipping salt at a profit, whilst everyone else failed. Heaps of salt were always ready to be shipped at a moment's notice'. They sold some of the salt to the United States, but mainly bartered their product for produce with the other Out Islanders and New Providence.[6] Smuggling also took place extensively between Ragged Island and Cuba.[7] In spite of the absence of money, Powles observed that at Ragged Island 'all the population seems fairly well off, and there is an appearance of comfort about their houses that is altogether exceptional'.[8]

In 1891 some 77 per cent of the total Bahamas' population of 47,565 lived on the Out Islands. Most Out Island settlements were strung out along either the leeward or windward coasts, to protect them from the rough weather of the ocean. Settlements varied in age, size and racial composition. The northern islands of Abaco, Spanish Wells, Harbour Island and North Eleuthera, which were settled by the Eleutherian Adventurers and/or by 'Yankee Loyalists', had settlement patterns which differed from those of the more southerly islands.[9] These islands were first settled by the Loyalists and predominately by Southern Americans. As Sharer has shown, the northwestern islands were more compact and geared towards maritime activities, while the southeastern islands tended to have settlements more densely settled and spread further apart, being almost entirely oriented towards agriculture. The former held eighty-five per cent of the European-descended population while the latter were predominantly black.[10] Settlements in the southern islands more resembled those that Erna Brodber spoke of in urban Kingston, Jamaica[11] than those in the northern Bahama islands. The people usually lived not in a single house surrounded by a garden, but in a 'yard' or compound.[12] Some family compounds actually became settlements, for example Seymour's at Cat Island and Simms on Long Island. Different 'yards' often made up a settlement and would also be called after the surname of the family, for example, 'Darling Yard' in Colonel Hill, Crooked Island.[13]

In some islands, there existed small townships such as Dunmore Town, (Harbour Island), New Plymouth (Abaco), and Governor's Harbour (Eleuthera) in the north, and George Town (Exuma), Clarence Town (Long Island) and Cockburn Town (Watlings or San Salvador) in the south. These towns served as chief ports and the seat of the Resident Justice or Commissioner. They had churches, libraries, rectories, schools, the court house and jail, a market place and a rudimentary road system.[14]

Out Island settlements were usually self-contained and isolated and might have more contact with Nassau for trade purposes than with a neighbouring village. Just as each island was quite a distance from the others, so too was each settlement; inter-communication was very difficult.

There was a lack of good roads and transportation between the distant settlements was by foot, horseback, small sail boats or schooner. Anglican priests and Methodist ministers repeatedly wrote of the arduous journeys and long distances walked between settlements on rugged roads.[15]

It was often difficult to locate suitable horses or ponies, many of which were small, 'scraggy and ungroomed'. Saddles, stirrups and girths were scarce and even horses found the rocky, sandy, bushy paths hard to negotiate. Sailing in small boats around shallow and rocky coasts from settlement to settlement was uncomfortable and dangerous.

There was no cable or telephone communication between Nassau and most Out Islands or between communities until after the First World War. The news of the war was received in Clarence Town, Long Island, ten days after hostilities began. Travel in the late nineteenth and early twentieth centuries was mainly by sailing vessels. A fortnightly steamship communication had been established between Nassau and several of the Out Islands including Abaco, Eleuthera, Cat Island, Long Island and Inagua – but the majority of people still travelled by a sailing vessel, especially the Mail Boat. The Mail Boat was a vessel chartered by the government to carry the post.[16] However, it conveyed much more than correspondence and parcels. Its decks were usually packed with all sorts of produce, sheep, pigs, fowls, barrels of sisal and sponge, as well as people.[17] Often the boat was dirty and the cabins stuffy. Moreover, sailing could provide real hardships and if conditions were not favourable there could be serious delays. A head wind, calm, or scorching sun made the sea journey tedious. Head winds, for example, could cause a journey from Bimini to Nassau, which took twenty-two hours sailing on the outward journey, to take ninety hours on the return trip. Rough seas or dead calms equally hampered travel. A journey which usually took three days to Inagua could take eleven days with a lack of suitable winds.[18]

On arrival at an island settlement, passengers usually disembarked into a small row boat, which conveyed them to land. Docks and jetties were rare. If the tide was too low to accommodate the boat, passengers were carried for the last part of the journey on the back or in the arms of a strong local man.

Separation by water, poor communications and the lack of efficient transportation, made for neglect in the Out Islands. The Bahamas, like Barbados and Bermuda, retained the outdated old representative system. Theoretically, the colonial Governor, a Crown appointment, who was responsible for administering the colony, had great power. In practice, however, the lower branch of the House of Assembly comprising twenty-nine elected members and representing fifteen districts controlled most policy through the constitution and amendments of legislation of all kinds. The Nassau mercantile elite, who dominated the House of Assembly, often had differences with the colonial establishment. Moreover, they were indifferent to the plight of Out Islanders and the latter could not usually afford to sit in the legislature. Out Islanders therefore lacked representation to put forward their interests.

Very often, because of crops ruined by drought or flooding, Out Islanders were reduced to near starvation. Only in instances of crisis did the House of Assembly react. After a hurricane, emergency supplies would be sent, but budget allocation for the islands was meagre. There was never enough money assigned or any inclination to develop the type of infrastructure so badly needed. The Out Islands, which also suffered from inadequate schools, poorly trained teachers and a lack of supplies, drifted along isolated, and for the most part poverty-stricken.

Eager to control the affairs of the colony from the capital, the Nassau mercantile elite did little to promote land ownership in the Out Islands and perpetuated oppressive labour systems which had emerged in the Bahamas after the abolition of slavery. The ex-slaves turned to 'squatting, labour tenancy and to the share system'. Labour was also controlled by the credit and truck system.

Land tenure at the turn of the century was 'extremely confused'. The Crown only granted or leased land to those who could afford to develop it. Crown land regulations set the price beyond the reach of the majority of Out Islanders. Most people owned no land and four-fifths of all land belonged to the Crown. Many people turned to squatting while others farmed on 'commonages' – land held by the inhabitants in common, or on 'generation lands' – land transmitted through the family, often informally, titles to which often never existed.

Moreover, because of the thin, rocky soil, and the 'slash and burn' method of agriculture, farmers were obliged to move their fields every one to three years. It was therefore almost impossible for squatters, because of the mandatory period of sixty years' occupation of Crown Islands,[19] to obtain legal title to a piece of land that they had farmed. However, many squatters did not realize this and as William Rodgers has demonstrated for Abaco, according to folk land tenure beliefs, a man owned any piece of land that he had farmed unless someone else had farmed the land after he had abandoned it.[20]

The limited ownership of land greatly affected the lives of Out Islanders, since agriculture, (which included subsistence farming for food crops and pineapples for export), along with sponge fishing, were the mainstays of the Bahamian economy in the late nineteenth and early twentieth centuries. Some Out Islanders did purchase land, but property was owned mostly by private absentee proprietors who, through agents, operated their estates mainly by labour tenancy and the share system. The latter was a system that had developed after the end of slavery whereby the landlords supplied the land and in turn the tenants, who provided the labour, gave a share of the crop yield,[21] usually a half or a third.

In the immediate post-emancipation years, the absentee proprietors had no supervision costs. By the late nineteenth century, however, because of the success and prosperity of the pineapple industry, landlords took a greater interest in it. The tenants began to rely on them for credit, pineapple slips, manure and fertilizer. Advances in cash and kind were subtracted from the sale of the pineapples produced and the labourer often ended up in debt to the landlord who 'maximized' his profit by using a cheap labour force.[22]

Those peasant farmers who owned land usually lacked capital and had no means of transportation. On a visit to the Out Islands in 1896, Governor Haynes Smith observed:

> ... their labour was thrown away because they could get no transport to a market and that the produce rotted on the ground or sometimes (as I saw) where it had been carried to the shipping places it rotted in heaps on the sea shore.[23]

By the late nineteenth and early twentieth centuries, sponging was the leading industry in the Bahamas. Many Out Island men signed on sponging voyages which lasted from five to eight weeks depending on the catch. Most boats were owned by Nassau merchants who outfitted them. The Out Island fishermen, who were desperately poor, usually signed up on the truck system. The merchants supplied food for the men on the voyage as well as provisions for their wives and families. These goods were often supplied at a high profit to the merchant, and often a loss to the fishermen since payment was recovered at high rates of interest. The outfitters often supplied provisions in kind, such as flour, sugar, tobacco, and articles of clothing which the fishermen might not necessarily want. Powles observed:

> Probably the fisherman does not want the goods, or, at any rate, he wants money more to leave with his family; and in order to get it he sells the goods at about half the price at which they are charged to him. I was about to say half their value, but this would be grossly incorrect, for the goods are usually worth next to nothing.[24]

On returning from the voyage, the sponge fishermen were paid after many deductions had been made. As Governor Blake observed, 'Be the year bad or good, the closing of the account rarely leaves any but the smallest margin in favour of the debtor. There is hardly any circulation of money in the Out Islands'.[25]

Powles commented in 1888 that 'there was very few among the working classes of the Bahamas who know how to handle cash at all, except domestic servants and skilled work people'.[26]

The truck and credit systems permeated most industries and ensured the merchants' control of labour. Out Island salt-rakers, shipbuilders and pilots were paid in truck. Similarly, the truck system was also used in Inagua and Long Cay to pay labourers employed with American and German steamship companies. Bahamian labourers were employed to load and discharge cargoes at West Indian and Central American ports.[27] Governor Haynes Smith noted 'that the labourers engaged to serve on board the different steamers were paid on their return by the local agent in doles of truck and at unconscionable prices...'[28]

Governor Ambrose Shea believed that the only way that Bahamian labourers could gain independence from 'the pernicious credit system with its paralyzing influence' was through the development of the sisal industry using foreign (mainly British) capital.[29] Shea not only succeeded in cajoling Bahamian farmers into planting sisal, he also attracted a number of foreign investors to the Bahamas. With capital investment and government support, large areas of Crown land were either sold or leased. By 1890, the sisal industry had become firmly established. One investor was Joseph Chamberlain who had a 20,000 acre plantation near Mastic Point, Andros, operated by his son Neville. Besides Andros, sisal was also grown at Savannah Sound, Eleuthera, Long Island, Exuma, Rum Cay, Cat Island, Inagua and Abaco. Shea noted that there was a steady decline of the truck system, since on the plantations, the labourers were paid weekly in cash.[30] By the mid-1890s, optimism had turned to despair, and although there were substantial exports of sisal between 1898 and 1902 during the Spanish-American war, by 1912 all the large plantations on the Out Islands had failed and were abandoned.

Isolation compounded by oppressive labour systems imposed by the dominant Nassau mercantile elite, and the failure to establish a staple crop,

"Characteristic Home of Sponge Fishermen"
in Nineteenth and Early Twentieth Century Bahamas
(Courtesy of G.B. Shattuck, ed., The Bahama Islands, 1905)

kept the Out Islands poor and undeveloped, with most Out Islanders living at the same economic and social level.

Traditionally, the people from the nearby black settlement of The Bluff in North Eleuthera visited Spanish Wells during the day to sell their produce and to work. They could not, however, stay overnight. Stark observed of Spanish Wells and North Eleuthera that 'race prejudice runs higher than anywhere else in the colony ... on board "The Dart" the mail schooner plying between Harbour Island and Nassau, no passenger of colour is allowed to enter the cabin'.

Bi-racial communities for the most part were older and closer to Nassau. Some bi-racial settlements such as Dunmore Town, New Plymouth and Governor's Harbour, had more diverse occupations and also had some attributes of a town as described earlier. Each was the educational, political and commercial centre of its district. For example, Dunmore Town and Governor's Harbour had medical doctors in 1897.[31] Again, race rather than class, separated the people. Dunmore Town, New Plymouth and Governor's Harbour all exhibited residential segregation. At Dunmore Town, for example, the whites lived near the Bay or on the hill overlooking it, and had substantial houses, while the blacks lived in small wooden cabins raised from platforms made of rocks. Their houses were located in the back of the whites or to the east of them.[32]

In Governor's Harbour, coloured and black people lived on Cupid's Cay (a small cay between the harbour and mainland separated from the latter by a narrow ridge of sand), while the white people had houses on the mainland. Houses of the whites were scattered along a slope which rose quite steeply – about 150 feet – and overlooked the harbour.[33] Powles described the white area in 1887:

> The houses on this hillside are white and clean, standing each of them in its own garden and the whole place, thanks to Mr. Preston's energetic superintendence of public works, looks very like a pretty little English watering-place.[34]

Similarly, in New Plymouth, the whites lived on the harbour side – the 'best part of the town' and in 'more eligible dwellings'. Socially, blacks accepted their inferior status. Economically, whites stood a greater chance of doing well. While most people of both races were poor and worked together as farmers and fishermen, some whites were better off economically and were described as 'fairly well-to-do'.[35] They were shippers of pineapples, owners of boats, small ships and businesses.

At Dunmore Town, Harbour Island, in the 1880s, whites such as 'Hoppie' Higgs and Joseph Albury established three small sugar mills which processed sugar cane for inter-island trade and local consumption. 'Hoppie' Higgs operated a small grocery store and William Munroe, a sail loft where it was said the best sails in the Bahamas were made.[36] Blacks, besides farming, raised chickens, worked for whites and the local Board of Works in the town. One of their chief tasks was carrying water from wells dug on the north beach.

There was little social life among the people in bi-racial settlements, each family living very much apart. People of both races attended government schools and the Anglican and Methodist churches. At Dunmore Town, whites had the opportunity, not available to blacks, to attend private schools, six of which were said to have existed on Harbour Island in 1899.[37] While church was a common meeting place for both races, there was segregation in their seating patterns. For example, in New Plymouth, in 1889, the Anglican priest reported: 'White people sat by themselves occupying the front benches on the northside' while the remainder of the church 'was occupied by black and coloured people'.[38]

Similarly, at Dunmore Town, Powles wrote of the rife discrimination in the Methodist church in the late nineteenth century. On one occasion, five coloured men entered the Methodist church through the white man's door and walked up the aisle. The service abruptly discontinued until they were evicted. They were charged and convicted the next day by the Resident Justice who fined them for 'brawling'.[39]

The all-black settlements displayed more cultural homogeneity than the bi-racial. The race question was not generally a burning issue, and where considerable miscegenation had occurred in the past, or where no whites remained, social stratification was based not on race but on social attitudes and associations based on colour.[40] Henry Taylor in describing his experience as headteacher in the Pompey Bay area in Acklins during the early 1920s, relates that there were two groups:

> One group lived at Delectable Bay, and the other at Pompey Bay. The two settlements were over two miles apart. The school-buildings were situated between the two settlements. The inhabitants of Delectable Bay were generally dark-skinned while the people of Pompey Bay were all light to dark browned complexion. There was a colour and class prejudice among them, that I was not faced with at Long Island... The pupils of the school who came from Pompey Bay did not want to sit with or near the pupils from Delectable Bay. They did not play together and kept themselves distinctly apart at all times in two separate groups. The Delectable Bay students were pressured by the Pompey Bay students not to use the front door of the school.[41]

In all-black settlements some people were held in higher esteem than others. Perhaps Peter J. Wilson's theory in *Crab Antics* for the black community of Providencia can be applied to the elite in black Out Island communities. They not only had 'reputation', a characteristic held by the majority of the people, but also gained some 'respectability' which separated them from the rest of the community.[42] At the Bluff, Eleuthera, for example, Powles met a 'head man of the village' who 'seemed to have assumed that position by tacit consent'.[43]

A large number of black catechists assisted the Anglican clergy in the Bahamas. The catechists were licensed to read prayers, preach, baptize and marry. Black Baptist ministers had similar privileges both in the British Baptist Missionary Society and in the native Baptist churches. The ministers were especially important in Cat Island which had the most successful Baptist mission on the Out Islands in the late nineteenth century. Indeed Henry Taylor wrote of Long Island:

> Each of the catechists or ministers was a leader in his community, and was held in respect by all those around him. Their words were accepted, and they in turn did everything possible to demand the respect of others in the community. For one of the inhabitants to rise to a position of leadership in his church showed that he was an outstanding individual and was respected not only by the members of his own congregation but also by all the other congregations.[44]

Midwives and bush doctors also held a special social status in their respective communities, black, white or bi-racial. Aunt Celia, 'the medicine woman of Eight Mile Rock' in the early 1900s, was known for her effective cures from 'medicines' grown in the 'bush'. Amelia Defries marvelled at 'the remarkable soundness of her knowledge', and was 'cured' of her ailment 'in an incredibly short time'.[45] Sarah Kerr of Clarence Town was also well respected as a midwife and medicine woman. She believed that 'God make bush for every sick'. If she failed to cure you there was no hope and a visit to Nassau would be pointless.[46]

People in all-black settlements, like those among the coloured middle class in Nassau, won respect for their successes in business. For example, the Gibson brothers of Savannah Sound owned a large three-masted schooner called *The Brothers* and 'traded direct with the States, without allowing the blighting shadow of Nassau to cross their path'. Powles also commented on the social graces and the apparent exposure to the outside world of one of the brothers, 'not only did he talk intelligently on general topics, but was well posted in European and American politics'.[47]

School teachers and Commissioners were also highly respected and almost revered in all settlements. Powles observed at Savannah Sound that the schoolmaster here, 'Symonette' by name, is a full-blooded African, whom the inspector admits to be one of the best masters he has in his employment.[48] Black Commissioners, however, were not welcomed in white communities and black Out Islanders would not graciously accept a dark-skinned coloured person in that post.[49]

Insularity and racial attitudes moulded Out Islanders' views towards marriage and kinship ties. One of the greatest fears of the white population with its feelings of superiority, was that miscegenation would take place. In fact, while it was prevalent in Nassau, it was not common in the Out Islands.

Dr Clement Penrose, one of the Johns Hopkins University Team who visited the Bahamas in 1903 on behalf of the Geographical Society of Baltimore, was perhaps prejudiced when he attributed the 'shocking condition of degeneracy at Hope Town' to the constant intermarrying of the white inhabitants.[50] Penrose observed that Hope Town at that time had about 1000 pure whites and twelve coloured people. There was no evidence of racial intermarriage. Almost all the white inhabitants could trace their ancestry to a Loyalist widow, Wyannie Malone, who arrived in Hope Town in 1785 with her four children. New blood was brought in early by 'Joe' John Albury of Harbour Island and Nathaniel Key of St Augustine, Florida. Thereafter, their offspring intermarried so closely with the descendants of Wyannie Malone that in a short time, 'the relationship between the three families was very close'.

A diagram of the Malone family tree, constructed with the assistance of the older inhabitants of the settlement and the clergyman, proved that there was indeed an 'enormous amount of intermarriage between the various members of the Malone, Russell, Albury and Key families of Hope Town'. Penrose concluded that 'early in the history of the Malone family indications of degeneracy were absent; but they began in the fourth generation and rapidly increased afterwards until they culminated by the presence of five idiots in one family'.[51]

Similarly, Spanish Wellians, though limited in number, (scorning the mainland blacks), persistently intermarried to retain their racial integrity. In 1903, Dr Penrose claimed that this close intermarriage had resulted in an unusually large number of cases of locomotor-ataxia, cataracts and other eye diseases. Dwarfs were also common. He added: 'We noted, also, that the mental acumen of many of the inhabitants of this place was rather low'.[52]

Whites in bi-racial settlements also intermarried. Wesley Mills, a Professor at McGill University, commented in 1887, 'Among a white population that does not travel, that does not receive accessions,... the play of "sexual selection" must be of the most restricted kind, and with corresponding results'. He described most of the whites as having 'the stamp of weakness and anaemia'.[53]

Isolation also helped to preserve some of the traditions and customs of Out Islanders. Although most people by the 1890s were nominally Christian, in the predominantly black settlements, notably in Cat Island and Andros, African-rooted traditions were still strong. Powles, on a visit to Cat Island in 1887 commented, 'The people here are very superstitious, and what is called "obeahism" is very common among them'.[54] During the same period, F.B. Matthews, an Anglican priest, after visiting at least ten stations along the Andros coast, wrote that the people were still very superstitious.[55] Later in

1918, at Mars Bay (also in Andros), it was reported that 'superstition' was still 'rife, a relic of the old African witchcraft.'[56]

In the absence of physicians, clinics and hospitals, bush medicine was common and considered vital among all three types of settlements. 'Bush doctors' were often assisted by largely untrained missionaries, clergy or Resident Justices stationed in the communities. In the case of severe illnesses, patients had to go to Nassau. However, the long slow voyage and the overconfidence of the Out Island 'practitioners' could end in disaster. Governor Blake in the late nineteenth century attributed the high mortality at the Nassau Hospital to the fact that 'people rarely apply for admission until they have exhausted the means of cure known to the "bush" doctors or obeah men. In many cases they are moribund when they arrive'.[57]

Isolation contributed to the continuities of recreational activities, especially those that were essentially African traditions. The belief systems of blacks and their recreational activities were intertwined. Music, derived from the antebellum slave songs of the United States and from the hymns contained in the early Wesleyan and Baptist hymnals,[58] was very important in the lives of Out Island blacks. It was an essential ingredient in ceremonies, church rites and also in everyday life. During the wake, a custom 'held on the night when some friend is supposed to be dying', men, women and children of all ages sang mournful hymns and 'anthems' long into the night.[59] Blacks also gathered at sunset on other occasions such as the eve of Emancipation Day and Christmas to sing all night. Whereas wake music was sad, this type was merry and was called 'settin' up'. After midnight, refreshments of coffee and bread were served. After this came the 'anthems' or religious folksongs that had not been learned from a book, but passed down from one generation to another.[60]

Also popular among blacks was the tradition of story-telling which followed the singing. The folktales were divided into 'old stories' and fairy tales which had roots in Africa and Europe. Many came by way of the American south and the Caribbean proper and concerned animals and their thrilling adventures.

Dancing was another form of entertainment. In spite of the Church's move to suppress it, wherever there was a strong African element in the population, the holding of ring dances to some form of rhythmic accompaniment – singing, chanting, clapping the goatskin drum, or maybe a combination of these – was a favourite recreational activity. African derived ring dances, of three distinctive types, the fire dance, the jumping dance and the ring play, were held in black and bi-racial Out Island communities in Over-the-Hill Nassau and in outlying black villages such as Fox Hill, Adelaide and Gambier.[61]

Out Island communities had special celebrations on Emancipation Day and Christmas Day, but not on the same scale as in Nassau. In black and bi-racial settlements, celebrations bore similarities to the John Canoe parade in

Nassau. There was usually dancing, some form of 'rushing' to music using drums.[62] In addition to the John Canoe parade, in Eleuthera, entertainment was given by the different lodges on Christmas Eve. In 1897, the Gregory Town lodge, the Grand United Order of Odd Fellows, gave a programme including 'dialogues, recitations, addresses, songs and instrumental music before a large and attentive audience...'[63]

Emancipation Day, on August 1, was celebrated in black and bi-racial communities (as it was in Fox Hill, New Providence), in various ways. In 1888, at Cat Island, the Reverend Matthews reported that harvested produce and fruit were used to decorate the church. Festivities included a choral celebration in the morning, a 'parish feast' in the afternoon, and sports, including athletics and football. The day ended with a choral evensong.[64] At Harbour Island in the late nineteenth century, it seemed that the entire black population, smartly dressed, congregated on the whites' harbour-side area of Dunmore Town to celebrate Emancipation Day. The Friendly Society and the lodge, which assisted members when they were sick and ensured each member a decent burial, led the festivities.[65]

Isolation, poverty and the lack of opportunity, and not population pressure, caused many Bahamians to migrate in the late nineteenth and early twentieth centuries. Between 1901 and 1911 emigration, which had begun in the latter part of the last century, intensified. Increasing numbers of Bahamians, the majority of them Out Island males, emigrated to the United States settling especially in Miami, Key West and other parts of Florida. Those islands which lost most population in the early 1900s were Harbour Island and Eleuthera.[66] Although much of this migration was temporary, and some of the emigrants' earnings returned to their families, a fairly large number of Bahamians made permanent homes in Florida, especially in Coconut Grove near Miami and Deerfield Beach.[67]

Some of the out-migration was checked by the establishment in 1906 of Wilson City, a lumber town established on Spenser's Point near the south end of Great Abaco by an American firm based in Minneapolis and registered as the Bahamas Timber Company.[68] Described by Steve Dodge as a 'marvel in its time', Wilson City attracted workers from all over Abaco and from some of the other islands. Not only were the labourers paid in cash, they were exposed, for the first time, to many modern conveniences, such as electric light, installed in 1908, a year before the service began in Nassau. They also benefitted from the establishment of an ice factory, the envy of Nassau as well as the Out Islands.[69] Racial discrimination was reinforced by residential and social segregation in Wilson City. The homes of black Bahamian workers were separated from those of the white American families. The two races did not worship together, neither did their children attend the same school.[70]

In the southern Bahamian Out Islands, hundreds of Bahamian labourers were employed on ships taking stevedores for the purpose of loading and unloading cargoes in South American, Central American and West Indian ports. Bahamians were also employed in the building of the Panama Canal as workers on fruit plantations in Costa Rica and as woodcutters in Honduras and Guatemala. Some worked in Mexico and, between 1900 and 1912, a fairly large number were recruited as cane cutters in the Dominican Republic. While many Out Islanders returned home, some refused on the account of the improbability of again getting work.

Labour migration, despite the truck system, brought cash into circulation and especially benefitted Long Cay, also called Fortune Island, and Inagua until the outbreak of World War I in 1914. Paul Albury called the stevedoring centre of Matthew Town 'a magical place' with 'bustling commerce all combined to produce a throbbing, booming atmosphere'.[71] Matthew Town, Inagua, by the early 1900s had several commission merchants, importers and dealers in dry goods and groceries, some of whom had business with Haiti and were agents for firms in France and the United States.[72] Matthew Town was also one of the few settlements to publish a newspaper, the *Inagua Record*, in the early twentieth century.[73] Long Cay also became a bustling and cosmopolitan settlement, equipped with stores and commission merchants. Not only did money circulate, but also news. The steamers, which sometimes called as often as three or four times a week, brought a constant supply of American newspapers, not more than four days old.[74] In some cases these isolated southern Out Island ports were receiving European news as soon as Nassau was.

While labour migration created a 'boom' in the two ports of call, the populations of many Out Island settlements declined steeply during the first two decades of the twentieth century due to heavy out-migration. Nassau's prosperity in the 1920s also attracted Out Islanders and this movement into the capital further exacerbated the depopulation of the Out Islands.[75]

The dispersed nature of the Bahamian archipelago and its physical and economic separation from the British West Indian islands made for isolation. The Out Islands were seldom affected, as New Providence was, by the temporary 'boom' times. They remained extremely poor, isolated and often suffered devastation by natural disasters. These factors combined with the indifferent attitude of the Nassau mercantile elite, an ineffective colonial establishment and the lack of political representation, helped to perpetuate oppressive land tenure and labour systems. Isolation continued even after steamships and cable were introduced and after Wilson City closed and the stevedoring trade had ceased. In fact the migration to Central America and to Florida drained the Out island communities of their most vigorous inhabitants.

Intense racial feeling and deep-set colour prejudice, especially where blacks and whites lived in the same community, seriously affected social life and all forms of associations, particularly marriage. Isolation, while delaying change, helped to preserve Out Island cultural customs and traditions especially in the black settlements. For many Out Islanders, the nineteenth century way of life – 'backward and unprogressive'[76] – lingered on well into the twentieth century.

Notes

1. Gordon K. Lewis, *The Growth of the Modern West Indies* (New York and London: 1968), 62.
2. S. Selvon, *An Island is a World* (London: 1955). Cited in David Lowenthal, 'The Range and Variation of Caribbean Societies' in *Slaves, Free Men, Citizens. West Indian Perspectives*, (ed by) Lambros Comitas and David Lowenthal (New York: 1973), 197.
3. Lowenthal, ibid.
4. John Holm, 'African Features in White Bahamian English', *English World Wide*, 1:1 (1980), 54.
5. Ragged Island had one white family, the Wilsons. It comprised of two brothers and their families who along with the Resident Justice were the only whites. NQMP, 4: 13 (June 1889), 159.
6. L.D. Powles, *The Land of The Pink Pearl* (London: 1888), 276.
7. *Precis Report of the Resident Justice, 1890. Appendix to Votes of the House Assembly* 1891 (Nassau: 1891), 35. Interview with Oris Russell, September 25, 1984 Nassau.
8. Powles, *Land of the Pink Pearl,* 276.
9. See Thelma Peters, 'The American Loyalists and the Plantation Period in The Bahama Islands', (Unpublished PhD thesis, University of Florida, 1960), 62-3.
10. Cyrus Sharer, 'The Population Growth of the Bahama Islands', (Unpublished PhD thesis, University of Michigan, 1955), 40-3.
11. Erna Brodber, *A Study of Yards in the City of Kingston* (Mona: 1975). Working Paper, No. 9, 1975.
12. See *Strangers No More. Anthropological Studies of Cat Island, the Bahamas,* ed. Joel S. Savishinsky (Ithaca: 1978), 71.
13. Interview with Luther E. Smith, Nassau, Feb. 8, 1984.
14. Saunders, 'Social History', 123-25.
15. Saunders, 'Social History', 12.
16. *Nassau Quarterly Mission Papers (NQMP)*, X: 39, December 1895, 86. See also *NQMP*, VI: 23, December 1891, 73.
17. Ibid., Vol. V, No. 19, December, 1890, p. 84.
18. James A. Archer to Hartley, May 29, 1893, MMS, Bahamas Box 22, and *NQMP*, Vol. X, No. 40, March 1896, 117-19.
19. See Real Property Limitation (Crown) Act, 1874, *Statute Law of the Bahamas,* (Nassau: 1965), chapters 120, 148, 149 and 150.
20. William B. Rodgers, 'The Wages of Change: An Anthropological Study of the Effects of Economic Development on some Negro Communities in the Out Islands', (Unpublished PhD thesis, Stanford University, 1965), 97. See also, M. Craton, 'White Law and Black Custom: The Evolution of Bahamian Land Tenures, in *Land and Development in the Caribbean* (London: 1987), 88-114.

21. H. Johnson, *Bahamas in Slavery and Freedom* (Kingston: 1991), 55-66.
22. Ibid., 148-150.
23. Haynes Smith to Chamberlain, July 7, 1896, Duplicate Governors' Despatches No. 76, 1893-1897, f. 443.
24. Powles, *Land of The Pink Pearl*, 88.
25. Blake to Derby, August 12, 1884, Duplicate Governors' Despatches 1881-1887, f 282.
26. Powles, *Land of The Pink Pearl*, 98.
27. See Patrice Williams, 'The Emigrant Labour Business: An Important Industry in the Late Nineteenth and Early Twentieth Centuries?', *Journal of The Bahamas Historical Society*, 7: 1, (October: 1985), 9-14.
28. Haynes Smith to Chamberlain, July 7, 1896, C023/244/104-107. The credit and truck systems continued well into the twentieth century although there were efforts made by a 1907 Act to stamp them out.
29. Shea to Knutsford, May 28, 1890, C023/231/302-302a.
30. In 1898 sisal production was 1,092,814 pounds exported at a value of £13,374. *Blue Book*, 1898.
31. *NQMP*, Vol. XIII, No. 47, December 1897, p. 76. In 1912, Matthew Town, Inagua, also had a doctor because of the increased population due to stevedoring.
32. Saunders, 'Social History', 124-25.
33. *NQMP*, Vol. IV, No. 14, 1889, 193.
34. Powles, *Land of The Pink Pearl*, 219.
35. Powles, *Land of The Pink Pearl*, 204.
36. A Portfolio of Wood Engravings of Historic Spots on Harbour Island, The Bahamas by John De Pol.
37. Saunders, 'Social History', 124. See also *Precis of Reports of Resident Justice* 1899. Appendix to the Votes of the House of Assembly 1898-1900, 75.
38. *NQMP*, Vol. 4, No. 13, June 1889, 154.
39. Powles, *Land of The Pink Pearl*, 111-12.
40. Marc Tull, 'Colour Pride in Tarpum Bay. A Bahamian Community Reacts to Equality', in *Anthropological Perspectives on Eleuthera Island 1973-1974*, (Corning, NY: 1974), 68.
41. Henry M. Taylor, *My Political Memoirs*, (Nassau: 1987), 34.
42. Peter J. Wilson, *Crab Antics: The Social Anthropology of English Speaking Negro Societies of the Caribbean* (New Haven and London: 1973).
43. Powles, *Land of The Pink Pearl*, 208.
44. Taylor, *My Political Memoirs*, 17.
45. Amelia Defries, *In a Forgotten Colony* (Nassau: 1917), 82-3.
46. Interview with Henry Taylor, February 26, 1990.
47. Powles, *Land of The Pink Pearl*, 227.
48. Ibid., 228.
49. Cited Saunders, 'Social History', 127. See also interview with Fr. William Thompson, December 28, 1983.
50. C.A. Penrose, 'Sanitary Conditions in the Bahamas', in *The Bahama Islands* ed. by G.B. Shattuck (New York: 1905), 410-11.
51. Ibid.

52. Ibid., 409. See also Willoughby Bullock, 'Spanish Wells', *The Journal of the Royal Empire Society*, XXII: 9 (September 1931), 491.
53. T. Wesley Mills, 'The Study of a Small and Isolated Community in the Bahama Islands', *The American Naturalist*, XXI: 10 (October 1887), 882 and 884.
54. Powles, *Land of the Pink Pearl*, 238.
55. *NQMP*, Vol. VIII, No. 30, September 1893, 34.
56. Ibid., Vol. XXXIII, No. 131. December 1918, 79.
57. Blake to Granville, March 20, 1886, #32, *Duplicate Governors Despatches 1881-1887*, f. 419. See also *NQMP*, Vol. XI, No. 41, June 1896, 21.
58. Clement Bethel, 'Music in the Bahamas: Its Roots, Development and Personality', (Unpublished MA thesis, University of California, Los Angeles, 1978), 59.
59. Charles L. Edwards, *Bahama Songs and Stories* (New York: 1895), 17.
60. Ibid., 18.
61. C. Bethel, 'Music in the Bahamas', 126.
62. Neville Chamberlain to Ida Chamberlain, Andros, December 25, 1893, NC1/16/2/24.
63. *Nassau Guardian*, January 1, 1897. In the bi-racial settlement of New Plymouth, Green Turtle Cay, Abaco, New Year's Day was celebrated by the appearance of 'Old Skin' or Bunce who was carried in a wheel barrow covered in canvas along the streets of the town. A hawker proceeded the barrow telling stores how 'Bunce' was caught. Money was collected, after which Bunce, the origin of which is obscure, appeared and danced. He was usually dressed in strange costumes made from paper or rags. 'Junkanoo', Public Records Office (Archives) (Nassau: 1978), 15.
64. *NQMP*, Vol. III, No. 10, September 1888, 54.
65. From pictorial evidence in C. Edwards, *Bahama Songs and Stories*, opposite pp. 18 and 90.
66. Saunders, 'Social History', 22 and 184.
67. Ibid., 184.
68. The Bahamas Timber company obtained a 100 year timber license with respect to the Crown pine forests of Abaco, Andros and Grand Bahama. The firm, investing more than £300,000, established a modern mill and huge steam derrick and railroad on which to load and carry the felled timber to the mill. The timber was shipped to Cuba, Nassau and the United States. The mill closed in 1916. Several years later the company revived the lumber industry at Norman's Castle, Abaco. See Haddon Smith to Harcourt, Jan. 1, 1914, Conf. Grey-Wilson to Harcourt, May 14, 1912, C023/269/304-306 and *Colonial Annual Reports, Bahamas, 1916-1917*, 13.
69. Steve Dodge, *Abaco: The History of an Out Island and its Cays* (North Miami: 1983), 83.
70. Colbert Williams, *The Methodist Contribution to Education in the Bahamas* (Gloucester: 1982), 179.
71. Paul Albury, *The Story of the Bahamas* (London: 1975), 199.
72. Saunders, 'Social History', 180. See also Advertisements in Northcroft, *Sketches of Summerland*, (Nassau: 1901).

73. Sidney H. Pactor, 'Communication in an Island Setting: A History of the Mass Media of the Bahama Islands, 1784-1956', (Unpublished PhD dissertation, University of Tennessee, Knoxville, 1985).
74. Powles, *Land of The Pink Pearl*, 254.
75. The islands which suffered population declines between 1901 and 1921 included Crooked Island, Cat Island, Eleuthera, Grand Bahama, Harbour Island, Inagua, Long Cay and Rum Cay. See Reports on the Census 1901 and 1921.
76. Address by Sir William Grey-Wilson, Governor of the Bahamas before the Empire Club of Canada on October 25, 1911 in Empire Club Speeches 1911-12, ed. by D.J. Goggin (Toronto: 1913).

5

Emancipation and 'Over-the-Hill'

By an Act of Parliament in 1834, slaves were declared apprentices, slave owners compensated and provisions made to transform a slave society as smoothly as possible into a free community. Freedom was not completed; the ex-slaves still had to work for their former masters and personal freedom was limited; ex-slaves could still be punished (indeed the whip was occasionally used), and were not allowed to sit on a jury or hold any office except very minor posts. It was the Emancipation Act of 1838 which was to come into effect on August 1 of that year, which gave the former slaves full freedom. The apprentices were: '...released and discharged of and from the then remaining term of their apprenticeship' and were forever after free men and women.[1]

Emancipation Day passed quietly; no riots, bloodshed or disorder. No great rejoicing took place and even in Nassau, although Emancipation Day was 'hailed with joy' by the apprentices, there was 'no noise or tumult'. Instead all places of worship were unusually packed with the liberated class and 'singing was unusually lively', so reports a Methodist Missionary.[2] This very orderly transition out of legal slavery foreshadowed the slowness of change to come.

Theoretically the ex-slaves were free men. They enjoyed freedom from punishments, freedom to leave the abodes and plantations of their former masters and cultivate their own land and freedom to choose the type of work they wished. In short they could exercise freedom in their own interest. However, it was a formal type of freedom and for a long time although legally the whole basis of society was changed by the 1838 Act, real change was to be very slow. In fact, the act did not alter immediately the structure of the society as there still existed ruler and ruled, white and black, landowners and labourers. Politically, socially and economically the ex-slaves were still at a great disadvantage and only time would change their position. The ex-slaves had few political rights or social and economic opportunities, and therefore continued to be economically exploited.

On the positive side, however, the ex-slaves and apprentices had freedom of movement. They could choose their own work and leave their former masters and employers, although this was not practical in the majority of cases. The Bahamas at the time of emancipation was experiencing an economic downturn. There was general poverty and insecurity, even for many former slave owners. The cotton plantations because of the chenille bug and poor soil had for the most part collapsed; salt, another staple, was declining and wrecking was to be stopped by the construction of lighthouses in the 1850s, 1860s and 1870s.

There was little or no paid employment on the Out Islands, and many of the ex-slaves took to subsistence farming where land was available. Unfortunately, land tenure was very confused.[3] Some ex-slaves remained on the land of their former owners as squatters or tenant farmers, while others farmed commonages. Some remained on land transmitted through the family (generation lands), often informally, titles to which were often suspect. The system of quit-rent tenure (land leased from the Crown) did not succeed as rents were often not paid and land reverted to the Crown. Freed blacks were not given much instruction and guidance in their new status and had little idea of the most modern methods of farming. Most people on the Out Islands farmed for subsistence and lived slightly above starvation level, hardly yielding enough crops for export.

During slavery, a peasantry developed in the Bahamas with the liberated Africans forming the nucleus of that peasantry. Howard Johnson suggests that a class of creole peasants also emerged during that same period. Not all

'Grant's Town'
(Courtesy of the Department of Archives, Bahamas)

peasants owned land, some merely had access to it. Most ex-slaves remained poor and the power structure was basically the same, based on ownership and therefore the ex-slaves remained almost as subordinate to their masters as when they were slaves or apprentices.[4]

It must be said that many of the former masters were also poor even though they had social status and political power. The ex-slaves had neither, and were still very much bound to the Nassau merchants (who were mainly white) by the iniquitous 'truck system'. Little attention was paid to the development of social services. For example, popular education, which should have been given top priority, received scant attention. Private schools existed for the elite and although the Board of Education was established in 1835, it only provided for primary education. Moreover, schools were not numerous enough to accommodate the Bahamian population and many children never attended school. The public schools were to suffer for many years from the lack of qualified teachers, inadequate buildings, and an apathetic attitude by the government. Health and welfare services hardly fared better and the legacy of this neglect was felt for many years.[5]

Socially, the white elite dominated the society in every aspect and racially the society was deeply divided. Geographer/historian David Lowenthal stated: 'Indeed, emancipation increased racial prejudice; with slavery gone, colour criteria took on greater importance in West Indian society, not less'.[6] The distance between white, brown and black widened. The coloureds (or browns) wanted acceptance by whites, the blacks wanted self-esteem and a share of the material and social benefits and the whites wanted blacks and coloureds to remain docile and passive and retain the status quo.

But what did emancipation mean for those people living 'Over-the-Hill'?

First of all what do we mean by 'Over-the-Hill'? Different people have different interpretations. Dr Eneas calls it a 'concept' not a place. Generally when one speaks of Over-the-Hill', Grant's Town, Bain Town and a part of Delancey Town are usually included.

Grant's Town was settled in 1825 by a number of liberated Africans who were captured by the Royal Navy and settled first at Carmichael, then known as Headquarters, in the southwestern part of New Providence. These people were never slaves; some of them were apprenticed to leading citizens in the town, while others worked in the Nassau market. Between 1820 and 1829, Governor Lewis Grant instructed the then Surveyor General, John Burnside, to lay out a settlement behind the town of Nassau for the apprenticed Africans who were employed within the town. At that time, Grant's Town was bordered on the east by East Street, on the west by Blue Hill Road, on the north by Cockburn and Lees Street, and in the south by the Blue Hills. After emancipation, freed slaves also settled in the area.[7]

Bain Town, which has been immortalized through literature by Dr Cleveland Eneas in his informative book,[8] is located to the west of Grant's

Town. It was originally part of a 140 acre land grant to one Susannah Weatherspoon, and was sold to a black Bahamian businessman, Charles H. Bain in the late 1840s. He divided the land into allotments and sold them at moderate prices to blacks – both liberated Africans and ex-slaves. It is believed that Bain Town was named in his honour. Bain Town was bordered on the west by Nassau Street, on the east by Blue Hill Road, on the north by South Street and on the south by what is now Poinciana Drive. The area south of Poinciana Drive was called Contabutta and according to Dr Eneas, was settled by the Congos who were socially inferior to the Yorubas of Bain Town.[9]

Delancey Town, the southern part of which can be considered Over-the-Hill, is located to the west of the town of Nassau. Located behind Dunmore House which was Government House in the late eighteenth century, it stretched from West Hill Street in the north to South Street in the south, Nassau Street in the west and Hospital Lane in the east. The area was named after Stephen Delancey, then Chief Justice of the Bahamas, who purchased 150 acres of land from John Brown in 1789. Lots were laid out carefully as an extension of the Nassau grid, and were surveyed. Parcels were apportioned to families of slaves some of whom were provided with modest cabins.[10] This was an attempt by the white elite to segregate the races residentially. It seems that residential separation was introduced after the arrival of the Loyalists who passed laws requiring all persons of colour to be domiciled outside the limits of Nassau for better security. This was because of the large increase in the black population.

Although these three towns were separated by trees and bushes, the land between them was gradually cleared and by the late nineteenth century, the entire black district became known as 'Over-the-Hill'. Charles Ives in *The Isles of Summer* (1880) in referring to Grant's Town, Bain Town and Delancey Town talks of the 'Back of Nassau, over the hill'.[11]

To people living Over-the-Hill, emancipation meant first of all that they were free, but this freedom was a very limited one. Most Over-the-Hill people were very poor and depended on a livelihood from the white merchants of Nassau. Many worked as domestics for the whites and better-off coloureds of Nassau, and as labourers, gardeners, wreckers, draymen, wheelwrights, blacksmiths, stevedores, masons, carpenters and the like. Some owned petty shops or stands on the side of the road and sold fruit and vegetables which they grew in their backyards.

Others owned the quarter-acre allotments, which were sold at 10 shillings a lot in 1835, shortly after emancipation. Inhabitants were allowed to pay quarterly in money or in labour. Small wooden cabins most of which were thatched were built on the allotments.[12] However, most settlers could not accumulate cash as wages were very low.

Over-the-Hill people were lowest in the hierarchical social pyramid – the white elite being at the top, and the coloureds in the middle. They were expected to be docile, polite and to return to their area when work was over. White Nassau discriminated against them residentially, employment-wise and in the places they could attend socially. Although an infant school was opened in Grant's Town in 1835, it was inferior to that provided for whites. Health and sanitation services were non-existent or very poor.

As Michael Doran and Renee Landis stated in an article about the area in 1980:

> Over-the-Hill was intentionally set apart during colonial times as a defined community of slaves and indentured servants. Although slavery has passed into history, an original characteristic of Over-the-Hill is an adjunct to Nassau, not a part of it. The city is still the preserve of the white elite, while Over-the-Hill is still occupied by poor blacks perceived as social inferiors.[13]

Politically, at the time of emancipation, the voice of people living in the Over-the-Hill area was not important and would not be heeded for many years to come. In 1834 there were four black members of the House of Assembly. However, most of the inhabitants of Over-the-Hill and in the whole Bahamas, for that matter, were 'dependent on the merchants for their necessaries, and generally indebted to the latter, who could control their votes'.[14] As late as 1889, only six black members were returned to the House of Assembly. The House was still dominated by the white mercantile elite. The white elite maintained the majority and directed policy to suit their own interests in informal, as much as in legislative, ways[15] while most Over-the-Hill matters were settled by the elders of the area under the silk-cotton tree.

Despite the attitudes of the powerful white elite and its discriminatory treatment of the Over-the-Hill people, something positive emerged. Perhaps it was the very isolation of the people and the fact that they were mainly ignored by the whites that united them. As Dr Eneas said in a talk about 'Over-the-Hill', the people of Bain Town and Grant's Town were free men, and never allowed anyone to forget that fact; they 'brooked no interference' from Up-town in any form.[16] It is interesting to note that both the riots which occurred in Grant's Town in the nineteenth century (one in 1863 and one in 1893) were caused by outside interference. The first disturbance occurred when members of the West India Regiment tried to enamour themselves with Grant's Town women. The second incident was sparked off when the police force, which comprised many Barbadians, imprisoned an Over-the-Hill person much to the chagrin of the Grant's Town residents. Magistrate Powles said in 1888 that the people in Grant's Town could 'get drink at all hours without any interference on the part of the police ...'[17]

As Dr Eneas also pointed out, the people from Over-the-Hill had to fend for themselves and make their own way in life. Many kept their native languages alive for some time. Dr C.R. Walker Sr., who was interviewed in 1970, remembered that as a boy some of the older Africans sang and talked in their own languages. He mentioned the Yorubas (Nangoes), Congoes and the Mandingo tribal groups from West Africa. There were others such as the Ibos and the Hausas. He also remembered that the Africans kept alive certain customs including the jump-in dance, the fire dance and ring play; storytelling, the B'Bookie and B'Rabby stories; drumming and the Christmas festivities (later known as John Canoe or Junkanoo), the playing of the West African game Warri; the way of preparing foods (victuals) in the African style such as Foo-foo (a type of Okra stew), Accara (mashed boiled peas, okra and hot pepper made into a type of patty), My-my (mashed peas, highly seasoned and wrapped in almond leaves) and Agidee (a type of dessert made with grits, milk, sugar and nutmeg). The people of Over-the-Hill also kept alive for a long time the African way of cooking food on outside fires[18] and knew the use of bush medicine. Economically they were able to survive by thrifty habits and through the custom of accumulating money by means of the Asue and also by the setting up of vegetable and fruit stalls and petty shops at the sides of the road, a custom so prevalent in West Africa.

There was a Grant's Town market in the mid-nineteenth century near the Rhine Hart Hotel, but later the inhabitants found it more profitable to sell the produce from their gardens in the town. Later, they would be among the first straw vendors.

Another means of survival was through the formation of Friendly Societies. These societies protected members during their old age and in time of sickness. They also ensured that members received dignified burials. The Grant's Town Friendly Society was established shortly after emancipation on August 1, 1835. There was also a Congo United Society in Bain Town which was established in 1864-75 with headquarters on Brougham Street, and a Hausa Society later known as the Knight of King George Lodge.

Besides these Friendly Societies, Over-the-Hill people also took religion seriously and assisted in building Wesley Methodist, St Agnes, Bethel Baptist; St John's and later the Churches of God. Magistrate Powles noted that they were 'reverential by nature and swearing was by no means common among them'.[19]

Over-the-Hill residents were proud people. Poor they might have been, but their humble houses were neat and clean. They took pride not only in their houses but in their appearance. As Magistrate Powles observed in 1888:

> On Sundays and holidays the coloured women usually wear cotton dresses of various shades of blue, rose-pink, and white ... Occasionally you see a coloured lady grandly attired in silk, satin and velveteen, or even velvet, with a fashionable hat, and probably coloured stockings and tight white boots and shoes. They nearly always wear shady hats, mostly trimmed with white, with some colour introduced, and on the whole their dress is pretty and tasteful, and very suitable to the climate.[20]

Over the years a community spirit grew, each generation instilling its values on the next. Through hard work and sacrifice many Over-the-Hill people and their descendants became leaders in the society at large. Among the early settlers of Grant's Town were the Robinsons, Mitchells, Williams, Wallaces, Cunninghams, Adderleys, Thompsons, Eneas', Fergusons, McPhersons and Hepburns. Some of the Bain Town names include the Smiths, Deans, Perpalls, Tooths, Bains and Sawyers.

When the wind of change began to blow over the Bahamas in the 1950s and 1960s, Over-the-Hill residents were aware and were in the vanguard of that change. Political change, brought by the 'Quiet Revolution' in 1967 which was to give a new dignity and pride to black Bahamians, was led by Over-the-Hill people.

Notes

1. Laws of The Bahamas, 2 Vic. c. 1.
2. James Eacott, Eleuthera, to MMS., August 2, 1838. Bahamas Letters 1835, 1838-1840, MMS.
3. Michael Craton, *A History of The Bahamas*, 3rd edition (Waterloo: 1986), 197.
4. Howard Johnson, *The Bahamas in Slavery and Freedom* (Kingston and London: 1991), 15-26.
5. Gail Saunders, *Slavery in The Bahamas, 1648-1838* (Nassau: 1985), 213-14; Michael Craton and Gail Saunders, *Islanders in the Stream. A History of the Bahamian People*. Vol 2. (Athens: Georgia University Press, 1998), 25-31.
6. David Lowenthal, *West Indian Societies* (New York: 1972), 67.
7. Patrice Williams, 'A Guide to African Villages in New Providence, Department of Archives', (Nassau: 1979), 8; Department of Archives, Bahamas, *Settlements in New Providence: Exhibition Booklet* (Nassau: 1982); Gail Saunders, *Slavery in The Bahamas*, 197.
8. Cleveland Eneas, *Bain Town* (Nassau: 1976).
9. Ibid., 2.
10. Department of Archives *Settlements*, 16-21.
11. Charles Ives, *The Isles of Summer* (New Haven: 1880), 53.
12. Colebrooke to Glengelg, December 15, 1838, C023/94/461.
13. M.F. Doran and R.A. Landis, 'Origin and Persistence of an Inner City Slum in Nassau', *Geographical Review*, 70: 2 (April: 1980), 189.
14. J.M. Wright, 'History of The Bahama Islands', in G.B. Shattuck, *The Bahama Islands* (Baltimore: 1908), 521. Cited in Colin Hughes, *Race and Politics in The Bahamas* (St. Lucia, Queensland: 1981), 10.
15. Gail Saunders, 'The Social History of The Bahamas' (Unpublished PhD thesis, University of Waterloo, 1985), 42.
16. Cleveland Eneas, *The Bahamas Sunday Times*, March 27 – April 3, 1988, 4.
17. L.D. Powles, *Land of The Pink Pearl* (London: 1888), 151.
18. Saunders, *Slavery in The Bahamas*, 165.
19. L.D. Powles, *Land of The Pink Pearl*, 155.
20. Ibid., 151-52.

6

Aspects of Traditional African-Bahamian Culture in the Late Nineteenth and Early Twentieth Century

Bahamian society in the late nineteenth and early twentieth century was deeply divided by race. Emancipation had legally freed the slaves, but in spite of gradual changes since 1838, it had failed to alter the structure of the society fundamentally. The majority of the people, who were black, remained dominated and socially ignored by the white official and mercantile class. In New Providence there was a growing coloured middle class which was also ignored by the ruling clique, yet which, in turn, looked down on the labouring black classes. According to Lowenthal, West Indian society is shaped by three basic elements, 'class hierarchy', 'social pluralism' and 'cultural pluralism'.[1] West Indian classes are separated not only by differences in 'colour and status, power and wealth' but maintain different 'social patterns and social frameworks'.[2] This paper will examine traditions, belief systems, and leisure time activities of the black majority.

Hard economic times meant that little time was left to black and poor whites for recreation. Most Bahamians' time, in fact, was taken up with work activities and it was sometimes difficult to separate work and leisure.[3] The majority of Bahamians combined work and pleasure. This was particularly evident in the market places, especially the Nassau market. As Bryan demonstrated, markets in Jamaica were viewed as the 'clubs of the poor' and were used for meeting friends and being entertained by Sagwa.[3]

African-Caribbean women also used the marketplace for organizing the Yoruba derived 'Asue' (also known as 'sou sou', 'partner' or 'meet and turn') to save and meet financial obligations.[4] As credit facilities were almost absent for all but the established merchants and businessmen, the ordinary labouring citizen had to find ways of financing projects for themselves. The Asue was a widespread informal or folk system of saving money. As Dr Eneas explained in *Bain Town* only people who had proven themselves trustworthy 'kept' the Asue:

> Small groups of people would place in the hand of these 'asue keepers', an equal sum of money every week; this was called a 'hand'. Each week, one of the participants was given the sum total of all the 'hands'

and this was repeated each week until all 'hands' were drawn; and the process started all over again.[5]

The Asue existed in Nassau, but was not very common on the Out Islands because of the scarcity of cash.

Friendly and Burial Societies and later Lodges also served as insurance plans for the poorer classes on all islands. Howard Johnson argued that Friendly Societies also served as an 'organizational structure around which support could be rallied for matters of great importance to the black community'. The Grant's Town and Eastern Friendly Societies were established as early as 1834 and provided African cultural values that 'were directly in line with tradition underlying similar African origins'.[6] They existed mainly to provide funeral and sickness benefits. Their membership was almost exclusively black. From the 1870s, Friendly Societies grew rapidly and played an important part in the economic and social lives of African-Bahamians. Friendly Societies celebrated an 'Annual Festival', usually to mark Emancipation Day and made a presentation to the Governor. On August 2, 1880, they processed, accompanied by a band, to Trinity Methodist Church, a bastion of the white elite, and filled the chapel. This event, expressions of grievances in the media and the passage of resolutions addressing the complaints of blacks demonstrated social protest and gave African Bahamians an 'extended political role' in 'response to the formal political structures which were dominated by a small group of white Bahamians'. Johnson also argued that the Friendly Societies can be seen as embryonic political parties.[7] Women were an integral part of the Friendly Societies and Lodges which also offered 'comradeship' and a sense of belonging to the community.

In the Bahamas as in the Caribbean generally, religion was fundamental and central to social life. It was indeed a 'major link' between the urban and rural communities.[8] In the late nineteenth century, most Bahamians were at least nominally Christian. Women and men from all sectors took the church very seriously, the Bible often was the only accessible book. The church offered respectability and provided a form of social control in regulating public behaviour, setting standards of morality, providing organized activities for its members and involving both men and women in leadership roles. It also provided 'an important criterion for social mobility'.[9]

At the turn of the century, the majority of Bahamians attended either the Anglican, Methodist or Baptist Church. There was also an African Episcopal Methodist or 'Shouter Chapel' in Over-the-Hill New Providence. These churches, which for the most part catered to both races, although race and colour bias in church memberships developed, offered a myriad of activities and some responsibility to both sexes. The church gave men and women the opportunity to 'get out' and communicate with other churchgoers.

Although the churches had mixed congregations, most blacks attended those in the Over-the-Hill area, such as St Agnes (Anglican), Wesley (Methodist) and Bethel or St John's (Baptist). Where the congregation was mixed, whites had segregated seating patterns. Church-going was an occasion when women dressed in their Sunday best. Many black women who did not wear shoes or stockings during the week did so on Sundays.

Blacks and coloureds aspired to membership in the Anglican Church, the established church in the Bahamas until 1869, and the church of the British colonists. They were attracted to its High Church Ritualism. Unlike Christ Church Cathedral which remained low church, the parishes of St Agnes and St Mary's which catered mainly to blacks and coloureds offered the celebration of the High Mass with its use of candles, vestments, incense and processional marches. The ritual included the adoration of the Virgin Mary and Confession. The Anglicans in the High Church parishes were said to have 'out Romed Rome'.[10]

The Baptist faith which had been introduced to the Bahamas by freed slaves from America, with its emphasis on spiritual freedom and the opportunity to worship in one's own way, attracted few whites and the church soon became almost exclusively black. It was particularly strong in Cat Island and Andros which had large African populations.

Women as well as men in the Anglican, Methodist and Baptist Churches took leadership roles as teachers of Sunday schools, fundraisers at the annual bazaars and in Guilds (Anglican Church), class leaders, heads of prayer groups, Temperance Leagues and later in the Women's League (Methodist Church). The more affluent blacks held social events to raise funds. The *Tribune* for October 31, 1911 advertised that a 'Garden Fete in aid of the Wesley Church Organ Fund would take place on Friday, November 3 at the Garden of Mrs David Patton, Augusta Street. Fruit and flower stalls...refreshments, light and solid,...music in attendance. Admission 3d Children 1d'.[11]

Church took up most of Sunday. There was the morning service, Sunday School and evensong. Although men directed the affairs of the church, women were an important and integral part. They participated in almost all the activities except those at the altar.

While the white elite and coloured middle class put emphasis on formalized institutional structures and systems of belief, the black masses, including women, combined the 'traditional, evangelical and fundamentalist forms of Christianity with revivalism and spiritualism'. Their God was more 'accessible to direct persuasion' and they believed 'both in salvation by faith and in a spirit world where the dead possessed supernatural powers and mediated among the living'.[12]

In the Baptist and AME Churches women were particularly moved by the emotional sermon, rhythmic anthem singing traditionally accompanied by handclapping and the phenomenon of spirit possession, the 'supreme religious experience for the person of African origins'. It demonstrated 'the continuing integration and syncretism between European based Christianity and African religious belief'.[13]

Herskovits, who noted similar possession rites among black communities in Guiana, Brazil, Haiti, Trinidad, Jamaica, Cuba and the United States believed, as did Dale Bisnauth, that these practices owed their existence in the New World to a common source in Africa.[14]

Dancing was taboo in the Baptist and Jumper Churches, but both men and women welcomed the African inspired 'Rushin' similar to the antebellum 'ring shout' in the Southern United States and revival services in Jamaica. The 'Rushin', march, shuffle or dance in a counter-clockwise direction around the church with rhythmic bodily movements and handclapping, was common in black communities. It was performed during the singing of anthems and spirituals at the end of the regular service.

Parsons witnessed a 'Rushin' meeting on New Year's Eve in 1927. Women were intimately involved:

> The two front rows of girls sang 'Shine, Shine, Shine' 'Honey in the Rock' and other 'anthum' (sic). Both sexes, young and old, performed a strut or one-step dance around the benches, the women holding out their petticoats and the men, the flaps of their coats. Some of the paraders joined in the singing.[15]

This tradition, which was outlawed in the United States and subsequently disappeared, still survives in the Bahamas being particularly strong in Cat Island and Andros. Clement Bethel described it as a 'manifestation of a New World Africanism'. It is indeed an example of creolization and the struggle for survival under 'harsh and oppressive' conditions not only in slavery as Bisnauth contends, but also in freedom.[16]

Although nominally Christian, the black labouring population particularly on Cat Island and Andros, as in other Caribbean societies, retained African features in their religious practices into the early twentieth century. The memory of these beliefs and traditions was probably strengthened and augmented by the arrival and settlement of Liberated Africans between 1811 and 1860.[17] Both men and women believed in 'the efficacy of certain charms practices under the name of "Obi or "Obeah"' and participated in the 'old African witchcraft as practised by the slaves imported from the West Coast of Africa'.[18]

An Anglican priest accused some of the Baptists of being 'semi-heathen people' and 'very slightly acquainted either with the Creed or the Ten Commandments: living under obedience to their native elders, mixed with a superstitious dread of obeah and witchcraft…' Anglican priest, the Rev. M.M.J. Cooper, writing from Watlings Island, complained of the problem of Obeahism 'or the belief in the power of persons working under the influence of the witchdoctor to do just as they pleased with anyone whom they desire to hurt or…' to 'put one so' or to 'fix' or 'wuk witch'.[19]

The practice of obeah, a combination of superstition, medicine and worship, and the use of 'bush' medicine were an integral part of the lives of the black class of both sexes in the Bahamas. Although they were generally banned, these practices were socially important and can be seen as 'vehicles of protest and resistance'.[20] 'Obeah included any religious or magical practices...considered to be "African", including healing and conjuring of all types – securing success in love and family affairs, or favourable results in litigation, or injuring enemies.'[21]

Up to the 1950s, Grant's Town and Fox Hill were renowned for their obeah experts some of whom had learned their skills in Cuba and Haiti. Dr Eneas remembers that the people in Bain Town were very superstitious and true believers in Obeah. They were employed to do special jobs and make the potent 'fix' which was 'not to be messed with under any circumstances'. The most common sign of Obeah was a tree which was 'fixed' displaying the conspicuous green bottle stuffed with wet moss, leaves, twigs and sand, hanging from a branch. If the fruit was stolen or eaten from a tree so 'fixed' one would 'swell up and die'. There was no use going to a physician once you were fixed because 'doctor medicine' cannot cure Obeah. Ancestral spirits used to hurt people in the Bahamas, as in Jamaica, were known as 'duppies'.[22]

From slavery days, West Indians, including the Bahamian black labouring class, traditionally used the West African practice of herbal medicine, believed to be curative and to contain magical powers. It was particularly prevalent in Out Island settlements, where there were no doctors. European doctors and administrators commented on the high mortality rate and reluctance of Caribbean creoles to go to the hospital.[23] Governor Blake reported in 1886 that 'people rarely applied for admission until they had exhausted the means of cure known to the "Bush" doctors or obeah men'.[24]

Patrick Bryan demonstrated that in Jamaica like the doctors, the governors did not report on those home remedies that worked, and many of them did. Bahamians, like their Caribbean counterparts in the early 1900s, believed there was a hidden danger in doctor medicine. Amelia Defries told of her visit to 'Aunt Celia', the medicine woman of Eight Mile Rock, Grand Bahama who cured her of a chill or cold in two days, the usual time her cures are effected. Aunt Celia who boasted that 'nobody never dies of my treatment', picked her medicine in the 'Bush' and freshly boiled it for each patient.

For physiotherapy she used lard or melted tallow candle and sometimes mixed it with cow's gall and a 'large, big rusty old nail'; to heal wounds she boiled the Shepherd's Needle plant and 'pepper grass' for inflammation. Tooth decay was cured with cobbler's wax rubbed in daily to 'kill out de worrum what eats de teet away'. She also treated and had cures for sore throats, tumours, growths, skin problems, headache and typhoid fever.[25] Aunt Celia also served as a midwife and used birth methods similar to those of her counterparts in the Caribbean. After the birth of a baby, the mother and child remained in the house for nine days and only family members were allowed to visit. Some mothers stayed in the house and avoided hard work for three to six months.[26]

The survival of the practice of Bush Medicine was especially evident at the Smithsonian Folklife Festival in 1994 when Daisy Nottage, from North Andros, demonstrated the potency of her medicine concoction, 'Twenty One Gun Salute' by curing many Bahamian participants who became ill with influenza and even those who 'ain't sick' but just needed energy.[27]

African-Caribbean and African-Bahamian customs relating to death and burial differed from those practised by Europeans. The event of a death for the majority of Caribbean people was of general community interest. As Clement Bethel stated, 'the observation of death rites and ceremonies is central to the Afro-Bahamian mentality'. A tradition of 'holding wakes and, "setting-up" meetings over the dead' was observed throughout the Bahama Islands.[28] The custom varied in the different settlements. In some communities the wake was held before death when family, friends, Friendly Society and Lodge members gathered at the home of the ailing person. Edwards described a wake in the 1890s:

> The strangest of all their customs is the service of song held on the night when some friend is supposed to be dying. If the patient does not die, they come again the next night, and between the disease and the hymns the poor negro is pretty sure to succumb. The singers, men, women and children of all ages, sit around on the floor of the larger room of the hut and stand outside at the doors and windows, while the invalid lies upon the floor in the smaller room. Long into the night they sing their most mournful hymns and 'anthems', and only in the light of dawn do those who are left as chief mourners silently disperse.[29]

In most settlements the wake or 'setting up' was held after the funeral, usually in the church or at the home of the deceased. If held at home, after midnight, refreshments of coffee and johnny cake (a local bread) were served. There would also be a secret supply of alcoholic beverages for the men.

The funeral, because of the climate and lack of embalming methods, usually took place within 24 hours of the death. After the 'passing', men, usually from the Friendly Society or Lodge, built a coffin while others dug the grave. Women prepared and 'dressed' the body to be 'laid out' for burial. The coffin was carried in procession from the house to the church and the graveside. Lodge members turned out in full regalia to the accompaniment of a brass band and followed the coffin. As Clement Bethel noted, the music on the way to the graveyard 'is slow and mournful'. On leaving the cemetery, the tempo of the band livened up.[30] The funeral served as a meeting ground for old friends and was a highlight in the social life of the black majority.

Music was, and still is, an integral part of the lives of Caribbean people. What Hugh Paget wrote of Jamaican country people in the foreword to *Folk*

Songs of Jamaica can be applied generally: 'they work and play to music: it is the spontaneous expression in their own idiom of their joys and sorrows, their wit, their religion and their philosophy of life'.[31] Caribbean music, a creolization process blending African and European forms, began very early in slave societies. Bilby argued that blending occurred between European and African traditions as well as the 'varied traditions of a multitude of African ethnic groups'.[32]

Essentially, African traditions were present in the music of the majority of Bahamians. Music, derived from the antebellum slave songs of the United States and from the hymns contained in the early Wesleyan and Baptist hymnals, was important in the lives of the black men and women. Religious music was characterized almost exclusively by unaccompanied singing and secular music was associated 'with festive recreation and dance activities' incorporating the use of musical instruments.[33]

Religious songs or spirituals, important at social gatherings and wakes, included wake or 'setting up' songs with biblical themes. Rhyming songs (spiritual and secular), including fantasies or real-life happenings, gave an animated storyteller a back-up chorus. The rhymer or lead singer, usually a male, tells the story in verse and a chorus echoes basically the same refrain after each verse. Anthems or religious hymns closely resembling the American antebellum slave songs were brought to the Bahamas by the Loyalists. They incorporate call and response patterns with a lead soloist, male or female, and are accompanied by a syncopated beat. The Bahamian songs expressed themes of faith, hope and optimism 'rather than those of pessimism and sorrow' present in American negro spirituals.

Clement Bethel demonstrated that while religious music in the Bahamas was heavily influenced by Africa, it came almost exclusively by way of the United States mainland. Secular music on the other hand, with its strong emphasis on drumming and dancing, emanated more directly from Africa. Survival of the African-based traditions was partly due to the isolated and neglected black settlements and the continued practice by men and women both in New Providence and in the Out Islands.

Dance was another popular form of entertainment. Bethel argued that there were three distinctly different types of African-derived ring dances which were frequently practised, especially in Over-the-Hill, New Providence and in black settlements. Despite the Christian Church's effort to suppress such dances, the holding of ring dances to the accompaniment of the goatskin drum (the chief instrument throughout Africa), perhaps a concertina and two pieces of iron, was a favourite form of recreational activity.[34]

Each dance – the Fire dance, the Jumping dance and the Ring Play – was held upon the formation of a ring in which the participants, both men and women, stood in a circle around one or more dancers. There was always some form of accompaniment – singing, chanting, clapping, drum rhythms or maybe a combination of these. Solo dancing by both sexes took place at some point in the proceedings.[35]

A popular form of leisure among the Bahamian black labouring population was the telling of traditional folktales. Folklorists Edwards, Parsons and Crowley pointed out that 'Ole' stories were told in the evening, in 'yards' or in a house usually inhabited by families or individuals who had much in common. Storytelling and the telling of riddles, usually following singing, was a time when children and adults gathered at bedtime, lay on the floor or sat on rocks in the yard and listened to an adult, 'talk old stories'. Storytelling usually continued until midnight.[36]

Tales were divided into 'old stories' and fairy tales which had roots in Europe and Africa. Many came by way of the American South and the West Indies. Crowley argued that so many of the traditional Bahamian structures, themes and even stylistic devices are shared with other New World Negroes, it seems to indicate that they came to the New World together as part of the same cultural heritage. '… Africa still remains the most likely source of the old stories.'[37]

The characters of B'Rabby and B'Booky, popularized in America by Joel Chander Harris, were favourites occurring in Haiti, St Lucia, Trinidad, Jamaica and other Caribbean islands as do most other Bahamian characters. The B'Anansi West African trickster, a symbol of passive resistance and particularly popular in Jamaican folk tales, is also present in Bahamian folk tales. Very often 'old stories' included tales of ships and wrecks, of large hauls of fish, or various adventures, or misfortunes such as the cholera and the 1866 hurricane.[38] Both men and women were storytellers.

According to Crowley in the 1960s, storytelling although less frequent in New Providence, survived the 'advent of radios, motion pictures, and extensive literacy.'[39] In 1994, several storytellers, including some women, notably Mabel Williams of San Salvador and Kayla Edwards of Nassau, accompanied the contingent to the Smithsonian Folklife Festival. However, Patricia Glinton-Meicholas, another prominent storyteller who has published her work, is fearful that 'unless storytelling receives a fresh infection of creativity and recaptures its audience, the tradition will be lost to us'.[40]

Public holidays were scattered throughout the year. One day holidays were occasions for festive celebrations. These usually included Christmas and New Year, Good Friday, Easter Monday, King's Birthday, Whit Monday, Empire Day and Emancipation Day or August Monday.[41]

Emancipation Day was celebrated throughout the Bahamas on or around August 1 in various ways in the different settlements. Women were very much involved in these activities. Powles observed in Nassau that, every August, some of the Africans elected a queen (perhaps similar to the Shango Cult in Trinidad) whose will was law on certain matters. Northcroft noticed that 'processions, dances and entertainment of various sorts are held and sometimes the proceedings are kept up for nearly a week'. As already noted, Friendly Societies in Nassau traditionally marched to Government House on the eve of Emancipation to present past grievances. According to Dr Eneas, people also gave thanks in their various churches and afterwards gathered on the Fox Hill Parade or green for speech-making and 'generally merry-making'.[42]

None of the Out Island communities celebrated holidays as elaborately as the Nassauvians did. At Cat Island in 1888, the Reverend Matthews reported that harvested produce and fruit were used to decorate the church. Festivities included a choral celebration in the morning, a 'parish feast' and sports including athletics and football in the afternoon. The day ended with choral evensong. At Harbour Island, led by the Friendly Societies and Lodges, the entire black population, smartly dressed, congregated on the whites' harbour-side area of Dunmore Town to celebrate Emancipation Day.[43]

Fox Hill Day in New Providence traditionally followed a week after Emancipation Day and was quite elaborate. According to Dr Eneas, Bain Town people, who made preparations well in advance, moved to stay with relatives a week before the great day. Women did most of the preparations and participated in the church and Sunday School programmes which featured recitations, music and drama. They also were an integral part of the festivities which included plaiting of the Maypole, ring play and singing.

They supervised stalls with all types of food including the traditional African dishes such as accara, moi-moi, agidi and foo-foo. Other foods, popular even in recent times, namely coconut cakes, peas and rice, stewed fish and different kinds of native fruit, were also available. Liquor was sold to the men at nearby stalls. Women did not usually drink in public.[44]

Many Out Island communities celebrated holidays such as Empire Day by holding an 'Entertainment' or concert, actually a variety show, featuring every age rank in the community. These programmes, as they were also called, were usually lengthy affairs and included recitations, dialogues, songs (solos and duets) and drills. Women were usually among the organizers and also participated. Guy Fawkes Day, in remembrance of the ill-fated 'Gunpowder Plot', a custom peculiar to the English, was transferred to their colonies where it was adopted wholeheartedly. Although not a holiday it was celebrated in the Bahamas with some enthusiasm. On November 5 from a little after sunset, until well into the night, effigies were burnt 'in a revelry of shouting, singing accompanied by the beating of drums, clanging of cowbells and popping of fire crackers'.[45]

Christmas was traditionally a time for great festivities. Most of the activity, especially in Out Island communities, centered around the church. Christmas Eve and the New Year's Eve Watch-night services attracted most of the community, male and female. Both services usually ended with a 'rushin' meeting followed by dancing and 'spreeing' and much drinking, at least by the men. A week before Christmas there was 'feverish activity' when houses were cleaned and churches made ready. Special foods, especially bennie, coconut and pound cakes were made. Just before Christmas, whole families visited Nassau. While the men disposed of their sponges or other wares, the ladies shopped for clothes, dry-goods and other foods, unavailable on the Out Island settlements.[46]

Three days holiday had been given at Christmas to slaves in the Bahamas and they celebrated 'in their own way' usually ending with a 'gran dance'.[47] By the early 1890s, the urban, male and predominantly black John Canoe Festival was a popular feature of the season, not only as a way of letting off steam, but was also used by the Friendly Societies in the 1890s as 'an agent for social change (and protest) and a way of prodding the Government into action'.[48] 'Perhaps, Junkanoo', as Natalie Davis argued for Carnival 'could at once be social protest and social control...the elites may willingly allow such play in order to release tensions that could otherwise be threatening.'[49]

At the Out Islands such as Eleuthera and Green Turtle Cay off Abaco, Christmas festivities were slightly different. While John Canoe was held in Eleuthera, the chief amusement was an entertainment given by the different Lodges on Christmas Eve. In the bi-racial settlement of Green Turtle Cay, Abaco, New Year's Day was celebrated by the appearance of 'Old Skin' or 'Bunce' who was carried in a wheel barrow covered in canvas along the streets of the town where most of the population including women turned out. He later appeared and danced in strange costumes made from paper or rags.[50]

For the majority of Bahamians the nineteenth century way of life continued well into the twentieth. The late nineteenth century worldwide developments in electricity, communications and transportation although impacting positively on the Bahamas, only marginally affected the majority of Bahamians who lived in the Out Islands and in isolated settlements in New Providence. The lack of leisure time and electricity meant that the labouring black population had limited exposure to the American culture which impacted on the Bahamas, especially after Prohibition and the First World War.

Traditional popular culture remained strong in black rural settlements on New Providence and in the Out Islands. The recent performances of Bahamian tradition bearers at the Smithsonian Folklife Festival (1994) in Washington is evidence of the survival of traditional Bahamian culture. Research for the Festival revealed that relative isolation and poverty preserved the traditional popular culture with its strong African influences which through a process of creolization had developed a distinctly Bahamian style. The settlement of Liberated Africans in the Bahamas between 1811 and 1860 reinforced African-derived culture. The work of Rosanne Adderley, on the impact of Liberated Africans on Bahamian and Trinidadian societies, is most important in this regard. [51]

Notes

1. David Lowenthal, *West Indian Societies* (London: Oxford University Press, 1972), 91.
2. Lowenthal, 100
3. Patrick Bryan, *The Jamaican People 1880-1902* (London and Basingstoke: Macmillan, 1991), 209.
4. Olive Senior, *Working Miracles: Women's Lives in the English Speaking Caribbean* (Cave Hill, Barbados: University of the West Indies, Institute of Social and Economic Research, 1991), 146.
5. Cleveland Eneas, *Bain Town* (Nassau: 1976), 17.
6. Howard Johnson, 'Friendly Societies in The Bahamas, 1834-1910', *Slavery and Abolition, A Journal of Comparative Studies*. 12: 3 (Dec. 1991), 184-186.
7. Ibid.
8. Bryan, 207.
9. Dale Bisnauth, *History of Religions in the Caribbean* (Kingston: 1989), 100.
10. Gail Saunders, 'Social History of The Bahamas' (Unpublished PhD thesis, University of Waterloo, 1985), 89-90; M. Craton and G. Saunders, *Islanders in The Stream. A History of The Bahamian People*. 2 vols (Athens, Georgia: University of Georgia Press, 1998) 2: 112.
11. *Nassau Tribune*, Oct. 31, 1911.
12. Lowenthal, 115.
13. Clement Bethel, 'Music in The Bahamas: Its Roots, Development and Personality', (MA thesis, University of California, Los Angeles, 1978), 55-6.
14. Melville J. Herskovits, *The Myth of The Negro Past* (Gloucester, MA: 1970), 215-16. Cited in C. Bethel, 'Music in The Bahamas'.
15. Elsie Clews Parsons, 'Spirituals and Other Folklore from the Bahamas', *Journal of American Folklore*. 41: 162 (Oct.- Dec., 1928), 455-56.
16. Bethel, 'Music in the Bahamas', 84.
17. Gail Saunders, *Slavery in The Bahamas* (Nassau: 1985), 193-202; Howard Johnson, *The Bahamas in Slavery and Freedom* (Kingston: Ian Randle Publishers; London: James Currey, 1991), 30-54; Craton and Saunders, *Islanders in The Stream*. 2: 5-17.
18. *Nassau Quarterly Mission Papers (NQMP)*,XI: 43 (Dec. 1896), 79.
19. *NQMP,* XXXI: 122 (Sept. 1916) 41. See also Roscow Shedden, *Ups and Downs in a West Indian Diocese* (London: 1927): 145-6.
20. Frank Jan Van Dyk, 'Review of History of Religions in The Caribbean', by D. Bisnauth in *New West Indian Guide*, 68: 3 and 4 (1994), 339.
21. Bridget Brereton, *Race Relations in Colonial Trinidad, 1870-1900* (Cambridge: University Press, 1979), 156; See also Timothy McCartney, *Ten Ten The Bible Ten. Obeah in the Bahamas* (Nassau: 1976), 56.
22. *Harper's Magazine*, 132 (Dec. 1915); Daniel Crowley, *I Could Talk Old Story Good: Creativity in Bahamian Folklore* (Berkeley and Los Angeles: University of California Press, 1966), 17; Eneas, 9; Lillith Glover, *Ilun Peepul. A Jaunt Through Bahamian Culture and Folklore* (Nassau), 89-90.

23. Bryan, 185.
24. Blake to Granville, March 20, 1886. No. 32 Duplicate Governors' Despatches, Dec. 8, 1881 – July 25, 1887, 419.
25. Amelia Defries, *In a Forgotten Colony* (Nassau: Nassau Guardian, 1916), 81-6.
26. Ibid., 83. See also Keith Otterbein, *The Andros Islanders. A Study of Family Organization in the Bahamas* (Kansas: University of Kansas Press, 1966), 63-6 and Saunders, *Bahamian Society*, 28-9.
27. Interview with Daisy Nottage and Mabel Williams, Smithsonian Folklife Festival, July 4, 1994.
28. Bethel, 84.
29. Charles L. Edwards, *Bahamas Songs and Stories* (New York: 1942, reprint of 1895 edition).
30. Bethel, 90-91. See also *Bahamas Handbook*, 1970-1971 'The Bahamian Way of Death', 94-107.
31. Hugh Paget in the Foreword of *Folk Songs of Jamaica*, ed. by Tom Murray (London: Oxford University Press, 1951).
32. Kenneth M. Bilby. *The Caribbean as a Musical Region* (Washington D.C.: The Woodrow Wilson International Centre for Scholars). One in a series of 11 pamphlets entitled *Focus Caribbean*, edited by S. Mintz and S. Price, 3.
33. Bethel, 28.
34. Bethel, 62.
35. Ibid, 125-8.
36. Edwards, *Bahamas Songs...*, 17; Parsons, 'Spirituals and Other Folklore'; D. Crowley, *I Could Talk*, 11-2.
37. Crowley, 129; See also Helen L. Flowers, *A Classification of the Folktale of The West Indies by Types and Motifs* (New York: 1980).
38. Crowley, 106; G.J.H. Northcroft, *Sketches of Summerland. Giving Some Account of Nassau and the Bahama Islands* (Nassau: 1912), 71.
39. Ibid., 14.
40. Patricia Glinton-Meicholas, *An Evening in Guanima* (Nassau: Guanima Press, 1993) (Introduction).
41. No. 8. 26 Vic. C. 8 assented to 26 May 1863, declared Christmas Day, the Birthdays of the King or Queen, and the Prince of Wales' Dec. 3, in commemoration of the landing of HRH Prince Alfred at Nassau in 1861 and New Year's Day to be public holidays. By 1926, the latter holiday had been dropped and Good Friday, Empire Day, first Monday in August and October 12 had been added, 25 of 1926, Statute Law of The Bahamas (Nassau: 1929), 2032-6.
42. L.D. Powles, *The Land of the Pink Pearl* (London: 1981), 147; Northcroft, 66 and Eneas, *Bain Town*, 32; Angelina Pollak-Eltz, 'The Shango Cult and other African Rituals in Trinidad, Grenada, and Carriacou and their Possible Influence on the Spiritual Baptist Faith', *Caribbean Quarterly*, 39: 3 and 4 (Sept./Dec. 1993), 19-24.
43. *NQMP*, III: 10 (Sept. 1888), 54; Edwards, *Bahamas Songs* opposite 18 and 90; Saunders, 'Social History', 139.
44. Eneas, *Bain Town*, 32-3; Saunders, 'Social History', 107.
45. See Bethel, 'Music in the Bahamas...', 216 and Powles, *Pink Pearl*, 147.
46. Glover, 42-3.

47. Farquharson's Journal 1831-2, published as a *Relic of Slavery* (Nassau: 1957), Wed. Dec. 26, 1832, 36.
48. Bethel 'Music in the Bahamas...', 219
49. Natalie Davis, *Society and Culture in Early Modern France* (Stanford, California: 1975), Chap. 4. Cited Steven L. Kaplan, *Understanding Popular Culture*. 11 (Berlin: 1984).
50. *Junkanoo* (Nassau: Public Records Office, 1978), 15; Saunders, 'Social History', 138; Michael Craton, 'Decoding Pitchy-Patchy: The Roots, Branches and Essence of Junkanoo', Paper presented at the 26th Annual Conference of the Association of Caribbean Historians, 10-11.
51. Rosanne M. Adderely, 'New Negroes from Africa: Culture and Community Among Liberated Africans in The Bahamas and Trinidad 1810 to 1900'. (PhD dissertation, University of Pennsylvania, 1996).

7

The Blockade Running Era in the Bahamas: Blessing or Curse?

Until recently, historians and writers have not given a balanced and positive view of Bahamian history. As Peter Dalleo demonstrated in *Pirates and Plunderers? Rethinking Bahamian History*, 'few authors have attempted to construct a general treatment of the past, none have succeeded in providing a comprehensive history of the Bahamian experience'.[1] It is true, general histories have tended to rely too heavily on the 'boom and bust' interpretation of Bahamian history giving the impression that Bahamians were a lazy, immoral people with a 'wait and see attitude', profiting from the misfortunes of others, and relying on the 'bonanza' periods like piracy, wrecking, blockade-running and rum-running that resulted.

An examination of the blockade-running period and its effects on Bahamian society might throw a different light on the interpretation of Bahamian history. The period 1861 to 1865 was an important period during which the character of Bahamian society was being forged. Poverty was endemic and life for the majority of Bahamians was harsh, especially on the Out Islands. Most people fished or farmed (or did both) for a living, but the soil to a large extent was unyielding and so agricultural conditions were difficult.

In 1861 salt was the principal staple of the colony and this was supplemented by sponge fishing (which was to sustain the Bahamian economy for three-quarters of a century) and the growth and export of pineapples.

Work for Out Island peasants was harsh and the rewards few. Four-fifths of the land belonged to the Crown and there was no sustained scheme to systematically develop it under lease or grant. Many peasants fell within the category of squatters, having no legal tenure, or farmed 'commonages' while others lived and worked on 'generation lands'.[2]

Many peasant farmers operated on the share-crop system whereby they supplied themselves and the proprietors with food. Their tenure remained insecure because of the control of the mercantile elite over them. Moreover, peasant farming conducted on a share-cropping basis was affected by the

Nassau in 1862, showing a blockade-runner in the left foreground
(From a drawing in the *Illustrated London News*)

truck system which was a means of ensuring that peasant farmers remained constantly indebted to the owners. In a similar way, the pineapple, sponge fishing and boat building industries were also prone to such control. In New Providence, most people lived in the town of Nassau and its suburbs. Governor Rawson estimated that in 1861, about a third of the population of Nassau lived in the suburbs of Grant's Town, Bain Town and Delancey Town.[3] Sandilands at Fox Hill was the only sizeable village outside the town. There were smaller settlements of liberated Africans at Carmichael, Adelaide and Gambier where African dialects were still to be heard.[4]

The town of Nassau stretched from just west of Nassau Street in the west to the east of Mackey Street in the east with a few houses further east. The most built up sections of the town were on Bay Street between George Street in the west and Victoria Avenue in the east. Many merchants lived above their shops on Bay Street or had their residences on Shirley Street, or on the side streets such as East Street (north), Parliament Street, Charlotte Street, Frederick Street, Market Street and George Street. The better-off residents such as Judge Doyle and the Duncombes lived on the ridge on either West Hill or East Hill Street.

The Bahamas in the 1850s was beginning to be recognized as a health resort. In the 1860-1861 season (December to April) about 70 Americans visited Nassau for health reasons many of whom remained to become permanent residents. In 1859 a steamship connection between Nassau and New York was established and in the same year the government agreed to build the Royal Victoria (Nassau's first hotel) which was completed in 1861. In fact its first guests were to be the colourful Confederate sailors, blockade runners and federal agents.

In 1861, very soon after the outbreak of the Civil War, President Lincoln ordered a blockade of the southern ports of the United States. Britain declared its neutrality and promised severe punishment to those British subjects who violated it. However, the southern states needed to trade their cotton for goods, including guns. Due to its strategic position and its proximity to ports in the south, such as Charleston and Wilmington, Nassau became a transshipment area where goods bound for Europe and Confederate ports were traded.

The effects of the blockade were not felt in Nassau until 1862. During the first year of the war, running the blockade was fairly easy as the Union had not properly mobilized its forces. However, when it brought more vessels into service and stationed them off the southern coast, the blockade was tightened and Nassau became important as an entrepôt and neutral port, because of its proximity to the busiest southern ports during the blockade.

For the Bahamas, blockade-running increased trade significantly. As a result, the value of imports went up from 274,584 pounds sterling in 1861 to 1,250,322 pounds sterling in 1862, and the value of exports from 195,584 pounds sterling to over one million pounds sterling over the same period. The number of ships entering and leaving Nassau increased by over one hundred percent.[5] As Stark stated of those years less than three decades later:

> Everyone was wild with excitement during these years of the war. The shops were packed to the ceilings, the streets were crowded with bales, boxes and barrels. Fortunes were made in a few weeks or months. Money was spent and scattered in the most extravagant and lavish manner. The town actually swarmed with southern refugees, captains of crews of blockade runners. Every available space in or out-of-doors was occupied. Men lay on verandahs, walls, docks and floors. Money

Unloading cotton from blockade-runners at Nassau
(Courtesy of the Department of Archives, Bahamas)

was plenty, and sailors sometimes landed with $1,500 in specie. Wages were doubled, liquors flowed freely and the common labourer had his champagne and rich food. Not since the days of the buccaneers and pirates had there been such times in the Bahamas.[6]

It must be remembered that it was Nassau and not the Bahamas generally which benefitted. Only a few violators of the blockade were Bahamians. Those who profited most were outsiders, mainly speculators.

However, some Bahamians did benefit. Shopkeepers and merchants who imported goods which they sold to southern ports and locally at inflated prices to southern visitors and agents in Nassau made huge profits. Moreover, lawyers, the few that there were (only 11 were listed in the Almanack of 1876), also had increased business from the number of maritime cases. The most notable one was the case of the *Oreto*, a blockade runner, captured by the Federals in Bahamian waters. The case was tried in the court of Vice-Admiralty but was released for lack of evidence. It is interesting to note that the armaments of the *Oreto* were hidden at Green Cay.[7]

People considered to be in the lower strata of society – usually coloureds and blacks, also benefitted during these years. Skilled artisans such as shoemakers, blacksmiths and seamstresses were kept busy. Unskilled labourers, including Out Islanders who had migrated to Nassau because of the 'boom', worked as stevedores and draymen especially on the docks where they loaded and unloaded cotton and other goods on and off the visiting steamers. Wages for unskilled labour and for domestic servants doubled. An unskilled labourer could earn $1 a day as a stevedore.[8]

Nassau itself also benefitted in material terms as improvements took place in the town. More construction was promoted by the sudden flow of money. Bay Street was widened, kerbstones and lights installed and the sidewalks were curbed with granite from Union to Parliament Streets. The north side of Bay Street was reclaimed and warehouses and shops built, including John S. George, on the corner of East and Bay Streets. The prison on East Street was built in 1865 right at the end of the blockade. Buildings were said to 'spring' up like mushrooms after rain, while the value of land escalated by 300 to 400 per cent.[9] Rents also rose and it was said that warehouses, shops or offices could be rented annually for what their purchase price was six years before.[10]

Business and the ability to earn money generally increased in Nassau but while wages rose, so did prices. Food was mostly imported and became more costly; eggs, for example were 4 pence each while chickens were 3 shillings and 6 pence. Dry goods such as cloth, notions and some luxury items were sold at inflated prices to local wage earners. Due to high prices, it was impossible for the ordinary workers to save or to accumulate capital.

Socially, blockade-running had a deleterious effect on the Nassau community. Because of the availability of money and the general excitement,

British sailors became over-exuberant and some often became inebriated. This public show of drunkenness – it is said that the sailors often passed out and lay in a stupor on the streets in the town – was a bad example to local people. Moreover, many sailors often got rowdy and became involved in quarrels which resulted in brawls. Cases of petty crimes and disturbances became common.[11]

When the Civil War ended, Nassau's frenzied trade plummeted. Whereas in 1864 at the peak of the blockade-running era, the total value of imports was over five million pounds sterling and the total exports over four and a half million pounds sterling, two years later the totals were 328,622 pounds sterling and 261,976 pounds sterling respectively.[12] The Bahamian economy once more was dependent on its agricultural products and sponge fishing.

Who profited from this brief prosperity? As Gordon K. Lewis has demonstrated in *The Growth of the Modern West Indies*, the main beneficiaries were 'the foreign commercial agents, captains, pilots and gang leaders who left as soon as the brittle affluence of the Atlantic bubble(s) burst...'[13]

Locally, the white merchant class, which included Nassauvians, British residents and landed proprietors, who had previously lived in the Out Islands but had moved into Nassau, benefitted most. For example, John S. George, which was established in 1859 by an Englishman, John Saffrey George, who arrived in Nassau in the mid 1840s, expanded during the 1860s, survived the depression which followed and later switched from selling imported foodstuffs, luxury items and liquor to hardware products, although it was always a sponge outfitter.

Many of the merchant class were members of the legislature. In 1868, two-thirds of the members of the House of Assembly were merchants. In that year not a single resident of the Out Islands was a member of the House.[14] The mercantile elite thus consolidated its economic strength by being elected to the House of Assembly or being appointed to either the Legislative or Executive Councils where they wielded political power.

Some men of colour also profited. Building contractors and blacksmiths such as J.E. Dupuch, tailors, drapers, boot and shoemakers and saddlers were kept busy and some were able to expand their businesses. According to Governor Rawson, two men of colour had done so well that they were able to establish licensed retailed liquor businesses.[15] J.E. Dupuch, building contractor and blacksmith, later entered the House of Assembly (probably in 1875) the first member of the Dupuch family to do so.[16]

However, the vast majority of the population who were mainly black, and quite a number of poor whites who lived in the eastern part of Nassau, Abaco, Harbour Island, Eleuthera and Spanish Wells, remained extremely poor. Many Out Islanders who had migrated to Nassau during the 'boom' period returned to their homes and to their farming and fishing. No efforts were made to develop farming on a systematic basis and most Out Islanders, locked out of ownership of land because of high prices, were to suffer under the truck and share-cropping systems for many years to come. Cotton cultivation was revived at several islands such as Watlings, Exuma and Long Island, but by 1869 it had been abandoned owing to frequent droughts, insect attacks and low prices. The blockade-running era also helped to underline the social divisions in Nassau society which were based mainly on race. Perhaps the most profound effect of the blockade-running era in the Bahamas was the fact that once more a small minority of Bahamians whose ancestors had harboured pirates, wreckers and illegal traders, had brushed again with profitting from activities that were generated from outside, and that were illegal. The whole moral tone of the society was in question.

In the 1920s Prohibition in the United States would again create a 'bonanza' period, once again to be exploited mainly by the small mercantile elite. While money from these brief periods of prosperity filtered down to the middle and labouring strata of the society, the boom periods did not benefit the majority of the population in the long term. Agriculture, fishing, and salt raking – the mainstays of the economy – were neglected and as Gordon Lewis boldly stated, 'sabotaged by the commercial mercantile class that found it more profitable to import foodstuffs from the United States than to subsidize the local food economy'.[17] Perhaps Governor Bayley was correct when he predicted in 1862, that Nassau, in fact the Bahamas, 'would never be the same when the Civil War ended'.

Notes

1. Peter Dalleo, 'Pirates and Plunderers? Rethinking Bahamian History' (Paper given at the Tenth Conference of Caribbean Historians, March 26 – April 1, 1978).
2. See Gail Saunders, 'The Social History of the Bahamas 1890-1953' (Unpublished PhD dissertation, University of Waterloo, 1985), 17-24.
3. Report by Rawson W. Rawson Nov. 9, 1867 C023/189/402.
4. Report on The Bahamas by J.J. Henry, Inspector Major, Station House, Nassau, Dec. 14, 1876. Enclosed in Secretary of State Papers 1831-1907 GOV/15/1, PRO Nassau.
5. Michael Craton, *A History of The Bahamas*, 3rd edition, (Waterloo: 1989), 228.
6. J.H. Stark, *History of and Guide to The Bahamas*, (New York: 1891), 95.
7. Governor's Office United States of America 1863-1872 Box 25, PRO, Nassau, Bahamas.
8. Report on The Blue Book 1862. Enclosed in Bayley to Newcastle, Oct. 15, 1863. Governor's Despatches 1862-1865, folio 197.
9. Gail Saunders and Donald Cartwright, *Historic Nassau* (London: 1979), 41.
10. Report on The Blue Book, 1862.
11. Report on The Blue Book, 1862.

12. Blue Books 1864 and 1866.
13. Gordon K. Lewis, *The Growth of the Modem West Indies* (New York and London: 1969), 311.
14. Rawson to Buckingham and Chandos, July 10, 1868, Governor' Despatches, 1867-1869, folios 292-299.
15. Rawson to Buckingham and Chandos, July 10, 1868, Governor's Despatches, 1867-1869, folios 292-299.
16. Etienne Dupuch, *The Tribune Story (London*: 1967), 19.
17. Gordon Lewis, 313.

8

Prohibition:

A Mixed Blessing for the Bahamas

In January 1919, the Eighteenth Amendment to the United States Constitution was ratified. The Volstead Act, passed in December of that year, introduced national prohibition, to take effect in 1920, outlawing the manufacture, sale, importation or transportation of 'intoxicating liquors'. While Congress agreed to an act banning the liquor trade, it did not provide sufficient funds for its enforcement. This oversight led to the emergence of a lucrative trade in bootleg liquor by a thriving underworld. The Bahamas, because of its proximity, became an important centre for the trans-shipment of liquor into the United States.[1]

Prohibition was a mixed blessing for the Bahamas. On the one hand it caused an unprecedented boom in the colony's poor economy which led to an improvement in public works and social services. The newly found wealth from bootlegging, coupled with the spillover of the land boom from Miami, was used also to boost the nascent tourist industry. On the other hand, while Nassau prospered, the Out Islands were neglected, and with them, agriculture and sponge fishing. The decade of the 1920s which saw much progress in the laying of the material foundations of Nassau, also witnessed the growth of many social ills.

The year 1919 was one of virtual depression especially for the Out Islands, brought about by a decline of the two main staples, sponge and sisal, the neglect of agriculture, a hurricane in September 1919, followed by a severe drought.[2]

Nassauvians also suffered owing to the disruption of shipping, and the subsequent closure of the two main hotels, the Royal Victoria and the Hotel Colonial. Dismal post-war conditions were accentuated by the prevailing high rate of exchange between the Bahamas and the United States, which affected imports.[3]

Prohibition changed this gloomy picture, at least for Nassau. The Volstead Act was difficult to enforce even with the help of several thousand customs agents and the American Coastguard service.[4] Nassau, with its excellent harbour facilities, was ideal for the movement of liquor. So were the scattered and isolated islands and cays closest to the American coast – some as near as 50 miles. Bimini and Grand Bahama monopolized the trade. The decade of the 1920s witnessed a vast movement of alcoholic beverages from the Bahama Islands to the mainland. Additionally, the Customs Act of 1919 had imposed relatively heavy duties upon imported alcohol. With the great increase in trade, there was an unprecedented rise in the revenue.[5]

By October 1921 the colony had undergone a transformation. From early 1920, Nassau's harbour was swarming with ships unloading thousands of barrels of liquor from English and Scottish liquor manufacturers.[6] The wharves and some streets were soon crowded with barrels and cases of liquor, while women and children were employed to roll barrels off Bay Street to the nearby warehouses, which quickly multiplied. By the end of 1920, 31 bonded warehouses had been constructed, to store a total of 37,400 cases and 13,700 barrels[7] imported so far. Liquor imports were so phenomenal that residents leased their cellars to help provide accommodation for the increasing supplies.[8]

Whereas in 1919 the Bahamas' income was £81,049, in the following year, it more than doubled, totalling £202,296. During the next three years, it steadily rose, peaking in 1923, when the value of liquor exports was £1,065,899 – twice that of 1921 and five times that of 1920.[9]

Accommodating legislation assisted this boom in the economy. The Tariff Amendment Act (No. 2) of 1920, allowed an 80 per cent drawback

**Barrels of liquor on Bay Street in Downtown Nassau
1920s and early 1930s during Prohibition**
(Photograph by Stanley Toogood. Courtesy of the Department of Archives and Linda Huber)

on liquor exported from the Bahamas, provided that proof could be shown that liquor had been landed outside the colony and would not be mixed with other spirits.[10] Three years later a Tariff Amendment Act[11] reduced customs duties on whisky imported from the Empire by 50 per cent.[12] The majority of liquor exports from the Bahamas were nominally consigned to the small French island of Miquelon, off the coast of Newfoundland.[13] Much of the liquor which entered the Bahamas and then left it, was never registered.[14]

After 1923, the total customs duty on whisky declined and so too did the general revenue. This was mainly due to the increased vigilance and speed of the prohibition flotilla.[15]

The British public as early as March 3, 1920 was aware of the Bahamas' change of fortune. *The Times* on that day reported that Prohibition had:

> transformed the Bahamas Government's financial position as if by magic from a deficit to a comparatively huge surplus, provided labour for large numbers of unemployed Bahamians and put more money in circulation in this little British colony than has been the case for many years.[16]

Internationally, much to the *Nassau Guardian*'s editor and owner, Miss Mary Moseley's chagrin, the Bahamas soon earned a notorious reputation as a bootlegging haven.[17] Its role in rum-running also received increasing attention and criticism from the American Government and came to be regarded at the British Foreign Office as a threat to Anglo-American relations.[18] The Americans on several occasions accused Bahamian customs officials at West End, Grand Bahama, Bimini and Nassau, of issuing two sets of clearance papers to American ships involved in illicit smuggling,[19] and also of illegally transferring the ships' registries.

A Federal Prohibition Agent declared that a Mr M. Cole, a Customs Officer at Nassau, explained to him how two sets of clearance papers could be obtained. The first ones were issued with the liquor shipment. An hour later, the person to whom they were issued would return and state that he had discharged his cargo of liquor on the high seas. Then another set of papers for 'in ballast' in any American port would be issued. The Agent then hinted of corruption among Bahamian officials. He stated that 'Mr. Cole did not say that there would be any money required outside the regular fees but intimated that he and the boys expected to be taken care of'.[20]

Such claims of irregularities were strongly denied by Bahamian officials. Governor Cordeaux assured the Colonial Office that the part the colony played in the 'gigantic' smuggling of liquor into the United States was infinitesimal. He argued that the bulk of the profits went to Americans who bore the risk of landing it undetected on the American coast.[21] It is clear however, that Bahamians did nothing to discourage the bootleggers. In fact, they aided and abetted them. Finding it too risky actually to run the liquor, most Bahamians involved in the trade confined their activities to the legitimate occupation and safer business of selling wholesale to foreign bootleggers within the limits of the colony, either from liquor stores in Nassau, or from hulks or floating depots at sea.[22] As Major Bell recorded in his fascinating book, *Bahamas Isles of June*:

> It was not the business of the dealer who possessed liquor to inquire wither it was bound; that was the business of the Customs and the buyer. The men who made the greatest fortunes in Nassau never sailed a ship nor sold to any person in the United States a pint of booze. They did not have to go so far; buyers flooded their offices, took the liquor direct to chartered ships and sailed away.[23]

There is little doubt that some Bahamians were involved in the illegal smuggling of liquor into the United States. At least one Bahamian, who later was to become prominent in Bahamian politics, actually ran the liquor or allowed his boats to be used in liquor smuggling. Captain R.T. Symonette, Mariner of Current Island was named in a list of a 'Return of ships' registered in the Bahamas involved in the trade. By 1923, according to his first wife, Mrs Nellie Symonette, he had become a man of inconsiderable (sic) means perhaps worth a million dollars.[24] The trade, however, was dominated by Americans. In 1920, William McCoy, better known as 'the real McCoy' arrived in Nassau. With the help of a legally registered company, the British Transportation and Trading Company, registered in November 1921, in Nassau,[25] he embarked on a lucrative bootlegging career. It is said that he ran over 175,000 cases of liquor from the Bahamas to the American mainland.[26]

By 1921 the atmosphere of Nassau changed. Bootlegging activities had intensified, and Bill McCoy was joined by many other colourful but shady characters, with nicknames such as 'Tampa', 'Ranger', 'Squinty', 'Goldie', and 'Suggsy', who were in Nassau to buy liquor and to prevent any fraudulent sales to organizations which employed them.[27] In McCoy's words, Nassau was:

> well launched on her third and most prosperous era of activity...The big money clan rushed in upon her. Adventurers, businessmen, soldiers, including a renegade officer or so, sailors, loafers, and at least one minister, they sought to make their fortunes by keeping America wet. Bay Street...was no longer a sun drenched idle avenue where traffic in sponges and sisal progressed torpidly. It was filled with slit-eyed, hunch-shouldered strangers, with a bluster of Manhattan in their voices and a wary truculence of manners.[28]

The Lucerne Hotel on Frederick Street, Nassau, was the headquarters of the bootleggers. It also had among its clientele, Sir Daniel Tudor, Chief Justice, other English officials[29] and perhaps the odd Bahamian white. Much drinking, dancing and noisy partying took place there at the nearby Hotel

Allen. Etienne Dupuch, editor and owner of the *Tribune* spoke disapprovingly of the 'orgy at the Lucerne', and the group of excursionists who partied every night, dancing, in his words 'a dance abomination' – the Charleston.[30] The climax of the partying was the Bootlegger's Ball held in late July.

Peace was generally kept throughout Nassau. It was true that the usually quiet streets were 'enlivened' by bootleggers playing poker 'for $100 dollar bills on piles of empties', and that school teachers 'out for a lark' and women tourists were apt to rub shoulders with such men. But as Bell emphasized, 'There was no roughness to speak of, and no killings, though guns were out time and again when rival gangs met'.[31]

Mary Moseley was incensed at the English and American newspaper reports which accused Bahamians of collusion with the bootleggers.[32] Her protests did not pacify the American authorities or the supporters of Prohibition. Their attention was soon focused on Bimini, Gun Cay and West End, Grand Bahama, which were gaining reputations as centres of the liquor smuggling trade. Bimini and West End were made ports of entry and quickly gained notoriety. The island of Bimini, from early in 1920, was used as a base to smuggle liquor into the thirsty United States. Bahamians, even while obeying the letter of the law, colluded with the whisky smugglers.

Bimini, because of its proximity to the American mainland, especially Miami, became a well known 'wet' spot for Americans, who came by boat and airplane as often as twice a week to drink and have fun. West End, Grand Bahama, was used by the Americans in a similar way. The settlement also had several legally established liquor stores.

The harbour at Gun Cay[33] also facilitated business between Bahamians and American bootleggers. Bahamian schooners owned by licensed liquor dealers in Nassau, anchored inside the cays, almost permanently. From such vessels, whisky and other alcoholic beverages were sold. Schooners and power boats from Nassau refurbished their dwindling stock.

Bahamians, primarily whites, were involved as liquor merchants. Some coloureds also sold liquor but on a smaller scale. Whites, coloureds and blacks were involved in running the liquor from Nassau to the various cays and ports. Black women were involved in a small way in Nassau. Besides rolling barrels, they were employed by liquor merchants to sew the special triangular shaped burlap sacks in which the liquor was packed. These sacks, each containing six bottles, were easily disposed of and handled.[34]

The Bahamas' newly acquired wealth was expended mainly in financing sorely needed large public work projects in Nassau, financing hotels, and generally making the island of New Providence attractive to tourists. Something was also done to improve social services. Before the end of the decade, a pipe-borne water supply and sewerage system for the city of Nassau had been completed.[35] Great progress was made to improve the material well-being of the city, but some, such as Etienne Dupuch, thought that too much development happened in too short a time, and that expenditure on it was out of proportion compared to that spent on the stable industries.[36]

In 1923, after some debate and public comment, a start was made on dredging the harbour to make it a deep water port and to provide a deeper entrance and larger turning basin for visiting ships. This operation was completed in August 1928, enabling the harbour to accommodate vessels of up to 27 feet draught. A warehouse and customs shed were also built to accommodate passengers. Completed in July 1928, the wharf later was named the Prince George's Wharf in honour of a visit by His Royal Highness Prince George, who landed at Nassau on October 1, 1928.[37]

A new electricity power plant and a cold storage plant were installed in 1922 and the communications system was extended during the decade. In order to cope with the increasing motor traffic in Nassau, roads were greatly improved, many of them being 'oiled'. The ownership of a car soon became a status symbol, and the Sunday drive the favourite pastime among the elite and the well-off coloureds.[38] As the 1920s progressed, materialism and the love of money became important to many in the society. Whereas six cars had been imported in 1918, 297 were brought into Nassau in 1922.[39] The Out Islands, however, had few cars. With the exception of Eleuthera, there were hardly any roads which were suitable for wheeled traffic.

Relatively speaking, great improvements were made in all communications during the decade. While the telephone system was being extended in New Providence in the 1920s, most of the Out Islands were without lines, or like Eleuthera, Cat Island and Long Island, had only their main settlements linked by telephone. Many more Out Islands benefitted by an extension of the wireless telegraph, which by 1925 was installed at Governor's Harbour and Harbour Island, Eleuthera, Bimini, Inagua, Hope Town, and Norman's Castle (Abaco Lumber), Abaco and West End, Grand Bahama.[40] For the majority of Out Islands, though, communication was still difficult. Haziel Albury related that anyone from Man-O-War wishing to send a telegram had to travel by sail boat to Hope Town.[41]

The Bahamian Government concentrated on improving the communications between Nassau and the outside world, especially the United States. By the end of the decade, Nassau had established a weekly passenger and freight service during the winter months, and a fortnightly service to and from New York during the summer by the Munson Line, which was under contract to the Government.[42] There was a monthly freight service from England via Bermuda and a service connecting Nassau with Halifax, Canada, Bermuda, Jamaica and British Honduras. There were also frequent sailings from Miami to Nassau, a voyage of fifteen hours. Perhaps the most important innovation was the introduction of a daily air service by Pan American Airways. A seaplane carrying 24 passengers began a regular service during the winter months between Miami and Nassau on January 2, 1929.[43]

Such developments, concentrated in the capital, were aimed at assisting the expansion of the tourist industry. By 1929 Nassau was well established as a resort, owing to its unrivaled winter climate, fine bathing beaches, fishing, yachting, tennis, golf and its 'old-world atmosphere'. Additionally, the Government during the 1920s adopted a more aggressive policy towards 'selling' the Bahamas. The Development Board, chaired by R.H. Curry, who was the leading steam-ship agent, spent thousands of pounds in advertisements, maps, books and pamphlets to attract wealthy Americans and Canadians.[44] The Government made certain that adequate facilities were available. Sporting activities such as lawn tennis flourished by 1929.

Guests were ensured accommodation in the major hotels – the New Colonial, the Fort Montagu, completed in 1926, and the more traditional Royal Victoria. There were also smaller hotels such as the notorious Lucerne and Allen. There were several boarding houses and some private families accepted paying guests. Some tourists leased furnished houses for the winter.[45]

Attracted by the knowledge that liquor was available in Nassau, 'tourists came in by waves and floods'.[46] Some of the foreign elite were lured by the exclusive Porcupine Club on Hog Island and the posh Bahamian Club opened on West Bay Street in 1920. The Bahamian Club's owner was an American, C. F. Reed, who was granted permission to operate roulette tables, the first gambling facility to be opened in the Bahamas.

Bimini and Cat Cay also attracted tourists and investors. Their proximity to the United States and their fine game-fishing and yachting soon made them popular resorts for wealthy Americans. At Bimini the exclusive and palatial Bay Rod and Gun Club, built by American investor Thomas J. Peters at the cost of more than a million dollars, was opened in January, 1920.[47]

American investors began buying estates and cays, building homes and laying out developments on Hog Island and the New Providence mainland. With land changing hands at an unprecedented rate, its value increased enormously, especially on New Providence.

American speculation and development brought new optimism to Government, and also raised the value of land. Property on New Providence and the Out Islands in the early 1920s changed hands rapidly, and large tracts of Crown land which had lain dormant for centuries were bought by Americans and local speculators. In fact, Governor Cordeaux, in speaking about the 'tremendous boom' in real estate expressed his fear of Americanization and his reluctance to sell or lease much Crown land:

> I don't like the idea of parting, though its difficult to refuse genuine development schemes. Americans are buying every available inch of

private land in New Providence and paying enormous prices for it – and there will soon be nothing British left except the Flag!⁴⁸

On New Providence, America and British investors acquired large tracts of land, mainly on the western side of the island. One company, the Nelson-Bullock-Nelson Company, real estate developers of Miami, purchased the Clifton and the Old Fort Estates, together with neighbouring properties, with plans to develop them. The W.E. Brown Land Company bought much of the J.S. Johnson sisal plantation in order to lay out Westward Villas along the western road.⁴⁹

A similar development in the west which catered to whites only was the Grove Estate, also known as Vista Marina Subdivision, owned by G.R. Baxter, an Englishman who settled in Nassau.⁵⁰ Some development also occurred east of the town and at the eastern end of the island including 'Shirley Slope', and 'Buen Retiro'. Houses also began to appear 'Out East'.

Land developments were also taking place to accommodate blacks and coloureds, some of whom had recently migrated from the Out Islands. Most developers were foreign, but among the outstanding local entrepreneurs was L.W. Young. Realizing the lack of housing for Out Islanders arriving in Nassau, he developed 'Walton Ville' in the southern district ⁵¹ and 'Kemp's Addition' in Grant's Town, south of Young Street. Mason's Addition was another subdivision developed for the coloureds and blacks, many of whom were also Out Islanders. Chippingham, originally known as Rainbow Village, was developed by H.N. Chipman, and settled mainly by Out Islanders and West Indians. Captain J.S. Engler of Miami, hoping to lure many Bahamian residents in Miami back to the Bahamas, subdivided 'Nassau's Master Suburb', naming it Englerston. Situated in the far south, this land at that time was uninhabited. Captain Engler offered 'homes on easy terms'.⁵²

While the increased revenue resulting from Prohibition was used mainly in the development of public works to assist the tourist industry, smaller amounts were invested in expanding and improving educational and health services.

The major innovation was the establishment of a government secondary school, the Government High School. Brought about after some public pressure, including that of black politicians like Thaddeus A. Toote, and R.M. Bailey, the idea for the institution originated with the Board of Education which intended that the school be used to train teachers for the Government's primary schools. Its curriculum was academic, and its students entered for the external Cambridge Junior Exams. In 1932 they began sitting for the Cambridge Overseas School Certificate.⁵³

Advances were also made in public health and the medical service. Major improvements, including the provision of a potable water supply and the sewerage scheme, however, mainly benefitted the elite. These two schemes covered the entire city area in the west, but not Grant's Town nor Bain

Town in the south. Sanitary conditions for the majority of the population were dismal.

Sir Wilfred Beveridge's report revealed the extremely unhygienic conditions existing, particularly in the Eastern District, Grant's Town and Bain Town, all primarily coloured and black areas.[54] The installation of pipe-borne water and sewerage would take time to change such conditions.

In the Pond District, for example, the majority of its inhabitants lived in wooden houses, obtained water from shallow and often polluted wells, and usually had outside pit-latrines. Garbage and litter collected as there was no organized system of garbage disposal. Animals roamed the yards.[55] Similar conditions existed in Grant's Town and Bain Town, the main residential areas for blacks.

The appointment of a Bacteriologist in 1923 helped to diagnose venereal disease and also to change the attitudes of the inhabitants, many of whom had regarded the infection lightly unless incapacitated. A man often referred to an attack as 'a little Gentleman's Fever which is nothing at all'. Although lepers and tubercular patients were not as yet segregated, there was recognition of the need to improve conditions.[56] Legislation was passed in 1928 providing for the establishment of a leper colony.

Childbirth was still a great risk and many midwives were unregistered and unqualified. A new Midwives Act passed in 1927 insisted that all practitioners be examined and registered.

Other innovations in health included the establishment of a dental clinic and X-ray Department in 1924, the posting of additional medical officers to the Out Islanders in 1925, and the voluntary establishment of an Infant Welfare Centre.[57] As usual, conditions on the Out Islands were worse than in Nassau. When a tooth decayed, an extraction was the answer.

In the early 1920s there were only two Out Island medical officers, stationed at Harbour Island and at Hope Town, Abaco. The majority of Out Islanders distrusted doctors, preferring to be nursed by relatives using home methods. When a doctor visited the school at Hope Town, many of the children, rather than be vaccinated, 'jumped through the windows'.[58] By the middle of the decade, three additional black doctors, W.A. Foulkes, Roland Cumberbatch and W.J. Miller, were posted to Inagua, Andros and Bimini, respectively.

Another important change was the voluntary establishment of the Infant Welfare Centre in December 1925. Organized by a Committee of elite ladies, it employed the assistance of an experienced Health Visitor from Canada, and received an annual sum of £300 from the Legislature. Clinics were opened in the St Agnes School in the southern district, at the Victoria School in the eastern district, and in the southwest at Quarry Mission. Established primarily to serve the coloured and black population, the Centres aimed to control the high infant mortality rate.[59] Dr Greaves, an Englishman and Dr Worrell, a Barbardian, gave their services free of charge.

While expansion was taking place in New Providence and so many significant improvements were being made, the Out Islands remained almost forgotten. Poverty, compounded by natural disasters, increased, and migration from the Out Islands to Nassau continued. This trend put more pressure on the already unsatisfactory state of public amenities in Nassau. Social problems in the capital therefore intensified during the decade, despite the improvements there.

The 1920s saw a general decline in the traditional agricultural pursuits such as pineapple and sisal growing and in sponge fishing. Influenced by large revenues accumulated from bootlegging, and the investment brought by the land boom, the House of Assembly concentrated its efforts on developing tourist amenities in Nassau while adopting an indifferent attitude to planning a constructive agriculture policy to assist the majority of the population still living on the Out Islands. The hurricanes between 1926 and 1929 exacerbated the situation.

The decline of the pineapple, sisal and sponge fishing industries was one of the important factors leading to the increased migration from the Out Islands to Nassau. The development of the tomato and timber industries, although important during the 1920s, did not compensate for the fall-off in the traditional products.[60]

Intensifying the depression in agriculture was a prolonged drought during the early 1920s. In the face of desperate straits, many Out Islanders had no option but to leave their homes. Before the passage of the 1924 Immigration Act in the United States many sponge fishermen and farmers had emigrated to Florida. Tightened United States immigration restrictions brought increasing numbers of Out Islanders to Nassau. The result of this internal migration and the effects of bootlegging on the capital were unemployment and underemployment, crime, juvenile delinquency and the growth of prostitution and illegitimacy.

Between 1921 and 1931 New Providence's population increased by 6,781, or 52.3 per cent. Whereas less than a quarter of the total population lived in New Providence in 1921, ten years later the proportion had risen to a third.[61] The islands losing most population in the decade were Cat Island, Inagua, Long Island, Harbour Island, Crooked Island, the Berry Islands and Rum Cay. Nassau received most of the migrants, but other islands such as Bimini and Grand Bahama which were involved in the liquor traffic also showed significant increases in population.

The flocking of Out Islanders to the capital created new social problems. In the area of employment, most of the newcomers were unskilled and numerous Out Islanders could find no steady employment.[62] The tourist industry, which should have created new jobs and new training skills for

Bahamian labourers, failed to do so because of the discriminatory policy of its management against coloureds and blacks. Most of the New Colonial's employees were imported.[63] It was not until 1925 that the hotel's management agreed to employ Bahamians as bellboys.[64]

While jobs became scarcer towards the end of the decade and wages were reduced, the cost of living remained high in Nassau. It was generally accepted as being one of the most expensive places in the world.

Increasing poverty among migrants and residents living in a seemingly prosperous and carefree city often led to crime. The decade witnessed an increase in stealing, housebreaking and burglary.[65] Violent crime, almost unknown in Nassau, began to be noted. Murder trials however, remained a rarity. For example, when Octavius Forbes was tried for murder in the Supreme Court in November 1924, large crowds assembled outside the court house. Perhaps the presence of bootleggers and gangster types, most of whom carried guns, affected Bahamians with criminal leanings. Additionally, some Bahamians who had engaged in bootlegging brought guns back from the United States.[66] The presence of so much newly acquired money in the face of poverty affected some, including three Bahamian men who were convicted of breaking into the public vault in March 1926, and stealing gold and silver to the value of over £15,000.

Juvenile crime was also on the increase. As early as 1923 a Commission was appointed to enquire into the establishment of an Industrial or Reformatory school.[67] Its report and numerous newspaper accounts[68] revealed that juvenile vagrancy and crime were common in Nassau. Drinking and the use of bad language were also on the increase. Between 1921 and February 1923, 112 juvenile offenders, ranging from ages nine to fourteen, had been brought before the Magistrate's Court charged with larceny and breaches of the Vagrancy Act.[69] About 20 of the boys were habitual offenders and gave the police constant trouble. There were a similar number of female offenders and troublemakers; many turned to prostitution in order to make ends meet.

Interrelated causes and effects were an increase in poverty, illegitimacy, the lack of parental control and the influence of bootlegging. Many children appearing in the Magistrate's Court were illegitimate, and came from one-parent homes. The rate of illegitimacy in 1922 for the whole colony was about 30 per cent. In comparison to some other Caribbean colonies, such as Jamaica, where it was about 75 per cent for the same period, the Bahamas' rate was not excessive. However, in the southern district of New Providence, that is Over-the-Hill, the illegitimacy rate was 72 per cent.[70]

Numerous children, described as 'waifs and strays' were simply left by emigrating parents with relatives or friends in Nassau. Themselves very poor, they were unable to care properly for the children. Those Out Islanders who remained in Nassau did not always register their children in school, and they subsequently took to the streets. Truancy was common, both in Nassau and the Out Islands.[71]

In spite of the awareness of the growing problem of juvenile vagrancy and crime, the Reformatory Bill brought before the House of Assembly in May 1921 was rejected. But as time elapsed, the problem of juvenile crime intensified. It was not until 1928, however, that the Government established the Boys' Industrial School, 'a euphemism of the reformatory for juvenile offenders'.[72]

Bootlegging affected the Bahamas profoundly. It changed social values and widened the gap between the classes. Creating a white *nouveau riche* group, Prohibition provided the 'financial foundation of their status as the social and political ruling class of the island...'[73] It also determined that the basis of the Bahamas' economy from the 1920s onward would have a strong commercial, rather than an agricultural, bias. The new wealth created a cleavage between whites, but even the growth of a white middle class did not change the colour situation. With the advent of a strong American influence, the colour line hardened.

Economically, the whites grew stronger and their intolerance of foreign competition by the Chinese, Greeks, Jews and Lebanese could be seen in their efforts to impose controls over immigrant competition. A series of Acts between 1928 and 1931 restricted immigration to the Bahamas and limited the participation of the trading minorities to certain businesses. Some of the coloured middle classes had also benefitted from the temporary boom and many had businesses on Bay Street. Those who benefitted least were the black labouring class.[74]

All in all, Prohibition had a pervasive effect on Bahamian society. Before the 1920s, an entrenched mercantile white elite had little real capital. Their colour, more than their wealth, separated them from the coloureds and blacks. Bootlegging profits, augmented by those from the land boom, brought quick money into Nassau, creating a new monied class which was mostly white. *Nouveaux riches* soon consolidated their wealth in successful businesses, and safeguarded themselves against immigrant competition. To ensure their positions and power, they sought seats in the legislature. Values were subtly changing. The newly rich liquor families might not have been accepted easily by the established elite, but as Bell stated in 1934, 'money ruled. Mammon was king – those who did not pay him reverence were too few to matter.'[75] Social distinctions between whites widened. Class was now distinguishable by wealth as well as colour.

Similarly, as already noted, the colour line grew more rigid. American investment, following the wake of bootlegging and the Florida land boom, brought more than just money to the Bahamas. With the advent of Americans such as Frank Munson, came the Jim Crow attitudes and system of segregation practised in the new hotels and exclusive clubs. Because of the growing importance of the tourist industry and the dependence on American investment, the white elite did little to stop the increasingly blatant discrimination against coloureds and blacks in public places and educational establishments.

The brief prosperity of the Prohibition years was marked by the consolidation of commercial enterprise and the improvement and modernization of public facilities and communication in Nassau. While concentrating on the expansion of the tourist industry, the legislators greatly neglected agriculture, and took an indifferent attitude to the faltering sponge fishing industry. The brief bonanza not only set the economic and patterns but also delayed political and constitutional progress in the Bahamas. General neglect of the Out Islands, compounded by the devastating hurricanes, resulted in increased migration of destitute Out Islanders to the capital. When the Wall Street Crash came in 1929, many Bahamians were already experiencing desperate poverty once again.

Notes

1. Michael Craton, *A History of the Bahamas* (London: Collins, 1962), 264; Michael Craton and Gail Saunders, *Islanders in The Stream. A History of The Bahamian People* (Athens: University of Georgia Press, 1998): 2, 237-252; Paul Albury, *Story of the Bahamas* (London: Macmillan, 1975), 176. See also Gail Saunders, 'The Social History of The Bahamas 1890-1953' (Unpublished PhD thesis, University of Waterloo, 1985), 241-312; David W. Noble, David A. Horowitz and Peter N. Carroll, *Twentieth Century Limited* (Boston: 1980), 206-207.
2. *Colonial Reports Bahamas, 1919-1920*, 40. Allardyce to Milner, Jan. 16, 1920, Confidential, CO 23/286/46-48.
3. By November 1919, the rate of exchange had reached 17 per cent, and by December 17, 23 per cent. See Philip Cash, 'Colonial Policies and Outside Influences: A Study of Bahamian History 1919-1947' (MA thesis, University of Wales, 1979), 48. At this time 80 per cent of Bahamian imports came from the United States and only 6 per cent from the United Kingdom. See *Colonial Reports Bahamas, 1919-1920*, 5.
4. Cash, 'Colonial Policies and Outside Influences', 58. See also David W. Noble, David A. Horowitz and Peter N. Carroll, *Twentieth Century Limited* (Boston: 1980), 207.
5. Cash, and Michael Craton, *History*, 265.
6. Bishop Roscow Shedden, *Ups and Downs in a West Indian Diocese* (London: 1927), 170.
7. *Nassau Guardian*, Feb. 4, 1920. Cordeaux to Milner, Feb. 15, 1921, CO 23/288/142. Cited Philip Cash, 'Colonial Policies and Outside Influences', 64.
8. Shedden, *Ups and Downs*, 171. See also H. Van de Water, *The Real McCoy* (New York: 1933), 93-94.
9. *Bahamas Blue Books, 1923-1924*, 178.

10. Craton, *History*, 268.
11. See *Statute Law of The Bahamas, 1929*, Vol. II, Ch. 106.
12. *Votes of the House of Assembly, 1923* (Nassau: Nassau Guardian, 1923), 428.
13. Cash, 'Colonial Policies and Outside Influences' and Craton, *History*, 268.
14. Craton, *History*, 268.
15. Telegram, Geddes of Foreign Office, September 20, 1923, A5907/903/45. F.O. 371 7297. Cited Cash, 'Colonial Policies and Outside Influences', 74.
16. *The Times* (of London), March 3, 1920.
17. *Nassau Guardian*, Sept. 1, 1921; Sept. 14 and 19, 1922; Jan. 13 and 23, 1923.
18. Cash, 'Colonial Policies and Outside Influences', 67-72. The 3-mile limit was also to become a prominent principle in later diplomatic manoeuvres involving liquor smuggling.
19. Telegram. Geddes to Curzon, August 4, 1921. Cited Cash, 67, 68, 71, 72.
20. Hughes to Geddes, June 26, 1922, CO23/292 Misc. Cordeaux to Churchill, Oct. 3, 1921, A297/170.45 F.O. 371-2274.
21. Cordeaux to Churchill, Oct. 19, 1921, CO 223/289/212 and 215-216.
22. Encl. Cordeaux to Amery, Dec. 31, 1925, Conf. CO 23/297.
23. Major H. MacLachlan Bell, *Bahamas: Isles of June* (New York: 1934), 190.
24. Grant to Churchill, Aug. 31, 1922, Conf. CO 23/291/215 and Hughes to Geddes, June 26, 1922, CO 23/292/Misc. Nellie Symonette to Devonshire, Dec. 29, CO23/294 Misc. According to Mrs Symonette he had made the money 'in the last three to four years in the whiskey business'.
25. Cordeaux to Geddes, April 2, 1923, CO 23/294 Misc. All the directors were American subjects except Bruce K. Thompson, a Bahamian who later became a successful liquor merchant.
26. H. Van de Water, *The Real McCoy*, 12. Because much of the liquor was diluted by purchasers and fortified by grain alcohol before it was sold, a figure of 700,000 cases would be a more accurate estimate of the amount actually sold in the United States.
27. Bell, *Bahamas Isles of June*, 186, and Cash, 'Colonial Policies and Outside Influences', 65.
28. Van de Water, *The Real McCoy*, 93-94.
29. Bell, *Bahamas Isles of June*, 184-186.
30. *Tribune*, Feb. 10, 1926, Jan. 22, 1925, Sept. 11, 1926.
31. Bell, *Bahamas Isles of June*, 184, 192, 193, 195.
32. *Nassau Guardian*, Sept. 14, 1922; Oct. 18, 1922. See also Sept. 1, 1921, Sept. 19, 1922; Jan. 13, 1923.
33. Gun Cay is a small, narrow islet located on the western edge of the Grand Bahama Bank, north of North Cat Cay. Between the two is a narrow passage with only sufficient water to permit vessels of light draught.
34. Interview with E. Basil North and Audrey North, July 31, 1984. See also Hughes to Geddes, June 26, 1922, CO 23/292 Misc.

35. The water supply system was completed on Sept. 30, 1928 and the drainage and sewerage system on March 31, 1929. See *The Year Book of the British West Indies, 1929*, 134.
36. Interview with Sir Etienne Dupuch, August 30, 1979.
37. *The Year Book of the British West Indies, 1929*, 134.
38. *Tribune*, July 17, 1926.
39. *Tribune*, June 27, 1925. There was a decline after 1922; 164 cars were imported in 1923 and 104 in 1924.
40. *Tribune*, June 17, 1925.
41. Haziel L. Albury, *Man-O-War. My Island Home*, (New Jersey: 1977), 89-92.
42. *The Year Book of the British West Indies, 1929*, 134.
43. *Colonial Annual Reports, Bahamas, 1931*. See also Colin Hughes, *Race and Politics in The Bahamas* (St Lucia, Australia: University of Queensland Press, 1981), 14.
44. Grant to Devonshire, Oct. 28, 1922, CO 23/291/340-345.
45. *The Year Book of the British West Indies, 1929*, 137.
46. Bell, *Bahamas Isles of June*, 191.
47. *Nassau Guardian*, Dec. 27, 1919, Jan. 3, 1920.
48. Cordeaux to Darnly, Private, Aug. 8, 1925, CO 23/296.
49. Mary Moseley, *The Bahamas Handbook* (Nassau: 1926), 30 and 35.
50. See for example, Conveyance, June 5, 1937 Between Guy Robert Brooke Baxter and Vendor and the Baxter Estate Ltd., clause 14: 'no lot or any part thereof or any interest therein in the Vista Marina Subdivision of the GROVE Estate shall be sold, leased or otherwise conveyed to any person other than a full-blooded member of the Caucasian race.'
51. Walton Ville was north of Wulff Road between Market and East Street South. *Tribune*, Jan. 20, 1923.
52. *Tribune*, Nov. 24, 1924. Captain J. S. Engler of Miami, Florida, developed Englers Public Market in Miami, which sold almost everything.
53. Colbert Williams, *The Methodist Contribution to Education in The Bahamas* (Gloucester: 1982), 67.
54. Sir Wilfred Beveridge, *Report on The Public Health and Medical Conditions in New Providence, Bahama Islands* (London: Waterloo, 1927), 41. Enc. In CO 23/359.
55. Beveridge, *Report on the Public Health*, 41-42.
56. Medical Report 1925-1926, Encl. CO 23/327.
57. Medical Report 1924-1925, Encl. Cordeaux to Amery, March 31, 1926, CO 23/297.
58. Chief Medical Officer's Annual Report 1923. Encl. Cordeaux to Thomas, March 21, 1924, CO 23/297.
59. Beveridge, *Report on The Public Health*, 37.
60. Saunders, 'Social History', 266-267.
61. *Report on The Census of the Bahama Islands, taken 26 April, 1931*, Nassau, 1931. New Providence's population numbered 12,975 in 1921 and 19,756 in 1931.
62. *Colonial Annual Reports, Bahamas, 1928*. Encl. CO 23/405.
63. *Nassau Guardian*, February 3, 1923.

64. *Nassau Guardian*, Feb. 21, 1925.
65. *Nassau Guardian*, Dec. 11, 1920; Aug. 23, 1923.
66. *Nassau Guardian*, Nov. 4 and 6, 1924.
67. *Report to Enquire into the Establishment of an Industrial School, Jan. 1923, Nassau Guardian*, 1923. Encl. Cordeaux to Thomas, March 12, 1924, CO 23/295.
68. *Nassau Guardian*, Jan. 25, 29; Feb 17; May 14 and July 28, 1921.
69. *Report to Enquire into the Establishment of an Industrial School*, 23.
70. *Report to Enquire into the Establishment of an Industrial School*, Out of 137 births, 97 were illegitimate.
71. *Report to Enquire into the Establishment of an Industrial School*, 19.
72. Colbert Williams, *The Methodist Contribution to Education*, 68. See also PRO/EDU/5-26, 10.
73. Gordon K. Lewis, *The Growth of The Modern West Indies* (London: 1968), 311.
74. See Howard Johnson, *The Bahamas From Slavery to Servitude* (Gainesville: University Press of Florida,1996), 131-150. See also Saunders, 'Social History', 288.
75. Major H.M. Bell, *Bahamas: Isles of June*, 193.

9

The Changing Face of Nassau

The Impact of Tourism on Bahamian Society in the 1920s and 1930s

During the second half of the twentieth century, fundamental change took place in the Caribbean. Many former colonies became independent and sought to develop their own political, economic and cultural patterns. Despite this, the dependency on foreign investment remained. The tourist industry which developed in most Caribbean territories during this period, was an 'engine of growth' and the key to development and modernization.[1]

As Patullo also demonstrated, the development of tourism while raising the standard of living for many in the region, has also had a negative impact in some areas. The dependency on tourism and the change from elite tourism to mass tourism has had damaging effects on the economies, the socioracial relations, the fragile infrastructure, cultural development and the environment.

In the Bahamas as in Jamaica, Barbados and Cuba, tourism on a small scale was developing in the nineteenth century. However, it was during the interwar years, 1919 to 1939, that there was a tremendous growth in tourist travel internationally. North Americans travelled to Europe and within the United States especially to Florida and California which offered sunshine and warmth. Some ventured to the more 'exotic' Caribbean and Atlantic islands of Bermuda and New Providence (Nassau) in the Bahamas.[2]

The Caribbean, as Paradise in European imagination, had come full circle – 'from Paradise to wasteland and back again'.[3] Frank Taylor stated that by the early twentieth century, the Caribbean, particularly Barbados, Jamaica, Cuba, the Bahamas (and Bermuda), 'began to be transformed into playgrounds' for itinerant Europeans and Americans in search of 'health and enjoyment'. The once tropical plantations, thought to be unfit for whites, 'were being touted as veritable gardens of Eden'.

The Bahamas was emerging as a 'rich man's paradise' from the mid-nineteenth century and tourism further expanded during the bonanza years of Prohibition in the United States (1919-33). Additionally, the decline in the traditional agricultural and sponge fishing industries and the possibility of

Paradise Bathing Beach, Nassau, Bahamas 1920s and 1930s
(Photograph by 'Doc' Sands. Courtesy of the Department of Archives and the C. Thackray Charitable Trust)

quick money encouraged the colonial administrators and House of Assembly to embrace the tourist business.

There is no detailed account of the tourist industry in the Bahamas. General historians[4] mention the industry briefly. Ian Strachan's (1995) recent doctoral dissertation has proved useful, as has, especially from a comparative perspective, Frank Taylor's *To Hell with Paradise* (1993).[5] Important sources, besides the traditional Colonial Office papers, include newspapers, travelogues, postcards, touristic magazines and oral history interviews.

This paper describes how Bahamian tourism developed in the 1920s and 1930s and analyses the impact on the socioeconomic and political life of the colony, including race relations and its effect on the white, coloured and black entrepreneurs. It concludes by comparing Nassau then to contemporary times there, and in the wider Caribbean.

The Development of Tourism in the 1920s and 1930s

As early as 1740, Nassau had gained a reputation as a winter and health resort for 'invalids' and from others from the United States and Canada seeking a change and warmer climate. However, up to the nineteenth century, tourism still existed on a very small scale and had limited impact on the economy. During the 1850s, the Government began to actively promote tourism. It made contracts with the shipping companies and financed the building of the first hotel, the Royal Victoria.[6]

Tourism remained a small industry, yet at the end of the nineteenth century there was another concerted effort to promote tourism. Governor Hayes Smith, eager to attract visitors from Florida which was becoming a popular resort for American northerners, negotiated with Henry M. Flagler, wealthy oil magnate, developer of South Florida and owner of the East Coast Railway and a large number of hotels.[7] Flagler was instrumental in boosting the development of tourism. He bought the Royal Victoria Hotel, agreed to build and maintain another hotel, the Colonial (opened in 1900) and to connect Nassau with his system of hotels and railways in Florida. This contract with Flagler and the very important Hotel and Steamship Act of 1898 gave the colony a winter passenger service between Nassau and Miami and a high standard of hotel accomodation.[8] These hotels provided splendid facilities for the wealthy visitor who wintered in Nassau. This type of visitor began the season which was to set a pattern for the tourist industry until the late 1940s.[9]

Much of the success of the tourist industry in the 1920s and 1930s was due to the upswing in the economy during Prohibition in the United States. Nassau, a trans-shipment port for smuggling liquor into the United States, benefited greatly from rum-running profits. Revenues increased as a result of the dramatic rise in liquor exports.[10]

Facilities were expanded and improved at the major hotels – the new New Colonial, the Fort Montagu, completed in 1926, and the Royal Victoria. There were also smaller hotels such as the Prince George (after the mid-1930s), Lucerne and Allen, with notorious reputations for housing rum-runners, and several boarding houses. Some private families accepted paying guests while others leased furnished houses for winter.

The Colonial Hotel was destroyed by fire on March 31, 1922. The government and the Development Board, determined that there should be

The British Colonial Tennis Courts in the early 1900s.
(Courtesy of the Department of Archives)

little or no adverse effect on tourism, contracted the Munson Steamship Line to quickly rebuild it. With a low interest government loan and imported West Indian and Cuban labourers, the company rebuilt it in six months. The hotel opened for the best season ever in February 1923. Aesthetically, the new structure was an eyesore. It was designed in the Spanish-American style, imported from South Florida, representing the first break with the traditional colonial Georgian architectural style.[11]

Like most expatriate officials Governor Sir Bede Clifford (1932-37) was at first sceptical about making tourism the mainstay of the Bahamian economy and attempted to improve agricultural production. However, he realised that tourism could quickly bolster the flagging economy and replace the revenue lost on exports boosted by Prohibition profits. As he recalled in his memoirs, he advised his Executive Council: 'Well, gentlemen, it amounts to this – if we can't take the liquor to the Americans we must bring the Americans to the liquor'. The Governor saw it as 'a choice between the tourist industry and bankruptcy'.[12] In other words, the liquor in Nassau attracted tourists 'in waves and floods'.

Clifford, therefore enthusiastically embarked on a policy to encourage tourists. In 1932 he had negotiated a tighter contract with the Munson Company, which had hitherto rendered unsatisfactory service and had let the New Colonial Hotel fall into disrepair. Under the new contract, the government would take over the hotel if the service did not improve.

The Government ensured that adequate and attractive facilities were available concentrating developments in the capital, mainly downtown Nassau. Sporting activities such as lawn tennis flourished by 1929. Frequent

Golf Links of Nassau, Bahamas early Twentieth Century
(Photograph by 'Doc' Sands. Courtesy of the Department of Archives and the C. Thackray Charitable Trust)

tournaments were held at the hotels or the Nassau Lawn Tennis Club. Golf links were built at Fort Charlotte and the Bahamas Country Club at Cable Beach. International golfers visited Nassau to participate in such tournaments as the British Colonial Open, which offered $5000 in prizes in 1935. In that year Nassau established itself firmly on the southern golfing circuit.[13] Other activities were fishing, duck and wild pigeon shooting. Big game fishing flourished at Bimini and Cat Cay, and like the mid-1930s Lyford Cay, through the efforts of Harold G. Christie, had also become known for the sport.[14]

Sea-bathing on the white coral sand beach at Hog Island was also a popular pastime.[15] Funds were allocated to establish a 'bathing beach' (for tourists only) on crown land opposite the New Colonial Hotel, while Fort Charlotte was restored and its grounds cleared for sight-seeing. Guides outfitted in costumes of the 1790 aeneid period gave tours. A pamphlet, *Historic Forts of Nassau*, written by Harcourt Malcolm, speaker of the Assembly and local historian, was sold there at one shilling. Profits from this sale and admission charge of two shillings were to be used for further restoration of historic monuments.[16]

Other tourist attractions included the white dominated horse racing and horse riding. Early in the decade an improved track for horse racing was built at the Montagu Park Race Course, also known as Hobby Horse Hall, located behind Cable Beach. The first races were held in January 1934, initiating a sport which was to become increasingly popular among ordinary Bahamians as well as well-heeled tourists.

The Miami-Nassau Ocean Race and the Spring Championship Races of the International Star Class Yacht Racing Association were inaugurated in Nassau in 1934. They were promoted mainly by Roland T. Symonette, Commodore of the Nassau Yacht Club (which he had founded in 1936).

Another attraction was the Williamson Photosphere. John E. Williamson, the pioneer of undersea photography, supported by the government, in 1939 developed the unique Seafloor Post Office located in the Photosphere. Visitors bought specially produced stamps and observed the 'wonders of the deep' in the clear Bahamian waters.[17]

Some of the foreign elite were lured by the exclusive Porcupine Club on Hog Island, the Bahamian Club on West Bay Street and others such as the Cat Cay and Bimini Rod and Gun Clubs. The Bahamian Club, which opened in 1920, was the first gambling facility in the Bahamas; its American owner, C.F. Reed, was granted permission to operate roulette tables. However, during the season, it was generally used by American and Canadian visitors to entertain their friends at dinner and supper. Many of the local elite were honorary members but they hardly ever patronized it.[18]

The infrastructure was greatly improved during the 1920s and 1930s from profits of the sale of alcohol. Wealth was expended mainly in financing sorely needed public works and communications, and in making Nassau more

The Landing Place, Nassau, Bahamas, 1930s
*(From a postcard. Courtesy of the Department of Archives
and the C. Thackray Charitable Trust)*

attractive to tourists and investors. Water, telephone and electricity supplies were improved and expanded. There was limited telephone service to the Out Islands but the wireless telegraph system was extended. A new electricity power plant and cold storage plant were installed in 1922.[19] By the end of the 1920s there was a modern pipe-borne water supply and sewerage system. To facilitate shipping, Nassau's harbour was dredged and deepened and a concrete wharf was constructed just north of Rawson Square. A warehouse and customs shed were also built to accommodate passengers. A new pier was constructed at Clifton, south-west New Providence, where ships could unload passengers and cargo during stormy weather which occasionally made Nassau harbour dangerously rough.

The once quiet streets were changing as the number of cars imported increased from 6 in 1918 to 297 in 1922. Thereafter, it continued to increase steadily. Ownership of a car became a status symbol and the Sunday drive the favourite pastime of the white and coloured elite. This growth in the number of cars, complaints about speeding and reckless driving, and the rise in the traffic accidents stimulated public criticism and the need for more traffic regulations.[20]

In order to cope with the increasing motor traffic in Nassau, the road system was extended and tarred by 1928. This was in contrast to the Out Island which, with the exception of Eleuthera, had very few roads which were suitable for wheeled traffic. Some, such as the *Nassau Guardian*'s editor, Mary Moseley, disliked the 'oiled' streets and bemoaned the new process, expressing her fondness for 'white' Bay Street.[21]

International communications were improved and by the end of the decade, the Munson Line conducted a weekly winter passenger and freight service and a fortnightly summer service to and from New York. There were other services from Halifax, Canada, Bermuda, Jamaica, British Honduras and England via Bermuda. There were also frequent sailings from Miami to Nassau, but perhaps the most important development was the introduction of a daily air service by Pan American Airways. On January 2, 1929, a seaplane carrying 24 passengers began a regular winter service between Miami and Nassau. In the summer an eight-passenger aircraft serviced the island once or twice a week.[22] In addition a direct telephone link between Nassau, New York and Canada was instituted, primarily to allow tourists and especially businessmen to keep in touch with their financial interests.

Nassau had gained a reputation not only as a tourist but also as a seasonal resort for the wealthy, some of whom made their homes there during the winter months. It was also during the 1930s that the Bahamas first became known internationally as a tax haven, attracting foreign investment, not only in the capital, but on several of the Out Islands. Owing to its loose tax structure – there were no income, profits, capital gains, nor real estate taxes – many investors were drawn to Nassau to escape taxation in North America and Britain.[23] By the mid-1930s Nassau was well established as a resort, owing to its unrivalled winter climate, yachting, 'old-world atmosphere' and the government's aggressive policy towards 'selling' the Bahamas. The Development Board, financed by the government and chaired by R.H. Curry, the leading steam-ship agent with vested interest, spent thousands of pounds in advertisements to attract wealthy Americans and Canadians.

The Effects of Tourism

The vigorous measures adopted by the Development Board to improve transportation and communication between the United States and the Bahamas and to develop other amenities brought increasing numbers of tourists to Nassau. Whereas 10,295 had visited during the 1922/3 season, over 25,000 stopped at Nassau between December 1934 and March 1935 and 57, 394 in 1938.[24] Revenues were boosted and much wealth accrued mainly to the white Nassau mercantile elite and foreign investors.

Economically, there were benefits but because of the nature of the Bahamian (indeed the Caribbean) economy, tourism had only a limited impact. The orientation towards the export market and the domination of foreign ownership inhibited the development of linkages between all sectors of the domestic economy. This was particularly pertinent in the Bahamas. There, the service sectors, tourism and financial services became the dominant activities with negligible development of secondary production and few linkages between any of the economic sectors.[25] Additionally, the absence of direct taxation and dependence on import duties led to an under-financed treasury in contrast to 'tremendously wealthy private empires'.[26]

The Bahamas benefited from the Florida land boom in the 1920s and 1930s. American tourists, many of whom were investors, bought estates and cays, built homes and laid out developments on Hog Island and New Providence. With land changing hands at an unprecedented rate, its value increased enormously especially on New Providence, although much land on the Out Islands was also leased or purchased. Bahamian realtors, led by Harold Christie, sold thousands of acres of land to foreigners. This was facilitated by local conditions such as poverty and shortage of money, local ignorance of the value of beach front properties, confused titles, and the inefficient services at the Surveyor General's Department and Registry.[27] The Colonial Administration's ambivalence towards such rapid development, perhaps hampered some sales.

In the 1930s, many palatial homes were built by expatriate residents. Among them were financier and banker Sir Herbert Holt and Lady Holt of Montreal, who began regularly visiting the Bahamas in 1935; financier, Sir Frederick Williams-Taylor and his wife, also originally of Montreal but recently settled in London; British aeroplane manufacturer Frederick Sigrist[28] from Berkshire, England, and Harry Oakes and his family who had several residences. They lavishly entertained each other and the local elite. In 1935 Nassau was described as 'the social centre of the south' where 'the society of Palm Beach and other Florida resorts mingled with the fashionable colony here in a gay whirl of parties' sometimes prompted by Royal visitors.[29]

More modest land developments were also taking place to accommodate blacks and coloureds, some of whom had recently migrated from the Out Islands. The developers were mainly foreign[30] with some outstanding local entrepreneurs like L. Walton Young who developed areas in southern New Providence, like his foreign counterparts, away from the increasingly pristine centre of Nassau.[31]

There was uneven development in the Bahamas. While Nassau experienced rapid development, the Out Islands, where the majority of people lived, were generally neglected. *Tribune* editor, Etienne Dupuch, commented in 1924, 'we have almost bankrupted the Treasury to build a hotel, a golf course and provide a steamship line while the people of the Out Islands starve.'[32] This situation, aggravated by tightened United States immigration restrictions after 1924 and a series of severe hurricanes in the late 1920s and early 1930s, accelerated migration of Out Islanders into Nassau. Between 1921 and 1931, New Providence's population increased by 6,781, or by 52.3 per cent. In 1921 less than a quarter of the total population lived in New Providence. Ten years later, the proportion had risen to a third.[33]

The migration to the capital created new socioeconomic problems. Most of the newcomers were unskilled and therefore unable to find steady employment.[34] The tourist industry brought in more money and should have created new jobs and training skills for Bahamian laborers, but did not because of management's discriminatory policy. The majority of people derived only a 'small share of profit' from tourism as the hotels and foreign residents imported most of their staff.[35]

Etienne Dupuch argued that the New Colonial, far from creating jobs, gave rise to competition. After much protest from cab drivers and boatmen, the hotel-sponsored transportation for guests to golf courses and the Hog Island Beach ceased and locals were hired. Bahamian bellboys were not employed until 1925.[36]

Governor Charles Dundas tried to rectify this situation by opening the Dundas Civic Centre, supplied by public subscription, to train blacks as cooks, waiters and domestic servants. They would be qualified for the lowest paid jobs which were available to blacks and coloureds and at which they might be capable.[37] The Montagu Hotel hired graduates of the Centre for the 1932-33 season to work as bartenders and Bahamian workers were supplied to the homes of the wealthy whites as well. Managerial positions continued to be filled by foreigners. Bahamian labourers also suffered from the high cost of living in Nassau. Jobs became scarcer towards the end of the decade and wages were reduced but the cost of living remained high. The combination of rich American tourists, prosperous bootleggers and real estate developers inflated the cost of living and made it difficult for British officials and Wesleyan ministers to maintain a satisfactory standard of living in Nassau.[38]

House rents for foreign residents were three times as expensive as those in Trinidad. It was much more for the majority of the labouring class and migrants. In 1938, unskilled labourers earned two to four shillings a day, while those with skills were paid between four and 20 shillings a day. Cooks and housemaids received 10-20 shillings a week for working about ten hours a day.[39] A labourer spent about 4 shillings a week on rent and 9 pence a day for his food. Food prices were especially high because of the decline in agriculture and the dependency on imports. Native-grown fruits and vegetables were scarce and expensive. Governor Dundas complained that there were 'not a few who now regard life as a cultivator beneath their dignity'.[40]

Labourers in the tourism industry suffered even more because of its seasonal nature. Many worked only three to four months of the year. Even in the winter when job opportunities became available, wages remained dangerously low and the black population barely survived. This demoralizing situation, tightening discriminatory policies and the transfer of other American values resulted in increased social problems such as vagrancy and crime.

In July 1935, when businessman and politician, Roland Symonette, was building the Prince George Hotel, 300 to 400 men sought employment. A near riot broke out when they realized that most of them would not be hired. Later that year, 800 unemployed men turned to Fort Charlotte for 40 available jobs. Unable to find work, many unashamedly took to begging, loitering, arson and theft. In the late summer of 1937, the Nassau and Montagu Theatres, both of which practised segregation, mysteriously burnt down. By July 1938, Governor Dundas admitted that there was 'a Nassau mob of about 1000 persons' consisting of 'young loafers, criminals and riff raff of that type'.[41]

In short, despite the growing optimism brought by the development of tourism, there were great social disparities within the Bahamian society. The growing restlessness, present in the Caribbean generally during the 1930s, culminated in riots and strikes. The Nassau riot of 1942, unlike those in the Caribbean, did not result in any immediate change in social conditions for the masses.

Despite the great advances in the health and material conditions in downtown Nassau, sanitary and health conditions for the majority of the population remained dismal until the 1960s. Major improvements of potable water and sewerage, excluded Grant's Town and Bain Town in the south, where the black majority resided. The House of Assembly, which at first had rejected the request of the Governor that a sanitary expert from England be employed, reversed its decision only after a number of American visitors became ill with typhoid fever.[42]

Sir Wilfred Beveridge, an eminent doctor and later one of the leaders of the Labour Party's great social reforms in Britain following World War II, praised Nassau's new water works and sewerage system then under construction. However, he deplored their limited extension and revealed the extremely unhygienic conditions of the Eastern and Pond Districts, Grant's Town and Bain Town. He was also shocked by the conditions in the hospital,

Native Market, Prince George Dock, Nassau
(From a postcard. Photograph by Freddie Maura. Mid-twentieth century. Courtesy of the Department of Archives and the C. Thackray Charitable Trust)

the prevalence of tuberculosis, venereal diseases, and neonatal tetanus, and horrified by public indifference, ignorance and poverty which led to substandard housing and overcrowding. These suburbs, not too far from central Nassau, suffered from congestion, flooding, uncollected garbage in which pigs, dogs and fowls rooted, and also open privies polluting both wells and cooking areas.[43]

Up to 1951 conditions virtually did not change. S.E.V. Luke of the Colonial Office wrote, 'Behind Nassau's picturesque old-world streets and the princely mansions along the East and West shores are slums as bad as any West Indian Colony, and far worse than anything Bermuda can show'. He added that 'it is disgraceful that conditions should exist in so rich an island'. Indeed over 71 per cent of New Providence housing still had no running water in 1953.[44]

Tourism and foreign investment especially affected the white elite Nassauvians, although the middle class also subtly became Americanized. Frank Taylor's[45] comment on the Jamaican situation, 'Along with the American tourist there had also come the American film, Hollywood values, and apparently Hollywood "vulgarity"' was also true for the Bahamas. A letter writer to the *Tribune* in March 1930 complained about the loudness, drinking and vulgar dancing by some of the staff of the New Colonial Hotel who were waiting to embark on the *Munargo*. The writer was shocked: 'What an example for our girls to see stockingless painted half-drunken dissipated young men and women displaying all around how far they have fallen into a state of utter depravity and disgrace'.[46] Undoubtedly, such vulgar behaviour, films and the radio, which became popular in Nassau during the thirties, had a profound effect on a section of the population. Another letter to the *Tribune* at the time, although perhaps exaggerating, stated that Nassau, under the influence of American culture, was going mad. The writer said young people of Nassau were frivolous, 'dancing, drinking and living a sporting life, in and out of season'.[47]

Besides keeping up with the most popular American dances the white and coloured elite were exposed to American foods and fashion. Preoccupation with materialism was growing and American imports also influenced dress codes. Styles became more casual and dresses were shortened from just above the ankle, usually to mid-calf length. Slacks were worn in the late thirties and make-up, although by no means universal, became more common. Men's styles also became less formal. Often, shirts with neckties were worn instead of the customary three piece dark tailored suit. As the search for the sun became a major force in the tourist industry bathing attire for both sexes became briefer (exposing the flesh) but was still modest.[48]

Drinking by both men and women had become an acceptable custom and an integral part of Bahamian society during the 1930s. Liquor interests increased after Prohibition and it became more accessible and inexpensive. Tourism, which attracted 'the fun-loving, heavy drinking' visitors and made liquor so accessible, had a profound impact on Bahamian drinking habits and the growth of alcoholism. Prostitution, which had been prevalent in Nassau since the early twentieth century, worsened as 'dance halls' and the sale of liquor increased. Prostitutes also frequented the wharves.[49]

Some persons at the time held reservations about the effects of the tourist industry. Alan Burns,[50] Colonial Secretary in Bahamas during the mid to late 1920s, expressed some scepticism, 'It was a glorious playground, but a very expensive place. The tourists poured money into the colony, but the people, both white and coloured, gave a great deal of their character in exchange for it'.

Prohibition and the development of the tourist industry had a profound effect on race and class relations. The white mercantile elite profited most from the tourist industry. This class traditionally included families such as the Malcolms, Duncombes, Adderleys and Moseleys. However, during the bonanza years of the 1920s it was expanded to include the *nouveau riche* group headed by Roland T. Symonette, Frank and Harold Christie and Walter K. Moore, all from poor backgrounds. Prohibition had brought quick money and provided the 'financial foundation of their status as the social and political ruling class of the island...'[51]

Money whitened. Roland Symonette, for example, a poor, light-skinned seaman from Current settlement, Eleuthera, actually participated in bootlegging and rose to a position of wealth and power in the mid 1920s. He, like the white mercantile elite generally, consolidated his position in legitimate enterprises and by election to the House of Assembly. In less than a generation the white community accepted him and his family. Wealth attracted power and authority and racial differences were linked to economic relationships. Now race became even more important in determining social status.[52]

The white mercantile elite controlled not only the strategic business enterprises but also the political machinery. The growing strength of *nouveau riche* politicians, united with the influential older elite, benefiting from corrupt election practices, made it increasingly difficult for coloureds and blacks to win seats. Politically the latter lost ground in the House of Assembly after 1935. Governor Dundas admitted in 1938, 'the corrupt practices of electioneering in this colony are notorious and not disputed by anyone'.[53] The secret ballot was not introduced to the Out Islands and permanently adopted in New Providence until 1946.

The gap between rich and poor and white and black widened in Nassau. 'The merchants of Bay Street ... saw to it that everything should be done to attract visitors who would spend money in their shops ...'[54] As a result, they restricted not only non-white participation but also legislatively controlled the immigrant minorities of Lebanese, Jews, Chinese and Greeks.[55] Foreigners, wishing to invest in the mid to late 1930s, usually first approached lawyer

A.K. Solomon, and after 1935, Stafford L. Sands, his brash and briliant nephew. Harold G. Christie then provided suitable land and Roland T. Symonette, who was in the shipbuilding and construction business, helped him to develop it. They also benefited from their interests in other lucrative enterprises such as the grocery, wholesale and liquor businesses. They, along with the Bethells, Kellys and Roberts, controlled the socioeconomic and political life of the colony.[56]

Some Bahamians were critical of the ruling elite's concentration on tourists and moneymaking to the detriment of the locals. An anonymous writer in protesting against another road diversion wrote:

> I can only come to the conclusion that we really need a thorough change among our so-called leaders today. They have sold Sunday for the almighty dollar; they have sold themselves for a mess of pottage and now they are trying to sell the last and only privilege that Bahamians have and pride, our walks along the waterfront. I wonder sometimes they don't ask ourselves (sic) to lock up ourselves in our homes at certain hours of the day so that tourists can have the rights and the privileges of the tourists for themselves.[57]

A small white middle class including teachers, civil servants and shop assistants, which was emerging after Prohibition, emulated the white *nouveau riche*. Not many young and ambitious white Bahamians wished to pursue further education and qualify professionally, except in the legal field. Commercial prosperity lured them into shopkeeping and other commercial enterprises. While wealth created a division among the Nassau whites, their colour and small numbers united them as a social group. Although they did not usually socialize, they assisted each other by finding positions or civil service jobs for white youngsters.

Coloured and black businessmen on or near Bay Street, many of whom had also benefited from Prohibition, pitted against wealthy white competition, were pushed off Bay Street in the 1930s. Those whose businesses survived the depression, underwent little expansion. Some coloureds, such as the DeGregorys and a number of upwardly mobile blacks, many of them originally from the Out Islands, like Herbert and Eugene Heastie, Edgar Bain and Ulrich Mortimer managed to keep their businesses going. Many established businesses over the hill.[58]

The majority of coloureds and upwardly mobile blacks, barred from holding jobs on Bay Street, turned to education for salvation. Fortunate pupils attended the Government High School, the first public secondary school established in Nassau in 1925. Others were able to attend schools abroad, particularly in the United States, England and the Anglophone Caribbean. Non-whites were increasingly employed in clerical level posts within the Civil Service and also as teachers.[59]

As in the Caribbean generally, the tourist industry made the racial situation worse. In the Bahamas, however, racial discrimination was more severe than in the other Caribbean colonies. The substantial white population (representing about 10 per cent or more of the population) and long historical ties with the southern United States led to antagonisitc race relations. With the advent of Americans such as Frank Munson – whom Dupuch described as a 'viciously prejudiced Man'[60] – came the Jim Crow attitudes. Discrimination was practised in public places and whites segregated themselves socially from blacks and coloureds, seeking to educate their children separately. The colour bar at Queen's College was rigorously upheld until the 1950s. Similarly, whites segregated themselves in seating patterns in church and in some cases kept separate Sunday Schools and even insisted on being buried in separate graveyards.[61] In the mid 1930s, a Methodist minister commented that in no other part of the West Indies was the colour situation so sad and the racial bitterness so deep as in the Bahamas.[62]

As Frank Taylor[63] demonstrates, racism was 'historically a built in feature of West Indian tradition of hospitality'. The development of and growing dependency on tourism and American investment during the 1920s and 1930s hardened the already existing colour line in the Bahamas. Like Jamaica and Barbados, the Bahamians suffered discrimination in most tourist related facilities, 'a mere reflection of practises current within the society as a Whole'. The flow of American visitors, money and ideas in the 1920s and 1930s reinforced and extended racial segregation. American and British investors and land developers bought large tracts of land in the western area including Westward Villas and the Grove Estate, also known as Vista Marina. Sales of properties were aimed at wealthy Americans and the Nassau elite. Even if coloureds or blacks could afford to purchase lots, they were specifically banned by restrictive covenants.[64] Similar developments occurred east of the town and included Shirley Slope and Buen Retiro. Additionally, as in Jamaica, the best beaches were reserved and, using public funds, were cordoned off for the exclusive use of tourists.[65]

The system of segregation was supported not only by the local elite but also by the governor at the time. Etienne Dupuch wrote later that Sir Bede Clifford 'felt that the tourist industry called for an "all white" policy…' Although he 'succeeded in stemming the downward economic trend … he did not realize the serious blow he had dealt to human relations in the colony'.[66]

Of course, the blatant discrimination did not go unnoticed. Three local black orchestra conductors, Bert Cambridge, Noel Maellet and Leonard White, complained that local orchestras and bands were considered good enough for local functions, but not for elite gatherings.[67] The hotels and clubs hired American bands during the tourist season in Nassau. If coloured and black musicians wished to hear a foreign orchestra, they had to seek special permission to enter the outside premises and listen at the windows.[68]

Bootlegging, followed by the development of tourism, changed social values and widened the gap not only between races, but also classes. The new wealth created a cleavage not only between whites but also between non-whites. It exacerbated the already ingrained self-hatred and inferiority complex held by non-whites. As in the Caribbean generally, the divisive element within the coloured and black middle class tended more to 'perpetuate than to eliminate colour prejudice'.[69]

Some coloured businesses also practised discrimination. Black's Candy Kitchen, for example, catered to all races but only whites or fair-skinned coloureds were allowed into its sit-down section. Some ambitious Nassau families, realizing the great advantages being offered to whites, gradually abandoned their coloured and black acquaintances and 'passed' for white. Association with whites and marriage to someone of European origin eventually led to acceptance by the white elite.[70]

Tourism's growth also stimulated the development and commercialization of local black entertainment and indigenous culture was also 'packaged' for tourists. Catering to visitors and locals alike, the nightclubs, which became popular in the 1930s also encouraged social drinking and prostitution. Two outstanding nightclubs, the Silver Slipper and the Zanzibar were built in Grant's Town in the 1930s. The former was foreign owned, while the Zanzibar was co-owned by black entrepreneurs Milo Butler, Bert Gibson, Preston Moss and Felix Johnson who catered to a varied clientele. Patrons attended in parties, usually fraternizing only with those at their own tables. The groups thus segregated their seating. Local black orchestras usually played at the clubs and 'native' floorshows were performed to please the tourists.[71] The Bahamian Goombay was popularized internationally by a member of the white elite, Charles Lofthouse. Black song writers and musicians, such as Alphonso 'Blind Blake' Higgs and George Symonette, also gained limited local recognition. Other less well known entertainers were Phillip Brice from Fox Hill, 'Cowboy' and 'Shorty the Serenader' who sauntered down Bay Street singing and playing for American visitors, especially when cruise ships were in port.[72]

Additionally, tourists and winter residents, with stereotyped ideas about the 'docility ...manners, superstitions, idiosyncracies, and modes of thought' about the 'natives' visited black settlements where they watched indigenous African-inspired dances and witnessed the 'Holy Rollers' at their prayer meetings, 'rolling more enthusiastically at the thought of the collection they would take up from the rich visitors'. Similarly young black boys dived for coins on the docks much to the amusement of tourists.[73] Tourism also had a profound effect on the development of straw work, an ancient Bahamian craft. The straw market proper started in the mid-1930s, behind Prince George's Wharf.

Conclusion

Downtown Nassau, in contrast to the black suburbs and Out Islands, changed significantly during the decades of the 1920s and 1930s. In order to please visitors, the infrastructure of the city was vastly improved and touristic and business facilities were constructed in the 'quaint and bustling' Bay Street area. By the end of the 1930s, Nassau boasted several hotels, two modern theatres, and many fashionable shops selling a variety of European and American goods which especially appealed to the tourists.

The growth of tourism during this period boosted revenues and generated jobs and wage labour for the New Providence workers. However, the greater wealth was domiciled in Nassau and more specifically in the hands of a small mercantile elite which controlled socioeconomic and political life. The black majority lived in poverty in a society in which social problems such as crime and vagrancy were increasing.

Modern tourism in the Bahamas and in the Caribbean is built on the foundation of the earlier development, but is very different from that in the 1920s and 1930s. Whereas the tourist industry then was seasonal and catered to the happy few, today the Bahamas and the Caribbean cater to large numbers of tourists.

In 1994, of the 13.7 million, Caribbean tourists about 3.5 million visited the Bahamas.[74] The change from elite tourism to mass tourism means that the Bahamas, a 'mature' destination, struggles to compete with the rest of the Caribbean which has embraced tourism in the light of the declining staple industries such as sugar, oil and agriculture.

Factors which have radically changed Caribbean tourism since the 1920s and 1930s are the introduction of big hotel chains, large scale gambling, and the cruise ship industry largely owned and controlled from outside the region. Expanding tremendously since the early 1980s, the cruise ship industry, especially, has outstripped land based tourism. However, while cruise ships bring in enormous numbers of tourists, there are questionable benefits to the Caribbean and its people and its long term effect on the region's land based tourism.[75]

As Patullo further demonstrated, competition between hotels and cruise ships is real. While hotels provide jobs for locals, cruise ships which operate in the Caribbean are free to employ who they wish. Most cruise ships are supplied by United States companies, not Caribbean ones. Moreover, cruise ships are polluting Caribbean waters and endangering the environment and because they supply their passengers with most amenities it has been argued that little is left to spend in ports of call.[76]

Tourism has also had a profound impact on indigenous culture in the Caribbean – its lifestyle, food, music, dress, architecture and celebrations.

The people of the Caribbean have imitated Americans and their ways and have subtly been Americanized.

While carnival in Trinidad has retained its own identity, it has changed over the years as it has been influenced by tourism. In the Bahamas, Junkanoo, a Christmas festival, which portrayed modest costumes of sacking, sponge and newspaper in the 1920s and 1930s, now displays elaborate costumes of cardboard, styrofoam and coloured crepe paper with groups hundreds-strong with drums, cowbells and trumpets and large brass sections. Although tourists are almost entirely excluded from participating in Junkanoo, their spectator role, at least in the earlier years, has been 'crucial to the survival of Junkanoo'.[77]

Additionally, economic benefits from tourism indirectly assist sponsors in getting large groups into the parade. Tourism created a dependency syndrome which was damaging socially, culturally and psychologically. Felix Bethel argues that '[I]t is clearly the case that as a result of tourism the Bahamas is chronically dependent' and not only economically.[78] Such a state of dependency has had a pervasive effect on its population and economic growth.[79] Indeed Gordon Lewis argued that '[t]his dependency on the wealthy United States tourist traffic, fundamentally parasitic, has incalculable consequences for the Bermudian-Bahamian (Caribbean) way of life. It has made of the ruling groups paranoid toursit-worshippers'. He further commented that life for the black majority was 'a grim struggle for existence in a deceptively idyllic Eden'.[80]

Lingering poverty and the inadequacies in Caribbean societies along with tourism have led to an increase in crime and drug addiction. No real solutions have been found by Caribbean governments to combat these deep-rooted social problems. Some local tourist leaders, who believe that unabated crime will destroy the tourist industry, have responded by creating all-inclusive resorts which are cordoned off from society and have tight security.

Changes introduced after the 'Quiet Revolution' in 1967 with its emphasis on the improvement of education and social services raised the standard of living for the black majority and led to the upward mobility of a large percentage of blacks. Despite this, the white mercantile elite has continued as the prominent beneficiaries of tourism, a 'monoculture'. Blacks in the Bahamas, as in the Caribbean generally, continue to occupy mainly servile positions in the tourism industry, catering mostly to a white clientele in an 'intrinsically ... neo-plantation enterprise'.[81]

Notes

1. Polly Pattullo. *Last Resorts: The Cost of Tourism in the Caribbean* (Kingston: Ian Randle Publishers; London: Cassells, 1996) 5-6.
2. Frank Taylor, 'The Tourist Industry in Jamaica, 1919-1939', *Social and Economic Studies*, 22 (1973) 1: 205-27.

3. Ian G. Strachan, 'Paradise and Plantation: The Economy of Caribbean Discourse' (Unpublished PhD dissertation, University of Pennsylvania, Philadelphia, 1995) 38.
4. See Paul Albury, *The Story of the Bahamas* (London: Macmillan, 1975); Michael Craton, *A History of the Bahamas*, 3rd ed. (Waterloo, Canada: San Salvador Press,1989). First published by Collins, 1962; Colin A. Hughes, *Race and Politics in the Bahamas* (St Lucia and London: University of Queensland Press, 1981).
5. Frank Taylor, *To Hell with Paradise: A History of the Jamaica Tourist Industry* (Pittsburgh: University of Pittsburgh Press, 1993).
6. Albury, *Story*, 221-222.
7. Haynes Smith to Chamberlain, February 23, 1897, C.O. 23/246/57.
8. Albury, *Story*, 225; Gail Saunders, 'Social History of the Bahamas' (Unpublished PhD thesis, University of Waterloo) 35.
9. Albury, *Story*, 225.
10. Saunders, 'Social History', 241-251; Craton, *History*, 250-255; Michael Craton and Gail Saunders, *Islanders in the Stream. A History of the Bahamian People*. 2 vols. (Athens, Georgia: Georgia University Press, 1994) 237-242.
11. Gail Saunders and Donald Cartwright, *Historic Nassau* (London: Macmillan, 1979) 44.
12. Bede Clifford, *Proconsul* (London: Evans Publishers, 1964) 194.
13. *Nassau Magazine* 2 (February 2, 1935): 12-13, 24.
14. *Tribune*, February 7, 1933; February 22 and March 5, 1937.
15. Grant to Devonshire, October 28, 1922 CO23/291/340-345; Aspinall, *The Pocket Guide to the West Indies: British Guiana, British Honduras, the Bermudas, the Spanish Main and the Panama Canals* (London: 1923) 253-254.
16. Clifford to Conliffe-Lister, December 30, 1932, CO23/463.
17. *Nassau Magazine* 2 (February 2, 1940) 8-9.
18. Cordeaux to Churchill, December 23, 1921, Conf. CO 23/289, 311-312.
19. See *Nassau Guardian*, September 30, 1922; *Colonial Annual Reports Bahamas*, 1928, 1931. Encl. CO 23/405, CO 23/454; *Tribune* June 17, 1925. In 1928 in Nassau there were 1000 subscribers which increased to 1,150 by 1931. Eleuthera by that year had 65 miles of telephone lines; Cat Island, 30 miles, Long Island, 45, connecting the major settlements.
20. *Nassau Guardian*, February 3, 1923; December 29, 1926; *Tribune*, April 15, September 23, 1923; July 17, 1926; January 11, 1927. New Traffic Rules were introduced early in 1927.
21. *Nassau Guardian*, August 20, 1921. See also *Colonial Annual Reports Bahamas*, 1931, Encl. CO 23/454.
22. Mary Moseley, *The Bahamas Handbook* (Nassau: Nassau Guardian, 1926) 35; Colin Hughes, *Race and Politics*, 253; Philip Cash, 'Colonial Policies and Outside Influences: A Study of Bahamian History, 1919-1947' (MA thesis, University of Wales) 210.
23. Anthony Thompson, *An Economic History of the Bahamas* (Nassau: Commonwealth Publications, 1979) 30.
24. *Tribune*, March 19, 1934; *Votes of the House of Assembly*, November 21, 1935 – June 1, 1936, Appendix A (Nassau: Nassau Guardian, 1936) 224; *Colonial Annual Report*, 1938 (London: HMSO, 1939), 18.

25. J. Kevin Higgins, *The Bahamian Economy: An Analysis* (Nassau: The Counselors, 1994).
26. Gordon K. Lewis, *The Growth of the Modern West Indies* (New York: Monthly Review Press, 1968) 320.
27. Saunders, 'Social History', 257; Craton and Saunders, *Islanders*. Vol. 2, 246.
28. Sigrist was a founding member of the Hawker Aircraft Company which manufactured the Hurricane, the single-seater fighter plane designed by Sidney Camm, and utilized so successfully in World War II.
29. See also *Nassau Magazine* 2 (April 1935): 4.
30. For example, Captain J.S. Engler of Miami, developer of Engler's Public Market in Miami, hoped to lure many Bahamian residents in Miami back to the Bahamas, and subdivided 'Nassau's Master Suburb' naming it Englerston.
31. Saunders, 'Social History', 259.
32. *Tribune*, January 23, 1924.
33. *Report on the Census of the Bahama Islands*, taken April 26, 1931.
34. *Colonial Annual Reports Bahamas*, 1928.
35. *Nassau Guardian,* February 3, 1923.
36. *Nassau Guardian,* February 21, 1925; *Tribune,* February 13, 1924.
37. Saunders, 'Social History', 340; Craton and Saunders, *Islanders in the Stream,* 264; Clement Bethel and Nicolette Bethel, *Junkanoo: Festival of the Bahamas* (London: Macmillan, 1991) 64.
38. Saunders, 'Social History', 269. Cordeaux to Amery, June 11, 1925, Conf., CO 23/296.
39. *Colonial Annual Report*, 1938, 19.
40. Dundas to Passfield, September 20, 1929, CO 23/415.
41. Dundas to Parkinson, July 11, 1938, Conf., CO 23/653. See also *Tribune*, September 5, 27 and 30, 1937.
42. Annual Medical and Sanitary Report, 1926-1927, Encl., CO 23/347.
43. Sir Wilfred Beveridge, *Report on the Public Health and on Medical Conditions in new Providence, Bahama Islands* (London: Waterlow, 1927) 48; Saunders 'Social History', 262.
44. S.E.V. Luke, Notes on the Bahamas, April 20, 1951, CO 23/889; *Report on the Census of the Bahama Islands*, December 6, 1953, Nassau, *Nassau Guardian*, 1954.
45. Taylor, 'The Tourist Industry in Jamaica, 1919-1939', 216.
46. *Tribune,* March 12, 1930.
47. *Tribune,* October 4, 1953.
48. *Tribune,* September 9, 1931; Nassau Magazine, 3:3 (February 1936), 15; James Walvin, *History as Tourism: Tourism as History* (Unpublished Paper, Heritage Tourism and Caribbean Development Conference, University of the West Indies, Mona, Jamaica, 1995) 16.
49. Sandra Dean-Patterson, 'A Longitudinal Study of Changes in Bahamian Drinking, 1969-1977' (Unpublished PhD dissertation, Brandeis University, Waltham, Massachusetts, 1978) 37. See also *Report of the Commission on Venereal Diseases* (Nassau: Nassau Guardian, 1918) 23.
50. Alan Burns, *Colonial Civil Servant* (London, s.n., 1949) 84.
51. Lewis, *The Growth of the Modern West Indies*, 311.
52. Hughes, *Race and Politics*, 22; See also chapter 1 of this book.

53. Dundas to McDonald, July 11, 1938, Conf., CO 23/653; Saunders, 'Social History', 232.
54. Burns, *Colonial Civil Servant*, 84.
55. Howard Johnson, *The Bahamas in Slavery and Freedom* (Kingston: Ian Randle Publishers; London: James Currey, 1991) 125-148.
56. Saunders, 'Social History', 352-353.
57. Philip Cash, Shirley Gordon, Gail Saunders, *Sources of Bahamian History* (London: Macmillan, 1991) 285.
58. Saunders, 'Social History', 359.
59. Saunders, 'Social History', 260, 279.
60. *Tribune*, December 16, 1983.
61. Cash, Gordon, Saunders, *Sources of Bahamian History*, 50-51, 144, 278-279. See also *Tribune*, January 6, 1938.
62. Wesleyan Methodist Missionary Society, Letters, Johnson to Burns, April 8, 1936.
63. Taylor, 'The Tourist Industry in Jamaica, 1919-1939', 213.
64. Saunders, 'Social History', 258.
65. Taylor, 'The Tourist Industry in Jamaica, 1919-1939', 213-214; Saunders, 'Social History', 328.
66. Etienne Dupuch, *Tribune Story* (London: Ernest Benn, 1967) 76-77.
67. *Tribune*, January 13, 1934.
68. Interview with Maxwell Thompson, January 17, 1984.
69. Sydney Olivier, *White Capital and Coloured Labour* (London: Socialist Library, 1910) 38-39; David Lowenthal, *West Indian Societies* (Oxford University Press, 1972) 72.
70. Saunders interview with Basil and Audrey North, August 10, 1984.
71. Saunders, 'Social History', 330-331; Craton and Saunders, *Islanders*, 265.
72. Burns, *Colonial Civil Servant*, 84; Saunders, 'Social History', 333.
73. Shelly B. Malone and Richard Roberts, *Nostalgic Nassau: Picture Postcards 1900-1940* (Florida: A.C. Graphics, 1991) 42; Anthony Dahl, *Literature of the Bahamas, 1724-1992: The March Towards National Identity* (Lanham: University Press of America, 1995) 64-65.
74. Patullo, *Last Resorts*, 11.
75. Patullo, *Last Resorts*, 157-159.
76. Patullo, *Last Resorts*, 161-165.
77. Nina Wood, 'Rushin' Hard and Runnin' Hot: Experience the Music of the Junkanoo Parade in Nassau Bahamas' (Unpublished PhD dissertation, Indiana University, Bloomington, 1995) 487.
78. Felix Bethel, 'Tourism, Public Policy, and National Development in the Bahamas'. In Dean Collinwood and Steve Dodge, eds., *Modern Bahamian Society* (Parkerburg, Iowa: Caribbean Books, 1989) 135.
79. William G. Demas, *Essays on Caribbean Integration and Development* (Mona, Jamaica: Institute for Social and Economic Research, University of the West Indies, 1976) 56-59.
80. Lewis, *Growth of the Modern West Indies*, 321, 327.
81. Frank Taylor, *To Hell with Paradise*, 175; Bethel, 'Tourism, Public Policy and National Development in the Bahamas', 99-138; Tom Barry, Beth Wood and Deb Preusch, *The Other Side of Paradise: Foreign Control in the Caribbean* (New York: Grove Press, 1984) 87; Taylor, *To Hell with Paradise*, 175.

10

The 1937 Riot in Inagua

The upheavals in the form of mass riots and strikes during the 1930s in the British West Indian colonies did not occur on a similar scale in the Bahamas. The Nassau Riot in 1942 during the following decade was a short-lived spontaneous outburst by a group of disgruntled labourers. Black Bahamian leaders failed to convert the riot into a political movement but an analysis of the disturbance[1] showed that it occurred against the background of narrow socioeconomic and political policies then rampant in the Bahamas.

Five years before the disturbance in Nassau, an incident erupted on Inagua, a remote island in the southern Bahamas. Following shortly after the Trinidad and Barbadian riots, the disturbance became known as the 'Inagua Riot'. This paper will explore the causes of the 1937 disturbance in Inagua. Such an analysis involves the examination of the disturbance and the events immediately prior to it.

To date no detailed examination of the Inagua disturbance has been published.[2] The incident is rarely mentioned in general histories. Colin Hughes and Philip Cash contended that it was essentially a clash of individuals.[3] Hughes gave the incident only a footnote and stressed that there were no similarities with the mass actions of the West Indian riots. Cash devoted more attention to the event and concluded that the 'events of the island of Inagua were given an importance unwarranted by the actual happenings…'[4] Margery Erickson, wife of Josiah (or Jim) who with his brothers revived the salt industry in Inagua in the 1930s, attributes the trouble to the personal animosity of certain Inaguans 'whose livelihood was threatened by the new prosperity' and 'who resented Jim's effort to improve Inagua'.[5]

Inagua[6] is about 596 square miles and is located within close proximity of Cuba and Haiti, with which territories it has traded from early times. It is the most southerly and third largest island of the Bahamas, lying 370 miles south of Nassau, the capital, which is located on New Providence Island. After the demise of the aboriginal Lucayans in the early sixteenth century, until the mid-nineteenth century, Inagua was largely uninhabited, unlike most of the major Bahamian islands which were settled between the mid-seventeenth and late eighteenth centuries. Inagua is believed to have been permanently settled between 1844 and 1849 when Matthew Town, its chief settlement, was laid out on the western end of the island.

Like the other Bahamian Out Islands, Inagua was governed by an Out Island Commissioner appointed by the central government in Nassau. Over the years, the Bahamas' House of Assembly, dominated by a wealthy white mercantile elite, had gained its independence and control of the purse. Like Barbados and Bermuda, the Bahamas retained the Old Representative System. Theoretically, the colonial governors wielded great power but the lower house of the Bahamas' bi-cameral legislature was a wholly elected body. It governed the Bahamas, maintaining influence over the economy and politics by favouring propertied interest, by excluding half of the population and by ignoring for the most part the Out Islands,[7] where until the 1950s most of the population lived.

Being in the dry belt of the Bahamian archipelago, Inagua naturally produced salt, which soon became the island's staple product. Until 1848, however, the Turks and Caicos Islands were the leading salt-producing and exporting islands in the Bahamas. After their separation from the colony in that year,[8] attention focused on the exploitation of Inagua's salt ponds and various companies were established during the mid-nineteenth century when the industry generally flourished.[9] The success of Inagua's salt industry was reflected in the growth of its population from 172 in 1847 to 1,120 in 1871, as shown by the *Blue Books* between those years and the Census Report taken in 1871.

By the early 1900s, however, the industry had collapsed. This was due partly to increasing production of mined salt in North America which caused a decline in prices, and United States tariffs which made it increasingly unprofitable to ship to the United States, the main consumer of Inagua's salt.[10] The economy in the late nineteenth and early twentieth centuries was being sustained by the steamship labour business which provided work for the male population.

Economic developments in Mexico and Central America needed much material and manpower. Steamship lines including the Hamburg-American Line, the Royal Netherlands Lines and the Atlas Company (which stopped at West Indian and Central American ports) picked up stevedore labour and contract workers to load and unload cargoes at the ports.[11] By 1882, Matthew Town had outstripped its main rival Albert Town on Long Cay, having become the 'main centre of labour recruitment' in the Bahamas.[12] Bahamian men from other islands gravitated to Inagua to find work.

At this time in the Bahamas most labourers were paid in truck. Initially steamship labourers were paid in cash but very soon the steamship companies changed to the local system of paying in truck and allowing the labourers credit and advances in food and drink. This exploitative practice was to continue well into the twentieth century. As Howard Johnson argued, 'The credit system and the indebtedness which it induced became an effective technique for mobilizing and maintaining a stable labour force, and payment in truck served to perpetuate the indebtedness'. He further argued that these systems were also methods for increasing the merchant's profits.[13]

Despite the truck system, the stevedore trade, helped only marginally by the cultivation and export of sisal, sustained Inagua's economy in the latter part of the nineteenth century and during the early years of the twentieth. In fact, Matthew Town was known as 'a magic port' in which one could find new opportunities and earn money. Its general appearance and active commerce gave it a 'booming atmosphere'.[14]

The appearance of a newspaper was a reflection of the increased trade between Inagua and the other islands of the Caribbean. Matthew Town was one of the few settlements in the Out Islands to publish a newspaper in the early twentieth century. A.H. Meallet, a local Inaguan, began a printing operation in Matthew Town in 1898 and a decade later began issuing the *Inaguan Record* which espoused the cause of the labourers. It was in print for five years but made little impact on the island's social or political life.[15]

With the advent of World War I, shipping was interrupted and steamship companies ceased calling at Inagua. By the 1920s and early 1930s, Inagua, like most of the Out Islands in the Bahamas, suffered from acute depression. Out Islanders flocked to Nassau to find work. Inagua's population declined by fifty per cent between 1911 and 1931, dropping from 1,343 to 667.[16] Demoralized because of the lack of work, some families left to seek a living in Nassau while others migrated to the southern United States.[17] On an Out Island tour in 1932, Governor Clifford described Matthew Town as 'forlorn and desolate...suggestive of a partially bombarded village well behind the lines.' He continued that the population, 'a queer mixture of Turks Islanders, a few of Haitian stock' and the rest 'Bahamian stock', found it difficult to feed and clothe themselves.[18]

By the mid-1930s, however, Inagua's stevedoring traffic and salt industry had been revived to a limited extent. Arthur L. Symonette, a local coloured merchant who was also a Justice of the Peace, spearheaded both operations. He ran a store and served as agent for the Royal Netherlands Steamship Company.[19] Evidence suggests that Symonette employed the truck system by which he kept the men indebted to him at his store. Margery Erickson wrote, 'No man could get a job on a southbound steamer except through Symonett (sic) and he employed only those whose families shopped at his store.'[20] When the stevedores returned to Inagua they found themselves in debt. Bills for goods that their families had 'supposedly' bought at the store while they were away meant that their wages went to pay their debts.[21] This caused much resentment and the labourers claimed that to supplement their wages they were forced to steal from the cargo of the ship and to smuggle rum and tafia from Cuba and Haiti. In 1936 the Inagua-based stevedores struck for higher wages.[22] Aware of Symonette's power and influence, a number of Inaguan men, who called themselves the 'Rulers' or 'Rock' of Inagua[23], united against him and forced him to cooperate with them. According to John Hughes Symonette was content as long as the bulk of the wages were used to purchase goods at his store.[24]

Inagua was unique among the Out Islands in that it had a labour union – the only one outside the capital. It had been organized in 1934 by Theodore Farquharson, son of an Acklins Islander who had migrated to Inagua. Having spent about 15 years in the United States, Theodore Farquharson had returned to Inagua in 1928 to take over his father's business, a general store. Described as 'an orator of the Hyde Park tub thumper type, with somewhat more education than the rest of his coloured brethren in Inagua',[25] Farquharson was perhaps instrumental in causing several work stoppages, but was not the instigator of the violent incident which occurred in 1937.

It was into such an atmosphere that the Ericksons, a New England family headed by Josiah Erickson, made their debut at Matthew Town in 1936. Arriving in mid-January to revitalize the salt industry, Josiah and his brothers Douglas and Wentworth established the West India Chemical Company, employing about 50 men and a few women.[26] The Ericksons, however, soon encountered hostility from the local people. Some prominent Inaguans, including Symonette, felt threatened by the new wave of economic activity which brought prosperity and new jobs. Until the coming of the Eriksons, Symonette was perhaps the most powerful man on the island through his shop and his control of the Royal Netherlands Steamship Company. With the revival of the salt business by the Ericksons, new avenues of employment opened up for Inaguans and Symonette or the other leading local families were losing their monopoly as employers and with it, their influence.[27] Moreover, a number of local Inaguans were suspicious of the newcomers, whom they saw as outsiders.

In December 1936 and early in 1937, a series of strikes, instigated by several of the leaders in the town including Nehemiah C. Alexander, a Baptist minister and shopkeeper, occurred. Demands were made for higher wages.[28] The Ericksons, already disliked by many of the inhabitants, thereupon retaliated by importing unskilled labour from Acklins, Long Cay, and Mayaguana.[29] Hostility towards them further intensified after they took over the steamship agency from Symonette. The influential group of men who called themselves 'the rulers of Inagua' or 'the Rock' and who had an uneasy alliance with Symonette were considered by Symonette to be his supporters. However they had intimidated and threatened him several times and he had been obliged to include two or three of them on all stevedoring voyages.[30]

Shortly after the strike in December 1936, a fight over a trivial incident occurred between Charles Kaddy, a white American truck driver for the West

Indian Chemical Company, and a local black stevedore, George Duvalier. When not employed, Duvalier loitered around Symonette's shop with his brother Willis. They had been born in the United States and had lived there for some time before returning to Inagua to live with their grandmother. They were believed to be among the so-called 'Band of Inagua Terrors'.[31] The latter, a group of lawless, reckless young men, many of whom had been charged with disorderly behaviour between 1934 and 1936, was led by Reginald Alexander, son of Baptist preacher Nehemiah Alexander. The ensuing fight, which erupted when Kaddy drove his truck into the side of Symonette's shop, very quickly developed into a brawl involving Duvalier's supporters, including his brother Willis, against almost the entire white staff of the company. All the participants subsequently appeared before Commissioner Fields[32] for disturbing the peace. Four members of each faction were convicted and fined two pounds each.[33] From that date it appeared that the Duvalier brothers continued to harbour a grudge against the Ericksons.[34] It was said that Willis Duvalier, at the hearing of the case, threatened that if there was further trouble with the Ericksons, he would 'shoot to kill'.[35]

For the next six months, Matthew Town was fairly orderly. In June 1937 however, Reginald Alexander, leader of the 'Band of Inagua Terrors', was found guilty by Commissioner Fields and fined five pounds for using obscene language to Euphemia Henderson, whose daughter he had courted.[36] Almost immediately afterwards, Reginald Alexander returned to the Henderson house, and accused Euphemia's daughter, Edna Henderson, of 'making a baby' for him. Mrs Henderson thereupon sued Alexander for twelve pounds damages, claiming defamation of her daughter's character. Reginald Alexander's sister, Mabel Alexander, paid the fine on June 27, 1937. Three days later, Euphemia Henderson's house was destroyed by fire. Arthur Ferguson, who was arrested on July 10, admitted that he had set the Henderson house on fire for two pounds, on instruction from Reginald Alexander. Both were charged with arson. Alexander, however, was granted bail. While in custody, an attempt was made to rescue Ferguson from prison. After a preliminary hearing, Commissioner Fields ordered both Ferguson and Alexander to stand trial in Nassau. The inquiry was completed on August 18.[37]

The next day, George Duvalier, a friend of both the accused, was arrested for assaulting Daniel Bain – the last witness to give evidence in the arson case. The Duvaliers disliked Bain because they believed he carried news to the Ericksons. While his trial was in session, Duvalier escaped from the courtroom. Corporal Edey, who had been sent to Inagua to investigate the arson case, and local constable Saunders, suspected by the Commissioner to be in collusion with the Duvaliers, ostensibly gave chase. While in pursuit of the suspect, Corporal Edey was attacked with a knife by Willis Duvalier, George's brother, and received a superficial wound over his right shoulder.

Commissioner Fields, while attempting to leave his office later on, was attacked by Willis Duvalier and only escaped injury by sheer luck.[38]

Fields eluded Willis Duvalier, and hurried to the Wireless Station to telegraph the authorities in Nassau. Meanwhile, Willis' brother George had acquired a gun and he followed Fields to the Wireless Station. After forcing the operator to leave, he then shot the Commissioner in the left forearm at close range. Believing Fields to be dead, Duvalier, still armed, ran to the Erickson's store and fired at Josiah Erickson. Fortunately for Erickson, the gun misfired. While Duvalier reloaded the weapon, Josiah and his younger brother Douglas escaped to their home.[39]

Hearing of the attack on the Commissioner, the Ericksons, securing arms, proceeded to the Wireless Station along with two American employees. On leaving the station with Fields whom they were surprised to find not fatally wounded, the whole party was attacked by Willis Duvalier. Both Ericksons, and their employee, Kaddy, received minor injuries. In fear of their lives, the Erickson party and the Commissioner spent the night at the Erickson household. Meanwhile, the Duvaliers had sought out an employee of the West Indian Chemical Company, John Munroe, a black labourer whom they considered a 'pimp' for the Ericksons, and shot him dead. They also set fire to the Commissioner's residence, the Wireless Station, the Ericksons' store and the Company's salt house.[40]

The next morning, August 20, the Ericksons, three of their employees, Dr Fields, and Corporal Edey fled Inagua in the Ericksons' motor boat. Their intention to contact an ocean line in order to relay a message to Nassau was frustrated when engine trouble developed. Drifting southwards, they landed in Cuba, and having no means of identification, were promptly arrested for possession of arms.[41]

Left in control of Matthew Town, the Duvaliers terrorized the inhabitants for two days, though causing little further harm. Neither the 'Band of Inagua Terrors' nor the rest of the inhabitants actually abetted them. It was reported that a number of inhabitants left the settlement of Matthew Town after the shooting of John Munroe, and went to stay at North East Point until they heard the Duvaliers had left the island.[42]

Those who stayed had not made an effort to stop their rampage either. On Sunday, August 22, after commanding the town for the weekend, the Duvaliers left Inagua in a small sailing boat. When the long overdue police detachment of eight arrived two days later, all was quiet.[43]

By October 12, 1937, both Duvaliers had been arrested in Haiti and brought to Nassau for trial. Found guilty of murder in the Nassau Supreme Court on November 3, 1937, they were executed less than three weeks later.[44]

When John A. Hughes visited Matthew Town early in 1938, he found no signs of unrest. It seemed that the truck system was no longer in operation.

Smuggling, however, continued on a small scale. The new Commissioner, Mr Malone, a white Abaconian, although disliked by Josiah Erickson for his alleged arrogance and colour prejudice, was said by Hughes, on the contrary, to have won the 'respect and affection' of the inhabitants.[45]

Before a detailed investigation was made and a report compiled, the incident at Inagua in 1937 was blown out of proportion by the press within and outside the Bahamas. The British press, cognizant of the unrest in the West Indies, elevated the events to an importance on a par with the riots in the southern Caribbean.[46]

Etienne Dupuch, editor of the *Nassau Daily Tribune* and then representative in the House of Assembly for Inagua, gave the disturbance headline and front page coverage. On August 25, he actually referred to the incident as a 'riot' and likened it to similar outbreaks throughout the British West Indies. He hinted that the cause of the unrest throughout the Caribbean was due to Communist propaganda and had nothing to do with wages. Even after it was officially confirmed that only two men (the Duvalier brothers) were the instigators of the disturbance, Dupuch still seemed skeptical.[47] Robert M. Bailey, a black tailor and political activist, expressed his skepticism in a letter to the *Tribune*. Exaggerating, he alluded to the seething unrest in the colony, specifically to the violence in New Providence, the 'burglary and incendiarism at Bimini', and the rioting and murder at Inagua. He asked:

> Can we believe that the Commissioner and fourteen heavily armed men, including five white Americans with large financial interests in the island, left a hilarious people only to try to get in communication with the capital, their wireless station being out of commission – burnt down – and there was no riot at Inagua?
>
> Can we believe that the law abiding residents of Inagua looked on with folded arms, while two men ran amuck, doing all this damage and made no attempt to overpower them...[48]

The mention of 'white' Americans was of some significance. Racial tension may have contributed towards the disturbance. Discrimination towards blacks and coloureds was rife in Nassau but was not so marked in the Out Islands where there was less class stratification. However, some Inaguans, including the Duvalier brothers, had spent time in the United States where prejudice was blatant and the existence of Jim Crow attitudes and the Ku Klux Klan and its lynching parties were threats to blacks. There is no evidence of racial discrimination practised by the Ericksons, but it is possible that the Inaguans may have encountered attitudes of white superiority displayed by the Americans, especially those employed in Inagua.[49]

Mary Moseley, editor of the *Nassau Guardian*, on the other hand, believed that the alleged riot was just a 'minor brawl', unconnected with labour disturbances in the British Caribbean. She attached little importance to colour prejudice but hinted that 'Erickson was a little suspect in consequence of his

American nationality.' She believed that the people of Inagua were far too sensible to indulge in any form of violence comparable to that which had appeared elsewhere in the West Indies. Moreover, in her opinion, the acts committed were 'entirely unworthy of Bahamians or any civilised people...'[50]

Who are we to believe? There is evidence which supports both sentiments. The argument that it resembled a mass riot is supported by Commissioner Fields' statement that at the time of his taking over the District it was 'in a state of unrest.'[51] He mentioned several strikes, the Inaguans' resentment towards the Ericksons for importing labourers from neighbouring islands and the anti-American feelings harboured by some of the Inaguans. In fact during the years 1935 and 1936, cases of unlawful and disorderly behaviour increased.[52]

Commissioner Fields also commented in his report on the events that Reginald Alexander, who had been charged with arson shortly before the disturbance, was the instigator of the activities and that his ' "band of Inagua terrors" was on the war path'. Fields implied that the local administration had no control over Inagua's population and could not even rely on the support of the local constable, Saunders, who seemed to be in collusion with the Duvaliers. After the murder of John Munroe, the Commissioner and the Ericksons spent a very uneasy night at the Ericksons' house, keeping guard all night and fearing an attack by the 'band of Inagua terrors.'[53]

Additionally, Fields' conclusions indicated that the undercurrents at Inagua were more serious than the administration admitted.[54] While Fields acknowledged that 'there was no actual riot', he added that 'it is equally true that had the Duvaliers been killed or dangerously wounded there would have been a riot and the hitherto passive band of terrors would have suddenly become very active'.[55]

Fields also remarked on the mainly passive participation of the Inaguans. He reported that the 'band of terrors' were active to a small degree. They helped to supply gasoline for the Residency, the Commissioner's home, tried to ascertain the strength of the numbers at the Ericksons' house and intercepted a message from the Ericksons' house to the Residency. As for the rest of the people, Fields was amazed:

> Though there were but two men on the war path there was not the usual crowd of curious spectators, the inhabitants of the settlement had suddenly seemingly retired to bed as though everyone had previously known all about it and was neither surprised nor alarmed when George and Willis became outlaws.

He concluded: 'While the rest of the inhabitants exhibited no willingness to help the Duvaliers, they equally made no effort and signified no willingness to stop them'.[56]

The argument that the Inagua disturbance was merely a clash of personalities and 'the work of the two men Duvalier alone' which Jarrett,

Colonial Secretary, and Acting Governor at the time of the disturbance, concluded in the official report, is also supported by strong evidence.

In Bahamian law, a riot occurs if three or more persons in a public or private place attempt or commit violence.[57] In the case of the Inagua incident, the murder, the attempted murder and the arson were actually performed by the two Duvalier brothers. George and Willis Duvalier resented the Ericksons, perhaps for racial reasons but more because of their intrusion and also because they took away Symonette's monopoly. They refused to work for the Ericksons. They had held a grudge against the Americans ever since the fight with Kaddy, one of their American employees. The Duvaliers considered John Munroe (whom they killed) as an informer to the Ericksons and showed animosity towards Commissioner Fields, who according to Governor Clifford 'failed to keep in touch with the local interest of the people and rather attached himself to the Erickson group'.[58] Moreover, Fields had convicted and fined them for the part they had taken in the fight against Kaddy and the Ericksons. The burning of the Erickson store and the salt house was directed against the Ericksons personally, while that of the Wireless Station and the Residency seemed to have been directed against Fields.

As H.O. Dalke, a social psychologist, has suggested in a study on race and minority riots, the likelihood of rioting and violence is very high 'in a transitional period, such as industrialization...'[59] The fact that the incident occurred in an area of the Bahamas where there was slight industrial development was perhaps significant to a limited degree. However, the lack of united action on the part of the inhabitants of Matthew Town, and the failure of the Duvaliers and their supporters to work havoc on the salt pans or kill more of the Ericksons' employees were also meaningful.

The riots and strikes that swept through the West Indies in the 1930s were caused by many factors. Oppressive economic conditions brought about by the Great Depression caused extensive unemployment, low wages and a high cost of living. Emigration outlets to North America were closed and labourers returned from South and Central America to join the unemployed.[60] These factors combined with dire poverty and squalid social conditions resulted in pent-up frustrations and distress which exploded in strikes and riots in the 1930s in the British Caribbean and in the early 1940s in Nassau, Bahamas.

Conditions which brought about the riots and strikes elsewhere in the British Caribbean were present in Inagua in the early 1930s. The Out Islands, which until the 1950s contained the majority of the population, were generally neglected by the reactionary Nassau white mercantile elite and little was done to improve the welfare of most of the people. However, by 1937, because of foreign investment, there was an upswing in Inagua's economy with increased salt exports[61] and high rate of employment. As Neil Smelser, a sociologist, argues[62] hostile outbursts may erupt if certain factors cause enough strain on a given society. Such factors include recent migrants or population invasions and new kinds of cultural contacts, new expectations and specific dissatisfactions. These factors were present in Inagua's society of 1937 and made for new tensions. The advent of the Ericksons and their employees and the revitalization of the salt industry heightened expectations which were not altogether satisfactory.

Why then was there no mass uprising? Inagua was a part of the far-flung Bahamian archipelago and was isolated from the main centres of the Bahamian population. Communication was difficult and transportation between the islands was often irregular. This made it hard to organize a national movement. The migration of Out Islanders into Nassau which began in the 1920s began to bring together the elements of dissatisfaction. It was not until the numbers were sufficient and the leaders available that there was a real demand for change.

In 1937 most Inaguans, at least the men,[63] were employed and were faring better than they had been in the late 1920s and early 1930s. Although there was some dissatisfaction and resentment towards the Ericksons' takeover of the salt industry and the stevedoring trade, the feeling was not universal. The fledgling trade union was extremely weak and no leader emerged. Additionally, the influential citizens at Inagua had ambivalent feelings towards Arthur L. Symonette, potential leader and most prosperous merchant at the time of the Ericksons' debut. They despised the truck system under which his labourers operated.

The Ericksons were seen as 'outsiders' and may have been resented as such. However, it must also be remembered that Matthew Town was quite a cosmopolitan settlement. Its inhabitants had traditionally been exposed to Europeans, other West Indians and Haitians. Many Inaguans had travelled to other West Indian islands, Central and South America. Some had lived and gone to school in Haiti.[64] Others had lived and worked for some years in North America. Inaguans had learned to mix with, and to tolerate, foreigners of both races.

The disturbance in Inagua in 1937 resulted from a personal vendetta. It occurred in a potentially explosive atmosphere but failed to develop into a political or labour riot. The causes of the Inagua incident were perhaps more deep-rooted than the government admitted. However, the isolated community of Matthew Town, although sympathetic towards the perpetrators, was unpoliticized and had no committed leadership. Moreover, it seemed content with the new wave of prosperity offered by the American investors.

Notes

1. See 'The 1942 Riot in Nassau' in this book, Ch. 11.
2. The riot in Inagua was examined in detail by Gail Saunders, 'The Social History of the Bahamas 1890-1953' (Unpublished PhD, University of Waterloo,1985), 309-374. This article is an expansion of the account given there. See also Michael Craton and Gail Saunders, *Islanders in The Stream, A History of The Bahamian People* Vol 2. (Athens, Georgia: Georgia University Press, 1992-1998), 270-271.
3. Colin Hughes, *Race and Politics in The Bahamas* (St Lucia, Queensland: University of Queensland Press, 1981), 19, and Philip Cash, 'Colonial Policies and Outside Influences: A Study of Bahamian History, 1919-1947' (Unpublished MA thesis, University of Wales, 1979), 239-240. For general histories see Paul Albury, *The Story of The Bahamas* (London and Basingstoke: Macmillan, 1983), 200 and Michael Craton, *A History of The Bahamas* (Waterloo: 1989).
4. Cash, 'Colonial Policies', 240; Hughes, *Race and Politics*, 19.
5. Margery Erickson, *Great Inagua* (New York: Capriole Press, 1987), 49.
6. Inagua is an Arawak Lucayan name which has survived intact. It means 'Small Eastern Land'. See Julian Granberry, 'Lucayan Toponyms', *Journal of The Bahamas Historical Society*, 13: 1 (Oct. 1991), 3-12.
7. The Out Islands are all those Bahamian islands outside of New Providence where Nassau, the capital, is located. Women were legally given the vote in 1960 and voted in the 1962 General Elections.
8. An Act for the Separation of Turks Island from The Bahamas, December 25, 1848.
9. The Heneagua Salt Pond Company, a Bahamian owned joint-stock company was formed in 1849 to cultivate the salt ponds in Inagua. During the next year, the Inagua Salt Pond Company owned by several inhabitants of Inagua was established. Later in 1865 a group of New Providence businessmen led by the Hon. Timothy Darling formed a joint-stock company that constructed a tramway to transport salt and also wharf facilities at Matthew Town. *Archives Exhibition Booklet*, 1980, 26-27.
10. Albury, *Story*, 198.
11. Howard Johnson, *The Bahamas, From Slavery To Servitude, 1783-1933*, (Gainesville: University Press of Florida, 1996), 113-115 and Patrice Williams, 'The Emigrant Labour Business. An Important Industry in the Late Nineteenth and Early Twentieth Centuries', *Journal of the Bahamas Historical Society*, 6: 1 (October 1985), 9-14.
12. Johnson, *From Slavery To Servitude*, 113.
13. Johnson, *From* Slavery To Servitude, 115.
14. Albury, *Story*, 199.
15. Sidney H. Pactor, 'Communication in an Island Setting: a History of the Mass Media of the Bahama Islands, 1784-1956' (Unpublished PhD dissertation, University of Tennessee, Knoxville, 1985), 307.
16. *Report of the Census of the Bahama Islands*, Taken on 26 April, 1931 (Nassau, Nassau Guardian: 1931).
17. Johnson, *From Slavery To Servitude*, 154-164; Raymond Mohl, 'Black Immigrants: Bahamians in early twentieth-century Miami', *The Florida*

Historical Quarterly (Jan. 1987) 271-297 and taped interview with Catherine A. Granger, Nassau, 1970.
18. Report of John A. Hughes, Feb. 23, 1938. Encl. Charles C. Dundas to Ormsby-Gore, March 18, 1938, CO23/638.
19. Sir Bede Clifford, to Conliffe-Lester, April 14, 1932, CO23/469.
20. Margery Erickson, *Great Inagua*, 49.
21. Erickson, *Great Inagua*, 49.
22. Encl. Charles C. Dundas to Ormsby-Gore, Feb. 21, 1938, Conf. CO23/638.
23. Encl. A.W. Erickson to Ormsby-Gore, Oct. 25, 1937, CO23/618. The so-called 'Rulers' of Inagua included among others, George Pickering, Albert Augustus, John Steele, James Baker, Charles Wildgoose, Maurice Daxon, Kenneth Williams, Bruce Mortimer and T.K. Palacious.
24. Encl. Charles Dundas to Ormsby-Gore. Report, March 18, 1938, CO23/638.
25. Encl. Charles Dundas to Ormsby-Gore, Feb. 21, 1938, Conf., CO23/638.
26. A.W. Erickson to Ormsby-Gore, Oct. 25, 1937, CO23/618.
27. J.C. Jarrett to Ormsby-Gore, Sept. 17, 1937, CO23/618.
28. Men earned two shillings a day, women earned one shilling and six pence a day. A.W. Erickson to Ormsby-Gore, Oct. 25, 1937, CO23/618.
29. Jarrett to Ormsby-Gore, Sept. 17, 1937, CO23/618.
30. Erickson to Ormsby-Gore, Oct. 25, 1937, CO23/638.
31. Encl. Dundas to Ormsby-Gore, Oct. 25, 1937, CO23/638.
32. Dundas to Ormsby-Gore, Feb. 21, 1938, CO23/668. Commissioner Fields was a coloured Trinidadian who was a physician by profession. He had been stationed at Inagua since 1926 and was well-liked by the Ericksons.
33. Encl. A.W. Erickson to Ormsby-Gore, Oct. 25, 1937, CO23/618.
34. Encl. Dundas to Ormsby-Gore, March 18, 1938, CO23/638.
35. *Appendix to Votes of the House of Assembly*, Oct. 18, 1937-21 Feb. 21, 1938, Nassau.
36. *Appendix to Votes of the House of Assembly, 1937-1938* (Nassau: Nassau Guardian, 1938), 200. Reginald Alexander had several previous convictions, ranging from discharging dynamite to using obscene and filthy language.
37. *Appendix to Votes of the House of Assembly, 1937-1938*, 207-208.
38. *Appendix to Votes of the House of Assembly, 1937-1938*, 211. Willis Duvalier apparently rushed at Fields with a knife. The Commissioner claimed to have talked him out of using the weapon.
39. *Appendix to Votes of the House of Assembly, 1937-1938*, 214.
40. *Appendix to Votes of the House of Assembly, 1937-1938*, 215-216.
41. *Appendix to Votes of the House of Assembly, 1937-1938*, 217-218. See also Telegram, Jarret to Ormsby-Gore, Aug. 24, 1937, CO23/618.
42. *Appendix to Votes of the House of Assembly, 1937-1938*, 221. J.A. Hughes Report. Encl. Dundas Ormsby-Gore, March 18, 1938, CO23/638.
43. Telegram. Jarrett to Ormsby-Gore, Aug. 23, 1937 CO23/618. A telegram was dispatched from Commissioner Fields, reporting the Inagua 'riot' and calling for police assistance. A police detachment was sent by a local steamship which developed engine trouble and was forced to put up at Rum Cay, another Bahamian Out Island. Another

boat was dispatched on August 20 to pick up the party. It reached Matthew Town on August 24, five days after the 'riot' occurred. Jarrett to Ormsby-Gore, Sept. 17, 1937, CO23/618. PRO.
44. *Tribune*, Oct. 13, Nov. 5 and 22, 1937. On the night before the execution, Commissioner Fields was staying with his friends, the W.B. Norths, who lived in Prison Lane, nearly opposite the Prison. He swore to the family that he saw someone at his window that night. (Interview with E. Basil North and Audrey V. North, Aug. 10, 1984).
45. John A. Hughes, Report, Feb. 23, 1938. Encl. Dundas to Ormsby-Gore, March 18, 1938, CO23/638.
46. The Inagua incident received much press coverage in England; accounts of the incident were published in the *Daily Express* on Aug. 26 and 27, 1937 and also on the latter date in the *Evening Standard* and *Manchester Guardian*.
47. *Tribune*, Aug. 25, 1937.
48. *Tribune*, Oct. 13, 1937.
49. For a discussion of race and class relations in Nassau see Saunders, 'The Role of the Coloured Middle Class in Nassau', Ch.1 in this book. Inagua was a mainly black community but had quite a number of white and coloured families. Each group generally lived at the same economic and social level, although leading families were recognized in the community.
50. K.E. Robinson. Note in connection with disturbances at Inagua, 1937. Encl. Jarrett to Ormsby-Gore, Aug. 23, 1937, CO23/618.
51. J.C., Jarrett to Ormsby-Gore, Conf., Sept. 17, 1937, CO23/618.
52. Police Charge Book 1938-1939. In 1934 there were 22 cases of disorderly behaviour or similar offences. In 1935 and 1936 there were 43 and 42 cases of disorderly behaviour respectively.
53. *Votes of the Legislative Council, 1937-1938* (Nassau: Nassau Guardian, 1938), 42.
54. Philip Cash, 'Colonial Policies and Outside Influences', 247.
55. *Votes of the Legislative Council, 1937-1938*, 42.
56. *Votes of the Legislative Council, 1937-1938*, 42-43.
57. *Statute Law of The Bahamas*, 1965. Penal Code. 48, 78.
58. Sir Bede Clifford to Beckett (Private), Aug. 30, 1937, CO23/618.
59. H.O. Dalke, 'Race and Minority Riots: A Study in the Typology of Violence', *Social Forces* (1952) No. XXX: 425.
60. Ann Spackman, *Constitutional Development of the West Indies 1922-1968: A Selection from the Major Documents* (Barbados: Caribbean University Press, 1975), 32-33.
61. Between 1933 and 1937 salt exports from Inagua increased from 80 bushels valued at £12 to 118,470 bushels valued at £1371. Encl. Charles Dundas to Ormsby-Gore, Feb. 21, 1938, CO23/638.
62. Neil J. Smelser, *The Theory of Collective Behaviour* (New York and London: 1962), 242-248.
63. The well-to-do women were housewives while some of the labouring class women worked in the salt ponds and on public works.
64. One example is the Ford family who spent about 10 years in Haiti. Vera Ford Cartwright, a former court interpreter, was educated in a Roman Catholic School at Port-au-Prince, Haiti.

11

The 1942 Riot in Nassau

A Demand For Change?

The Nassau riot of 1942 was the last in the series of riots and strikes that occurred throughout the British West Indies after 1934. These brought the very distressed conditions of the black labouring population to the attention of the Colonial Office, and the British government demonstrated its concern by the appointment of a Royal Commission which made a penetrating study of the area.[1] The Commissioners, however, did not visit the Bahamas. Instead, a contemporary investigation[2] which predicted that more trouble lay ahead generally in the West Indies, took a 'cheerful view' of the Bahamas situation owing to its relative prosperity. It failed to see that beneath the surface, as in the rest of the British West Indies, there were oppressive socioeconomic conditions under which the masses lived. Moreover, as the riot demonstrated, there was an absence of effective political and social organizations through which grievances could be vocalized.

There is a dearth of literature on the 1942 riot. General historians of the Bahamas, because of space limitations, have been unable to analyze the riot in detail. It has for the most part been described simply as a wage dispute.[3] However, the late political activist, Dame Doris Johnson, and former labour leader, Sir Randol Fawkes, both attributed deeper significance to the riot. They recognized it as the beginning of a political movement when the black labourers made real demands for social and political change.[4] Colin Hughes suggested that it was more of a 'symbolic' event which was later mythicized and used as a 'heroic movement' by the blacks, when a political movement had finally started.[5] In light of these arguments and the British West Indian situation, the immediate and long standing causes of the riot will be analyzed here. Such an analysis involves an examination of the riot itself, an investigation of the economic, social and political background, and the changes that resulted.

The entry of the United States into the Second World War brought mixed blessings for the Bahamas. On the one hand, it caused the collapse of the tourist industry and building construction which exacerbated the already serious unemployment problem. On the other, the Bahamas benefited because of its strategic position in the Atlantic hemisphere.[6] New Providence was chosen as the site of an Operational Training Unit under the joint auspices of the Imperial and United States governments. The installation which had to be built was supervised by the United States army engineering department and an American firm, Pleasantville Incorporated, began work on May 20, 1942 on two sites. One was just south of Grant's Town, the predominantly black section of Nassau, at the site of the small landing field that had been developed by Sir Harry Oakes.[7] The other was in the Pine Barren near the western end of New Providence. They were called the Main Field and Satellite Field respectively, and collectively, the 'Project'. The operation employed over two thousand men, many of them Out Islanders who had flocked to Nassau during the previous two decades in search of jobs.[8] The Project not only provided work for Bahamians but also caused an influx of many white American workers who were brought in as foremen, and they occupied the Hotel Colonial. Additionally, a detachment of a British army regiment, the Cameron Highlanders which had been at Dunkirk, arrived and occupied the Montague Hotel in early 1942, immediately before the start of the Project.

It had been agreed secretly between the United States and British governments that wages to be paid for labour on the Project should be at the local rates. For unskilled labour on building construction, Bahamian labourers received 4 shillings for eight hours. It was agreed that the wages for unskilled labourers on the Project should be deemed to be the wages for building construction, although these labourers were expected to do more skilled work for the same rate of pay as those employed in construction.[9] Although employment was scarce, and the Project could be regarded as 'an almost unhoped-for blessing', the labourers expected a wage higher than the local rate. Many of them had previously worked in the US and at the American base at Exuma for higher wages.[10] It was also rumoured by the American employees of the Pleasantville company that their company was willing to pay much higher wages to Bahamians but were prevented from doing so by the Bahamas government. American (white) employees were earning much more for doing identical work[11] and this caused dissatisfaction among the Bahamian labourers who had no effective means of expressing their grievances.

There were no political parties and no modern legislation dealing with trade unions or labour federations in Nassau.[12] However, a 'growing sentiment' during the previous ten years and a belief that something better should be done had led to the establishment of a Labour Union in 1936. Under the leadership of a white Bahamian, Percy Christie, the Union within a year had attracted about eight hundred members, mainly unskilled labourers. Not many artisans had joined. Instead, a number of skilled workers, who had wished to organize, formed a new organization. Both the Federation of Labour which they established in May 1942 and the Labour Union at the time of the riot were headed by Charles Rhodriquez, a coloured dry goods merchant in Grant's Town. On May 20, the labourers complained to Rhodriquez about their wages. He in turn outlined the labourers' grievance to the Labour Officer, John Hughes, who asked him to put the request in writing. On May 22, Rhodriquez called a meeting of skilled and unskilled labourers to discuss wages being paid at the Project, as a result of which a new scale of wages was unanimously adopted. A week later, on May 29, the letter requesting wages of eight shillings per day for unskilled labourers was delivered to the Labour Officer.

In the meantime, the House of Assembly had been dissolved and an election called for the middle of June. The Duke of Windsor had left the Bahamas for Washington on May 28 and the acting governor, Mr Heape, promised that an advisory board would be appointed to consider the new wage scale. This was communicated to the Labour Federation on May 30. The labour leaders seemed patient and unaware of any possible unrest. The delaying tactics of the government in response to the Labour Union's demands angered the labourers. On Sunday, May 31, a crowd of about four hundred labourers from Satellite Field, who had threatened the white Bahamian foreman, Karl Claridge, gathered in front of the offices of the Pleasantville company at the Main Field. There was no real leader, although Green, alias Leonard Storr, from Andros, who had recently signed on, was singled out. He was the most vocal, shouting 'We want more money'. The labourers lacked organization but managed to register two complaints: that they had not been paid when prevented from working due to rain and that they wanted higher wages. Mr Hughes, the Labour Officer, who chose to identify Green as the leader, addressed the crowd, promising to deal with the matter as early as possible and asked the crowd to disperse. Some did, but a number of the younger men remained. By this time, the Superintendent of the Nassau Police, Captain Edward Sears, along with a detachment of three or four policemen had appeared on the scene and tried to get the crowd including Green to leave the construction site. Sears was surrounded by the crowd which scattered only after he drew his revolver.

Despite efforts by the Labour Officer, the leaders of the Labour Federation and others to pacify the labourers, most of them refused to work on Monday morning, June 1. At about 8 a.m. the labourers assembled at the Main Field, and armed with machetes, sticks and clubs, marched through the southern district to town, singing patriotic songs including 'We'll Never Let the Old Flag Fall'.[13] One of the rioters, Napoleon McPhee, insists that they sang 'Burma Road Declare War on the Conchie Joe', 'Do Nigger, Don't You Lick Nobody, Don't Lick Nobody'.[14] This was unlikely as the song was composed later. Apparently they merely wished then to put their plea for higher wages to someone in authority. The labourers assembled at the Colonial Secretary's Office, obviously trying to obtain a satisfactory answer on the wage question. At 9 a.m. they were addressed by Mr Eric Hallinan, Attorney General, who urged them to choose a representative and send him to the Colonial Secretary or to the governor, and promised that their grievances would receive immediate attention. He added that the American authorities had wished to use only American labourers on the Project, but Bahamian workmen had done so well, that it had not been necessary. He therefore appealed to the crowd not to spoil the good impression that they had made.[15]

Obviously, the 'excited' and 'angry' crowd of black labourers, many of them young men from the Out Islands, received the wrong impression or purposely interpreted it the way they wished.[16] They understood that if they did not return to work, the government would replace them with American labourers. Within minutes, a rowdy crowd rioted up and down Bay Street, smashing windows and looting stores. A parked Coca-Cola truck on Bay Street provided a supply of missiles. By noon, Bay Street, the centre of white Nassau, lay in shambles. It had by that time been cleared by the police force led by Colonel Lindop, the Commissioner of Police.[17] Helped by the Cameron Highlanders, the labour leaders and other citizens, the police authorities pushed the crowd over to Grant's Town, the black section, where further rioting occurred. The angry mob directed their vengeance against property (mainly white), not persons. It attacked and looted bars owned by the Bay Street merchants in the 'Over-The-Hill' area and by 12:15 p.m., the Riot Act had to be read. In attempting to disperse the crowd in Grant's Town, the police and the soldiers were stoned and hit by bottles. Shots were fired and one man, Roy Johnson, was killed. Another, David Smith, was wounded and died later that day in the hospital. Five more Grant's Town men were serious wounded. In all, forty civilian rioters were treated for minor injuries. At about 12:30 p.m., the police and military withdrew from Grant's Town leaving four junior police officers in the seemingly quiet area. Trouble soon broke out when a hostile and inebriated crowd attacked the police station, burned an ambulance parked nearby and damaged the fire engine. Looting of the Grant's Town Library and Post Office was followed by general looting throughout the southern district.[18]

The labour leaders who did not back the riot or articulate demands other than for wage increases were again summoned to Government House. Percy Christie and Milo Butler visited the southern district urging that all clubs and liquor stores remain closed. By 8 p.m. on June 1, a curfew was instituted. Although Mr Adderley reported that it was fairly quiet on the evening of that day, the crowd had not been appeased, and between 10 and 10:30 a.m. on Tuesday, June 2, it attacked a grocery shop owned by Richard Holbert, a black merchant, and also the house of a black police corporal, B.J. Nottage. No reason has come to light why the rioters attacked either. Earlier, a mob marched all the way from Grant's Town to the Shirley Street pharmacy of Mr Cole who was white and looted it until the military intervened. Although a considerable amount of damage was done to property, the loss of life was not great. Three persons were killed as a result of the riots and curfew, and two subsequently died from wounds.[19] By June 8, with the curfew lifted by the Duke of Windsor, who had returned to Nassau on June 2, the city was back to normal and labourers on the Project had returned to work.

It seems that the rioters included a wide cross-section of the labouring class of skilled and unskilled workers, drawn mainly from Grant's Town and 'the Over-The-Hill' area, some of whom had criminal records. Many were young and probably migrants from the Out Islands. Randol Fawkes believes that there were also West Indians among the crowd.[20] Women were included in the riot at least on Tuesday, June 2, when the mob attacked the grocery shop of Richard Holbert.[21] Among those arrested was Alfred Stubbs, alias Sweet Potato, who burned the Royal Family in effigy. Another was Napoleon McPhee, a stone mason who, when asked why he destroyed the Union Jack, replied, 'I willing to fight under the flag, but I ain't gwine starve under the flag'.[22] In all, eighty persons appeared in court, twenty-two before the Supreme Court, fifty-eight in the Magistrate's Court. There were sixty-seven convictions. For breaches of curfew, forty-eight persons were tried and forty-seven were convicted. Sentences varied, the maximum being eight years which Green and Harold Thurston received. Both had previous convictions and were known to the police. Green, alias Storr, was considered to be the ringleader.[23]

There is no evidence to suggest that the riot was part of a planned conspiracy. Indeed, the Commissioners declared that the 'dissatisfaction on the part of the labourers does not appear to have been very articulate... the disturbances appear to have been completely unexpected by the labour leaders'.[24] Black anger had erupted spontaneously and then quickly died.

How does one account for this show of hostility by the black labourers which was directed mainly against the white establishment? An immediate cause besides the wages dispute might be attributed to the anxieties and tensions caused by the Second World War which put more structural strain on the society. Important factors which were present in the Bahamas in June 1942 and which may have caused this strain were recent migrants or population invasions and new kinds of cultural contacts; new expectations; deprivations in connection with food, unemployment, rising prices and falling wages; and specific dissatisfactions, for example employment opportunities, and rumours.[25] In considering long-term factors, it is important to understand the economic history and structure of the Bahamas in order to comprehend the conditions just before the riot. Poverty was the Bahamian norm.[26] There was always a scarcity of money but the Bahamas benefited from various outside influences which created a 'boom' and 'bust' characteristic in its economy with farming and fishing as the mainstay.

Although there were more longstanding industries in the nineteenth and early twentieth century Bahamas, such as sponging, pineapple, sisal, citrus and tomato, these one by one failed for various reasons, and agriculture was never put on a sound scientific base. Gradually, but especially after the First World War, agriculture was superseded by land booms, building booms and the development of the fledgling tourist industry which provided lucrative jobs.[27] The Out Islanders, mainly peasant farmers, flocked to Nassau. In 1921, 24.4 per cent of the entire population lived in New Providence, but by 1943 it had attracted nearly 43 per cent, an increase of over 126 per cent in twenty-two years.[28] These 'bonanza' type economies, while denuding the rural Out Island settlements of their population, boosted Nassau's economy and led eventually to the 'consolidation of capital business ethics'[29] in Bahamian society. When the adventurers and foreign commercial agents left, the Bahamian merchant class was provided with the foundation upon which to build fortunes.

On the eve of the Second World War with the collapse of the sponging industry, tourism backed by government financing, was developed as the major industry of the Bahamas. While tourism benefitted and was controlled by Nassau's importers, wholesalers, retailers and real estate dealers, most of whom were members of the House of Assembly, and who profited from the secondary investment brought by the outside capital; it also provided attractive wage employment in Nassau.[30] However, the tourist industry was seasonal and only provided three to four months' employment during the winter. Because of the precarious nature of tourism some labourers, especially Out Islanders, resorted to agriculture and fishing for the rest of the year. Agriculture, however, was for the most part neglected.

The outbreak of the war brought more hardship to the Bahamas. By 1941 the tourist industry had virtually ceased,[31] while the cost of living, due to the inequitable customs duties, had risen by well over fifty per cent since the beginning of the war. The findings of the Commission of Enquiry into the 1942 riots revealed (among other things) an alarming increase in the cost of living and a widening gap between wages and prices. A comparison of prices for 1938 and 1942 shows the following:

ITEM	COST IN:	
	1938	1942
Rice per qt.	3d	9d
Grits per qt.	2s ½d	4s ½d
Lard per lb.	8d	1s 1 ½d
Pork	8d	½s
Flour	1 ½d	2 ½d
Sugar	2d	3 ½d
Cheese	1s 6d	2s
Salt beef per lb.	8d	½s

Corned beef per tin	6d	1s
Condensed Milk per tin	5d	9d
Cotton per yard	6d	1s
Prints per yard	6d	1s 3d
Dill per yard	9d	1s 9d
Working Shirts	2s 6d	5s
Tennis Shoes	2s 6d	5s
	11s 8d	£1 2s 10d

A surplus revenue of £61,125 in 1941 did not accurately reflect the real position of the Bahamas' finances. The surplus was due primarily to the reduction in public works which were described as almost 'below the absolute minimum required to maintain public services'.[32] There were therefore fewer jobs for the estimated 9,000 wage earners in Nassau.[33] Moreover, the labourers suffered from very low wages, fixed by the Minimum Wage Act of 1936. In the face of rapidly rising prices, most workers found it difficult to make ends meet. The United States' entry into the war was the final straw. It is useful to examine the political background against which the riot occurred. The Bahamas' House of Assembly had for a long time been dominated by a wealthy white mercantile clique. Like Barbados and Bermuda, the Bahamas retained the Old Representative system of government. The governor and his advisors framed policies but it depended on the 'will of the House of Assembly' to carry them out.

Approximate Weekly Cost of Living, 1938

	New Providence	*Out Islands*
Food	11s	7s
Clothing	3s	2s
Rent	5s	2s
	19s	11s

Daily Wages in 1938

Unskilled Labourers (male)	4s
Unskilled Labourers (female)	2s
Carpenters	8s to 18s
Masons and Plasterers	8s to 24s
Painters	6s to 12s
Foremen	15s to 25s

(Source: Dundas to McDonald, Visit of Major Orde Browne, Jan. 11, 1939. C.O. 23/682.)

Over the years, the House had developed an independent spirit and controlled the purse. Very often it was difficult for the government to get its policies accepted through its three unofficial members who sat in the House of Assembly. Also, the cumbersome and out-of-date Board System, under which the main departments of government functioned, was controlled by members of the House of Assembly, that is by 'Bay Street'.[34]

In May 1942 all but five of the twenty-nine members of the traditionally independent House of Assembly belonged to this powerful white oligarchy.[35] Through the archaic constitutional system,[36] the mercantile group, many of them related by blood or friendship, cemented their power by occupying seats in the powerful House of Assembly and in the legislative and executive councils. Out Island representation and coloured participation were largely precluded by the high qualification[37] for membership and also by the prohibitive costs of election campaigns. Voting by secret ballot had been only temporarily instituted in New Providence in 1939 and elections were still held under the open vote system in the Out Islands. Illiterates voted openly after making a formal declaration, and there was said to be 'wholesale bribery and corruption'. In fact, most Bahamians, even if they qualified as voters, were not politically aware and did not know how to use the vote. Because of the lack of political organization and dependence on the white merchant class for employment, they were easily intimidated and often succumbed to the pressure of the rich and powerful.

Lacking a tradition of popular organized protest, the black majority in the Bahamas could do little about their socioeconomic and political subordination. However, by 1942, although lacking political organization, there was a vague growing racial consciousness among black leaders and also among some of the labouring population. Several external factors combined to create this new awareness.

Garveyism and the Pan-African movement, the influence of West Indians, the return of soldiers from the First World War and workers from the southern United States, all had an impact on Bahamian society. Although the growth of negritude and Garveyism made more impact in the United States than it did in the British Caribbean,[38] the essence of the Pan-African Movement, which praised blackness and gave dignity to the African heritage, filtered through to many West Indian leaders, some of whom passed it on to the ordinary people. Napoleon McPhee, a participant in the Nassau riot of 1942, remembers Marcus Garvey's visit to the Bahamas in 1928.

It is said that he delivered a public speech in the southern district.[39] Though there is no evidence to indicate that Garvey widely affected Bahamians, to most West Indians and especially Bahamians, themselves split by strong class and colour distinctions, Garvey's ideas were novel. The coloured and black middle class tended to imitate the whites and despised the black masses. However, Garvey encouraged blacks to feel some racial self-respect and demonstrated that political parties could be organized.

The beginning of the process which was to give West Indians a sense of pride and self-confidence was helped by the exposure gained by many Caribbean soldiers in the First World War. Among the large numbers of West Indians who served in the British West Indian Regiment during that war were about seven hundred Bahamians, most of whom returned. When overseas, they had come into contact with soldiers from the Dominions and England and were thus introduced to egalitarian and socialist ideas.[40] It is interesting to note that a Bahamian soldier, Sergeant Johnny Demeritte, who lost both legs in the war, was one of the leaders in a race riot in Liverpool before the troops went home.[41]

The West Indian influence caused a questioning of the social system in the Bahamas. At the end of the nineteenth century and during the early part of the twentieth century, hundreds of West Indians were brought into the Bahamas, some as policemen and many as skilled artisans who assisted in the rebuilding of an important tourist facility, the Hotel Colonial. A number of West Indians made their homes in the Bahamas.[42] The West Indians were generally better educated than Bahamians. The majority were skilled workmen with much experience in the Southern Caribbean and Central America. They had experienced the post-war 'wave of democratic sentiment' and a national spirit and seen the rise of leaders such as Cipriani in Trinidad.[43] In the Bahamas they were clearly dissatisfied with the oppressive conditions especially the blatant racial discrimination, and by 1931 there was a 'sudden appearance of race consciousness and group consciousness' which had never manifested itself before. Moreover, some West Indians had been vocalizing their discontent about the political and domestic problems in the Bahamas.[44]

Racial tension was an underlying cause of the riot. Bahamians suffered severe discrimination at home. In fact, until the late 1950s, blacks were barred from all hotels, were not allowed in some restaurants and movie houses and were only allowed to enter some churches by the rear door. Certain schools did not accept black children and many business firms were closed to them as places of employment. Thousands of Bahamians were further exposed to discrimination while working in the United States during World War I. At that time about 2500 Bahamians were employed in the USA in the construction of the new port at Charleston, South Carolina, most of whom returned home.

Evidence shows that many black middle class people were aware of the injustices in the society. Several of them had been educated in Britain or the United States, were talented and well qualified. However, they did not form a coherent bloc in either the 1942 or 1949 elections against the power of Bay Street. When the riot occurred they failed to take advantage of the situation and no leaders emerged. Even in the late 1940s, an official at the Colonial Office noted, 'The more vociferous coloured politicians exclaim against abuses and encourage racial ill-feelings but seem to have no common policy and no common ambition.'[45]

Members of the coloured elite, like A. F. Adderley and T. A. Toote, although deeply dissatisfied with the status quo, were too conservative to change it. They found it difficult to identify with the masses. Toote and Adderley, successful barristers, were considered 'upper class' among the coloured community. While Toote was considered by some to be more the poor man's friend, Adderley, who was perhaps the ablest member of the coloured community, was the third generation of Adderleys to serve in the legislature. As his law practice flourished, be became a highly respected figure in Nassau and in the courts by both blacks and whites. Governor Murphy believed that he had 'reached the stage in the evolution of a gentleman of colour at which his own community ceased to regard him as truly representing their outlook'.[46]

Milo Butler, a successful black merchant, was perhaps the most outspoken of all the black leaders. He had some support from the black masses but lacked a formal academic education. He was also inexperienced politically and needed an organized party in which to develop his leadership.[47] Dr Claudius Walker, a medical doctor who lived in Grant's Town, had contact with the masses. Possessed of a fine wit and winning personality, and being gregarious, he was more of an educator than a politician. Bert Cambridge, a musician, lived among the black labouring class, but lacked the necessary charisma.

These leaders were aware of the deep racial divisions in Bahamian society. Although they had been successful either in the professional or business world and had been elected to Parliament, they were themselves separated from the masses. At the same time, the rigid colour bar in the Bahamas separated socially even the most talented of the intermediary coloured class from the white community. The white power bloc objected to the admission of a coloured member to the executive council, not only because it felt less free to express views on certain matters, but for purely social reasons. Governor Murphy in November 1945 admitted that, if a coloured man was appointed to the executive council, members of the white community became apprehensive that they, and especially their wives, might meet him and his wife at Government House.[48]

Racial feeling was real. Dr Roland Cumberbatch, a Trinidad-born black physician, who himself had experienced discrimination[49] said that there was an underlying sense of injustice. He testified that when he approached Bay Street on the day of the riot, he met a crowd, some of whom remarked, 'No white man is passing here today'.[50] Maxwell Thompson, who was then a clerk in the government service, agreed that black and coloured people resented the discriminatory practices of the day, but there was little that they could do about them.[51] An English magistrate, Frank Eustace Field, who had lived in Nassau since 1941, said that on questioning the crowd in East Street on the day of the riot, he was told that 'the Conchie Joes'[52] had it coming to them for a long time. Sir Etienne Dupuch, controversial *Tribune* editor, believes that if Harry Glinton, a well respected black building contractor, had been given the job of liaison officer between the American contractors on the Project and the Bahamian labourers, instead of a white Bahamian, Karl Claridge, the riot would not have occurred.[53] Fear, perhaps justifiably, gripped some of the white population. Men were afraid for their wives and children and for themselves. Morton Turtle, a white Bahamian contractor who designed the office buildings at the Project and employed many black Bahamian labourers, disappeared on his boat for a few days just after the riot broke out.[54]

Additionally, some officials, including the Duke of Windsor and the American Vice-Consul, saw race as a strong factor in the causes of the riot. In fact, the Duke of Windsor was convinced that the riot resulted from 'strong racial feelings on both sides', and although he ordered the Commission to leave the question of race alone, he admitted that he personally disagreed profoundly with the policy of racial discrimination, and that the 'Bahamas wage rates was only an excuse to make a vigorous and noisy protest against the white population'.

The official American view was similar. In a confidential report, the American Vice-Consul stated, 'This outbreak has been a smouldering fire for years and there is little doubt that it is a colour question'. He continued, 'The pent-up fury of the mob wreaked vengeance against what in their minds was the oppressing forces, namely the white Bahamians as represented by business'.[55] Added to the oppressive and antagonistic racial situation were many social ills. Imperial labour adviser, Major Orde Browne, who visited the Bahamas in 1939, considered the housing generally good in comparison to the southern West Indies, but stated that certain areas left much to be desired. Overcrowding of the already small shacks had resulted because of excessive migration and the high birth rate among the population.[56]

Harold Beckett, a Colonial Office official who had visited Bermuda before coming to the Bahamas, disagreed with Browne's generally optimistic view. He thought that, by any standards other than West Indian, Grant's Town was a slum. Unlike Orde-Browne, he foresaw the labour trouble in New Providence. He was convinced that 'given a tourist slump and a Bustamante' there might be problems in the Bahamas. Dr Cumberbatch agreed that the majority of people lived in very squalid buildings and that the rapidly growing population was creating dire economic problems.[57]

Land was out of reach for the majority of the population. While some owned the land on which their houses were located, most were squatters who had no clear title. American capitalists were buying the best land in New Providence and were encouraged by the Bay Street politicians who stood to gain handsome profits. The black majority was either denied access to the land by a narrow Crown lands policy or simply did not know how to go about purchasing property.

Moreover, although the Bahamas was decidedly more healthy than the rest of the West Indies, there were still major medical problems. The infant mortality rate was extremely high and an alarming percentage of the population suffered from venereal diseases, tuberculosis and, to a lesser extent, from dietary deficiencies, especially on the Out Islands. A small staff of six medical officers was not sufficient to cope with these problems. Most of the Out Islands had no medical or nursing facilities at all.

The general level of education in 1942 was deplorable and not comparable to that in many other British West Indian colonies such as Jamaica, Trinidad and Barbados. Governed by an archaic Board System, the government's educational service with only one high school, had developed without very much professional or technical advice. Teachers were too few and were mostly unqualified and poorly paid. Facilities left much to be desired and hundreds of children, because of the distances between Out Island settlements, were not educated at all.[58] Until 1946 there was no Director of Education and no training colleges for the education of teachers.[59]

To the ordinary labourer, issues such as higher education were probably academic; basic education and health care for their children were more pressing issues. Along with the immediate tensions already mentioned, the lack of proper facilities in education and health, no doubt contributed towards the pent-up frustrations which exploded in the riot. But what were the immediate results of the riot? The Duke of Windsor, eager to stop further trouble, censored the press, ordered a curfew, forbade meetings in any streets or public places except with the permission of the police, negotiated a free mid-day meal for the labourers working on the Project[60] and a one shilling per day wage increase. The 'Bay Street Boys' blamed the riot on the government. In fact, by appointing its own select committee, the members of the House demonstrated their annoyance with the governor who had won the approval of the Colonial Office to appoint a Commission of Inquiry.[61] Both bodies recognized that the Bahamian labourers were dissatisfied with wages and discontented because the American workmen received higher wages for doing similar work. Finding fault with everyone but themselves for the riot, the select committee concluded that the government had failed to give sufficient information as to why wages were fixed at the local rate. It also contended (probably wrongly) that labour leaders agitated in order to make political mileage out of the disturbances, and that the American employees of Pleasantville Company had spread false propaganda among the workers about the rate of pay.[62]

Although perhaps deliberately conservative, the Russell Commission was more thorough.[63] Besides citing the immediate wage dispute and the part played by rumour in the riot, it also demonstrated that there were more deep-seated causes of discontent among the poorer and the labouring classes. It rightly cited the economic difficulties, political inequalities and the lack of social legislation and recommended, as did the select committee,[64] the passing of more adequate labour legislation. The Commission also called for an adjustment of import duties, the consideration of income tax and death duties, a land tax and the control of the sale of land, especially cultivatable acreage on the Out Islands. It urged that the population be educated in agriculture and fishing and that the Out Island conditions be improved in order to stop the drift to Nassau. The introduction of birth control, the permanency of the secret ballot in Nassau and its extension to the Out Islands was favoured by the commission, as well as constitutional reform.[65]

Both the Russell Commission and the select committee were shortsighted. Although the former was more perceptive, it dared not explore the explosive topic of race. Time would show that in spite of the Select Committee's recommendation of additional labour legislation, the House of Assembly's reactionary behaviour did not change essentially. Although Trade Union and Workmen's Compensation Acts were passed by the House of Assembly in 1943, the legislation was defective and severely restricted membership in a union.[66] Additionally, the House also refused to vote money for the then separate post of labour officer,[67] forcing the governor to resort to providing the salary out of Crown funds.

As far as a more equitable form of taxation and birth control were concerned, the recommendations did not get further than the executive council.[68] Both Windsor and Richardson, the governor's economic advisers,[69] supported an income tax policy, but Windsor saw no prospect that income tax would be acceptable to the legislature because of the view that it would discourage wealthy people from settling in the Bahamas.

Constitutionally, no major reforms were to come for years. The Vote of Ballot Act, to make the secret ballot permanent in New Providence and to extend it to the Out Islands, was not passed until 1946.[70] The life of the House of Assembly was reduced from seven to five years in 1962, two years after women were given the vote.

Protest and change were generally slow in coming to the Bahamas. The unrest experienced in the Caribbean was not felt in the Bahamas until 1942. The Bahamas, like the rest of the West Indies, had suffered from severe depression in the 1930s, exacerbated by the rigid United States immigration policy which closed an important migration outlet. Other outlets in Panama, Costa Rica and Cuba were also closed. Bahamians and other West Indians returned home during the depression years jobless and joined a population which was rapidly increasing. All these factors, combined with dire poverty, very low standards of living and squalid social conditions, resulted in pent-up frustration and discontent which exploded in strikes and riots in the 1930s in many British Caribbean colonies, and in the early 1940s in the Bahamas. Several factors were responsible for the minimal protest and slow political change.

Although the Bahamas has been shaped by many of the forces which shaped the West Indies proper, geographically it was isolated from the rest of the West Indies. Until the late 1930s, the majority of the population lived on the Out Islands making it difficult to organize a national movement. The poor soil and peculiar economic development made for radical departures in its socioeconomic development from the rest of the British Caribbean. Its powerful Bay Street merchant ruling class had a firm grip on its affairs, favouring a commercially-oriented economy which would especially benefit themselves and the capital city of Nassau.

Black and coloured leadership in the Bahamas was traditionally conservative and weak at the time of the riot. It failed to support the fledgling trade union movement and was generally ignorant of political organization. According to the evidence, black leaders tried to dissuade the rioters before and after the damage and bloodshed had occurred. Even Milo Butler, deemed a 'troublemaker' by the Americans, tried to pacify the rioters.[71]

Both the traditional and the newly educated black elite were dissatisfied with existing conditions, especially the rank discriminatory practices. As individuals, they were powerless to do anything about it. For most, who worked to safeguard their increasingly comfortable lifestyles, it would have been economic suicide to attempt to overthrow the system, and the absence of political parties or effective trade unions gave them little clout.

The riots and strikes in the British West Indies generally resulted in change, with political and constitutional advances taking place in most colonies in the 1940s and 1950s. New leaders emerged such as Bustamante in Jamaica and Grantley Adams in Barbados. The gradualist policy of the Imperial government was accelerated after the Second World War. Internally, there was a growing militancy in union-based and other political parties, nurtured by a new sense of nationalism and anti-colonial sentiment.

Many West Indian professionals and veterans who had become involved with progressive movements in London returned home after the war with new democratic ideas. They had seen whites performing menial tasks, and the whole idea of race relations took on a new meaning. Furthermore, the soldiers had been made aware of the nationalistic struggles for independence in India, Burma, the Gold Coast and Dutch Indonesia. The idea of Empire was losing its legitimacy.[72]

In the Bahamas, however, little immediate change occurred. Apart from the trade union legislation and the extension of the secret ballot to the Out Islands, very little was done to improve conditions between 1942 and 1964. The reactionary attitude of the House of Assembly, a complacent population lulled by increasing prosperity and the absence of dynamic and organized black leadership ensured this. Further, the absence of assertiveness by the Colonial Office,[73] which seemed afraid to interfere, along with the development of tourism as a main means of livelihood, delayed any administrative and social innovations for over two decades.

Additionally, the temporary but extensive migration by Bahamians to the United States also acted as a safety valve to delay change. In early 1943, the United States and the Bahamian governments signed a contract under which Bahamian labourers could be recruited to the United States to help work on Florida farms which, because of the war, lacked the necessary manpower. By May 1943 over 2,500 workers had left and, in August, the 5,000 quota was reached.[74]

The development of tourism and the subsequent boost to the economy which followed also postponed any alteration in the social structure. Led by Stafford Sands, a brilliant 'Bay Street' corporate lawyer, the House of Assembly turned its attention after the war to developing the industry. Tourism encouraged both construction projects as well as foreign investment in Nassau. Investors were lured by the absence of income tax and the lack of restrictions on the sale of land.

Banking facilities began to expand in the late 1940s to cope with the increasing financial interest. Superficially the colony appeared prosperous. Wages rose and living standards improved for the white and coloured elite. However, there was a general neglect of the majority of the population by a powerful wealthy minority, who through antiquated administrative and social structures maintained their control over the economy and the society. As Lewis argues, because of tourism and foreign private investment, many private wealthy empires resulted, and 'in effect, the Bahamian government was deliberately kept a poor government in a rich economy...'[75]

The 1942 riot in Nassau was a short-lived spontaneous outburst by a group of disgruntled labourers, and occurred against a background of narrow socioeconomic and political policies. The leaders of the coloured and black middle class in 1942 did not represent a united bloc in support of the black labouring class against 'Bay Street'. The black masses slept on, seemingly satisfied, unpoliticized, while the ruling white clique took advantage of the improving economy in Nassau, entrenching its power even more. On the other hand, black leadership took a long time to emerge and organize itself politically. Demand for change was over a decade in coming. The Progressive Liberal Party, which was in the vanguard of that change, was not organized until 1953.

Notes

1. See *West India Royal Commission Report 1938-1939*. June 1945 (Cmd. 6607), Sessional Papers, UK House of Commons 1944-1945, VI, 471.
2. Colonial Office: Labour Conditions in the West Indies, Report by Major G. St. J. Orde-Browne, London: Cmd. 6070, 1939.
3. See Michael Craton, *A History of the Bahamas* (London: 1969), 275, and Paul Albury, *The Story of the Bahamas* (London: 1973), 208-210.
4. Dame Doris Johnson, *The Quiet Revolution in the Bahamas* (Nassau: 1972), 15-28; Sir Randol Fawkes, *The Faith That Moved The Mountain* (Nassau: 1979), 21-36. See also M. Craton and G. Saunders, *Islanders in the Stream. A History of the Bahamian People* Vol. 2 (Athens: Georgia University Press, 1998), 286-292.
5. Colin Hughes, *Race and Politics in the Bahamas* (St Lucia: Queensland, 1981), 212-213.
6. Under the Destroyer-Bases deal in September 1940, President Roosevelt in an Executive Agreement promised over fifty destroyers to Britain. In return Britain gave sites for bases to the United States on Newfoundland and Bermuda on ninety-nine year leases and granted rent-free leases on ninety-nine years on six additional sites ranging from the Bahamas to British Guiana. The Bahamas' base site was on Exuma Island. See Thomas A. Bailey, *A Diplomatic History of the American People*, 6th edition. (New York: 1958), 718; *Robert Dallek, Franklin D. Roosevelt and American Foreign Policy, 1932-1945* (New York: 1979), 245-246; and Winston S. Churchill, *The Second World War*, Vol. II. Their Finest Hour (London: 1949), 354-368.
7. Sir Harry Oakes, who had discovered the Lake Shore Mine in Ontario, Canada came to the Bahamas in 1934 during the depression years. He bought land and invested a lot of money in various businesses. He also built Oakes Field, the first aerodrome in the Bahamas thus employing many local labourers who were suffering from the effects of the depression. See Michael Craton, *A History*, 270-272.
8. All Bahamian islands other than New Providence, location of the capital city, Nassau, were until the late 1960s referred to as Out Islands, that is out of Nassau.
9. Report of the Commission Appointed to Enquire into Disturbances in The Bahamas which took place in June 1942 (Nassau: 1942), 9. Also referred to as the Russell Commission. The Report of the Select Committee of the House of Assembly gives the date as May 6, 1942. See *Votes of the House of Assembly, 1942-1943* (Nassau: 1943), 311.
10. During the First World War, Bahamians had earned as much as $3.00 a day. See evidence from the Russell Commission, 9.
11. Select Committee in *Votes of the House of Assembly, 1942-1943*, 316.
12. Russell Commission, 10. The only law relating to trade unions in 1942 were the Combination Acts of 1825 and 1859. The English legislation on which these laws were based had been repealed in England over 70 years before. See Sir Randol Fawkes, *The Faith That Moved The Mountain*, 23.
13. See Evidence of James Sinclair, Roscoe W. Thompson, to the Russell Commission, 235-39.

14. Taped interview with Napoleon McPhee, Nassau, November 24, 1982.
15. See Evidence of Eric Hallinan to the Commission, 510.
16. Ibid.
17. Lt. Colonel Reginald A. Erskine-Lindop, an Englishman, started in the Service in the Leeward Islands in 1919. He served in Barbados before coming to the Bahamas in 1936. He had served in the Army during the First World War. Evidence of Lt. Col. Reginald A. Erskine-Lindop, to the Russell Commission, 28-53.
18. See Report of the Select Committee, Votes of the House of Assembly, 1942-1943, 311-315.
19. Russell Commission, 39-40.
20. Interview with Sir Randol Fawkes, November 22, 1982, Nassau.
21. Russell Commission, 31.
22. Fawkes, *The Faith That Moved The Mountain*, 25.
23. Russell Commission, 39-40: Supreme Court Criminal Minutes April 7 - July 30, 1942 and April 29 - August 1, 1942, and Magistrate Court Criminal Minutes April 15 - July 30, 1942, Magistrate Court Reference 7/104, Public Records Office, Nassau.
24. Russell Commission, 12.
25. Neil J. Smelser, *The Theory of Collective Behaviour* (New York and London: 1962), 242-248.
26. Albury, *The Story of the Bahamas*, 184.
27. Gordon Lewis, *Growth of the Modern West Indies* (New York and London: 1969), 319-322.
28. *Report on the Census of the Bahama Islands*. April 25, 1943, 2. Nassau Records Office.
29. Lewis, *Growth of the Modem West Indies*, 311.
30. Visit of Major Orde-Browne. Questionnaire on Labour and Report. C023/682
31. W.L. Heape to Cranborne. Estimates 1942, June 24, 1942, C023/720.
32. Heape to Cranborne. Estimates 1942, June 24, 1942. C023/720.
33. Dundas to McDonald. Visit of Major Orde-Browne. Jan. 11, 1939. C023/682.
34. Bay Street is the main street in Nassau. The mercantile white oligarchy who had businesses there or nearby came to be known as 'The Bay Street Boys'.
35. The five were coloured members, namely, Dr C.R. Walker for the Southern District, Mr Leon W. Young for the Eastern District, Mr Milo B. Butler for the Western District, Mr Leon G. Dupuch for Long Island, and Mr Alfred E.J. Dupuch for Inagua. Votes of the House of Assembly, September 29, 1940 – October 16, 1941.
36. See Bahamas Constitution C023/800 and Memorandum of the Bahamas Constitution C023/798. PRO, London.
37. The financial qualification for a member of the House of Assembly was the possession of real or personal property of the unencumbered value of £2.00. The property qualification for a voter was the ownership of land of the value of £5 or upwards, or the occupation of a house of the annual rental value or not less than £2 8s in New Providence and not less than £1.4d in an Out Island. See Russell Commission, 53.
38. See Locksley Edmondson, 'The Internationalization of Black Power: Historical and Contemporary Perspectives', *Is Massa Day Dead? Black*

Moods in the Caribbean, ed. by Orde Coombs (Garden City, N.Y.: 1974), 207. See also E. David Cronon, *Black Moses. The Story of Marcus Garvey* (Madison and London: 1969).
39. Taped Interview with Mr Napoleon McPhee, Nassau, November 24, 1982. See Tony Martin, *The Pan African Connection. From Slavery to Garvey and Beyond* (Cambridge, MA: 1983); and *The Marcus Garvey and Universal Negro Improvement Association Papers*, ed. by Robert A. Hill, vol 1 (California Press: 1983).
40. Morley Ayearst, *The British West Indies: The Search for Self-Government* (London: 1960), 33.
41. Colin Hughes, *Race and Politics*, 14.
42. See 'Report of a Select Committee of the House of Assembly. Progress of the Colony during the past five years 1888-1892, presented to the House of Assembly on March 7, 1893 and adopted on March 23, 1893 in C023/236 folios 145-151.
43. Report by the Hon. E.F.L. Wood, on his visit to the West Indies and British Guiana, Dec. 1921 - Feb. 1922. June 1922. UK Sessional Papers. House of Commons, vol. XVI, 353.
44. *Tribune*, July 1, 1931.
45. Colonial Office Note on the Constitution, 12. 8.1949, C023/858. Folio 2.
46. Personal letter. Murphy to Hall. Nov. 28, 1945. C023/799, folio 28. See also *Bahamas Handbook 1980*, 33.
47. Milo Butler was elected to the House of Assembly in 1939 for the Western district. He said that 'in a sense I represent the labour interests' but was not connected with the Labour Union or Federation. He claimed to be a candidate 'in the interest of the masses' and criticized government for their lack of knowledge about the masses who were very hard up. (Evidence to the Russell Commission of Enquiry 1942, 335-346). Mr Butler was also a witness before the Select Committee of the House of Assembly. (Report of the Select Committee, Votes of the House of Assembly, 1942-1943, 310). The staff of US Military Intelligence saw him as a 'Negro labour leader and trouble-maker'. Confidential. War Department; Survey of the Bahama Islands, 530.613. Prepared under the direction of the Chief of Staff by the Military Intelligence Service. War Dept. General Staff, April 6, 1942 RG 226. Records of the Office of Strategic Services 20671C.
48. Murphy to Hall. Personal letter, Nov. 28, 1945, CO23/799 Folio 28.
49. No black doctors were hired to work in the government hospital. Dr Cumberbatch was a government employee, but was appointed as a District Medical officer on the Out Islands. See Cumberbatch's Evidence to the Russell Commission, 476.
50. Ibid.
51. Taped interview with Mr Maxwell Thompson, Nassau, November 4, 1982.
52. 'Conchie Joe' is a term used to define a white Bahamian.
53. Sir Etienne Dupuch, *The Tribune Story* (London: 1967), 86.
54. Evidence of Morton Turtle and Mrs Turtle to the Russell Commission, 127-133; 97-98.
55. Confidential Background Report from the American Vice-Consul, John H.E. McAndrews, approved by the American Consul General, John W. Dye, June 30, 1942. Records of the War Department.

56. See visit of Major Orde-Browne, C023/682. The population had increased by 44.7 per cent in 52 years.
57. Evidence of Dr R. Cumberbatch to the Russell Commission of Enquiry, 476.
58. Dundas to Lloyd. Development and Welfare Programmes, March 27, 1940, C023/712/1.
59. Murphy to Seel, July 23, 1947, C023/873/1.
60. *Tribune*, June 9, 1942. The Duke of Windsor also broadcast several times over the local radio station. See *Tribune*, June 3 and June 9, 1942.
61. The Commission was appointed by the governor in October 1942 and it reported on November 26, 1942. The Select Committee of the House of Assembly was appointed on September 10, 1942 and reported in March 1943. The Duke of Windsor wrote to Stanley on March 24, 1943 that the Select Committee was appointed against his personally expressed wishes. However, it continued to function after the arrival of Sir Allison Russell, former Chief Justice of Tanganyika and the Chairman of the Commission. Other members of the Commission were two white merchants, Herbert McKinney and Herbert Brown, neither of whom were active politically but who were closer to Bay Street than to the labouring masses. Windsor to Cranborne, Oct. 6, 1942, C023/731/110. The members of the Select Committee were Stafford L. Sands (Chairman), Frank Christie, Asa H. Pritchard, Percy E. Christie, R.T. Symonette, Raymond W. Sawyer and Thaddeus A. Toote. Votes of the House of Assembly, 1942-1943, 330.
62. Select Committee, *Votes of the House of Assembly*, 330.
63. Howard Johnson in 'The Political Uses of Commissions of Enquiry (1): The Imperial-Colonial West Indian Context. The Forster and Moyne Commissions', *Social and Economic Studies,* 27, no. 3 (September 1978), 256-283, argued that the Colonial Office used the Commissions of Enquiry mechanism for introducing change in the colonies without appearing to impose Colonial Office solutions.
64. The select committee blamed the government for the riot and recommended that trade union and workmen's compensation legislation be introduced. It was the first time that a House Committee had recommended the establishment of labour legislation policy. See, *Tribune*, March 6, 1943.
65. See Russell Commission, 51-57.
66. An Act relating to Trade Unions, March 31, 1943, No. 9 of 1943 and an Act to provide for the payment of compensation to workmen for injuries suffered in the course of their employment were passed June 21, No. 25 of 1943. The Trade Union Act made provision for the registration of trade unions and the legality of strikes, but strikes were illegal if they had any object other than or in addition to the furtherance of a dispute within a trade or industry in which strikes were engaged or if a strike was aimed at coercing the government or if it inflicted hardship upon the community. Civil servants, domestic servants, hotel and agricultural workers were barred from union privileges. The Workmen's Compensation Act provided for compensation for injuries inflicted during employment. *Votes of the House of Assembly, 1942-1943*, 195.
67. That is, as a separate post from Chief Out Island Commissioner which was a joint post until 1943.

68. The governor and the executive council agreed that it was 'not wise to take any action' on the recommendation of birth control. See Executive Council Minutes, January 8, 1943 and also Windsor to Stanley, January 30, 1943, C023/733/20. In regard to income tax, Dundas, the Duke of Windsor's predecessor, had put the suggestion before the Executive Council but met strong opposition. The argument was that it would 'ruin the resort traffic of Nassau and split the whole community in twain'. Dundas to Lloyd, July 31, 1940, C023/692.
69. Professor J. Henry Richardson was appointed in early 1943 as economic adviser to the governor in Council. He was originally asked to stay on for two months, but in view of his valuable advice, it was agreed to extend his stay for the rest of the year. Windsor. Closing Speech to the Legislature, Sept. 14, 1943. *Votes of the House of Assembly, 1942-1943*, 587. See also *Review of Economic Problems* by Professor J.H. Richardson, C023/770.
70. General Assembly Election Act No. 19 of 1946.
71. Report of Select Committee, 5-6.
72. Selwyn Ryan, *Race and Nationalism in Trinidad and Tobago: A Study of Decolonization on a Multiracial Society* (University of Toronto Press: 1972), 70-71.
73. The Colonial Office's view was that in certain respects the 'white oligarchies' had been benevolent rulers and that in some respects conditions were better (in the Bahamas and Bermuda) for the coloured people than in Caribbean colonies. It did not really wish to interfere with the Bahamian constitution unless absolutely necessary. See Extract from note of meeting in Secretary of State's room, April 12, 1943 C023/744/2. See also, Stanley to Windsor, no date, C023/744/9.
74. Windsor to Stanley. Secret Dispatch, August 10,1943,CO23/760/5l.
75. Lewis, *Growth of the Modern West Indies*, 320.

12

The 1956 Resolution

Breaking Down the Barriers of Racial Discrimination in The Bahamas

Post-emancipation Caribbean societies inherited a rigid class/race stratification which persisted and was in some cases reinforced by the unequal distribution of wealth and power. The three-tier class-race structure, which existed well into the 1940s, and in some societies beyond, upheld the belief of European racial superiority and the inferiority of the Africans and their culture. The dominance of the traditional elite continued in economic matters, with the result that racism and colour prejudice directed against blacks and coloureds, and preoccupation with colour and shade, remained strong and were fundamental to the society.[1]

The Bahamas and Bermuda have been characterized by Gordon Lewis as 'Atlantic Outposts' similar historically to each other but 'apart from the West Indies and West Indians' and not considered 'as members of the family'. As Lewis has argued, the Bahamas and Bermuda were shaped by most of the forces such as European conquest, slavery and colonialism which moulded the West Indies. However, the absence of the sugar plantation with its impact on Caribbean slave societies and economies meant that the development of the Bahamas and Bermuda would be fundamentally different.[2]

Both colonies from early in their history developed economies that were maritime and commercial in character, thus separating them from the West Indies. Their commercial rather than agricultural economies, ties with the United States, isolation and poor communications, larger white population (the Bahamas' 10 per cent or over and Bermuda's 39 per cent or over in 1970), retention of the old representative system combined with the protracted political dominance of the white mercantile elite and a weak coloured middle stratum (at least in the case of the Bahamas) made for significant social and political differences.

Barbados' relatively large white community (comprising 4 per cent in 1970 compared to Trinidad and Tobago with 1.2 per cent and Guyana with 1.8 per cent) and retention of its early constitution also resulted in extreme conservatism and an entrenched system of racial discrimination. While the Bahamas and Bermuda remained 'strongholds of conservatism' the rest of the Caribbean, including Barbados, from 1935 witnessed an upsurge of militant working-class protest which led to social and political changes during the inter-war period.[3]

In the Bahamas there was a growth of colour consciousness during the 1930s to the early 1950s especially among Nassau's coloured and black middle class which, although despised by whites, considered itself superior to labouring blacks. Greater educational opportunities, travel, work experiences in the United States and the growth of tourism heightened racial awareness. Manifestations of this trend were evident in Milo Butler's demonstration on the commemoration of Emancipation Day in 1938, during the 1942 Nassau riot and in the mass appeal of the Progressive Liberal Party, the first political party, established in 1953. However, extreme conservatism and the lack of political and social unity among blacks meant that little headway was made in breaking down the barriers of racial discrimination in the Bahamas. The rapidly developing tourist industry was used as an excuse to maintain segregation in public places.

Prompted by two embarrassing incidents when eminent black West Indian travellers were refused accommodations in the racially segregated hotels and restaurants, Etienne Dupuch the well-travelled coloured proprietor and editor of the evening daily newspaper, the *Tribune*, tabled a resolution in the House of Assembly in January 1956 against racial discrimination in public places in the Bahamas. He also called for a commission of enquiry to investigate all matters relating to such discrimination.

While the 1956 resolution has been briefly described by several authors,[4] the question of why racial discrimination was tolerated for so long in the Bahamas has not been thoroughly explored. Colin Hughes in *Race and Politics in The Bahamas* succeeds in examining the relationship between race and political development in the Bahamas, but depends heavily on newspaper sources, not having access to Colonial Office, oral history, school and church records which we have utilized.

This paper attempts to examine the reasons for the persistent racial discrimination in the Bahamas. It describes the events surrounding the 1956 resolution and seeks to determine whether it was in fact successful in breaking down the barriers of the Bahamas' segregationist policies.

Geographically, the Bahamas is isolated from the Caribbean, being situated in the Atlantic. An archipelago, it is widely scattered, with islands being separated by as much as 600 miles. New Providence, with the town of Nassau, became the most important island from early in its history. The physical separation of the Out Islands from Nassau, compounded by poor communications, made for greater isolation, the development of strong local sentiments, individuality and deep conservatism.

The Bahamas and the United States have been strongly linked historically. North America has had a pervasive influence on the Bahamas which, like

Bermuda, maintained stronger ties with the American mainland than with the Caribbean. Gordon Lewis argues that their economies 'to all intents and purposes' were 'annexes of the continental economic system of the United States'.[5]

The early trade, legal and illegal, along with piracy and privateering, created seafaring links between the colonists of the islands and those of the mainland. These were strengthened during and after the American War of Independence. While the claim that the coming of the Loyalists transformed the islands may have been exaggerated, the change in the demographic balance of the population and the large influx of blacks, both slave and free, was of concern to the Old Inhabitants and to white Loyalists which led to tighter social controls and the hardening of race relations as demonstrated by the passing of harsh vagrancy laws and regulations. This resulted in residential separation of the races in Nassau and the Out Islands.[6]

In Nassau, as in most West Indian societies, social divisions developed by class and colour but in the Out Islands class lines were not as clearly demarcated. From the late eighteenth century, with the dismal outlook for a plantation economy, whites rapidly adapted to the lifestyle of the Old Inhabitants in Harbour Island and Eleuthera. In Abaco they established all-white settlements, such as Cherokee Sound, Hope Town on Elbow Cay, Man-O-War Cay, and Great Guana Cay on cays off the mainland. These endogamous isolated communities maintained closer social contact with the whites of northern Eleuthera than with the Abaco blacks who lived scattered along the mainland shore. Bi-racial settlements such as Marsh Harbour and Green Turtle Cay practised rigid social and racial separation.[7]

The substantial white population in the Bahamas, as Hughes has argued, made for significant differences with the West Indies. The white population in the Bahamas has always represented 10 per cent or more of the population.[8] This 'poor white' element of which Hoetink writes of the United States, was present in the West Indies, notably Barbados, the Saintes (a group of small islands under the administration of Guadeloupe) and the Bahamas. Poor whites in the Out Islands mirrored the prejudices of those in Nassau and did not mix socially with coloureds or blacks. The socio-racial structure in the Out Islands resembled the Deep South variant (where no intermediate social position for the coloureds was accepted), more than the North-West European Caribbean variant.[9] In Nassau, a coloured intermediate class, through education, land-ownership and 'respectability', was recognized in Bahamian society.

This apartheid-like situation was maintained, with a substantial number of white creoles preserving their racial purity. Bahamian whites segregated themselves socially and sought to educate their children separately, making no secret of their attitudes. At the Methodist High School, Queen's College, situated in Nassau, the lay members of the School Committee disagreed with the Missionary Society's policy to integrate the school. In 1948 it upheld its intransigent attitude arguing that the integration of the school would ultimately lead to intermarriage, which was to be avoided at all costs.[10] In the same year, a group of parents, in reaction to the new policy, established the exclusively white St Andrew's School, in reality a limited company, which numbered amongst shareholders the parents of every child enrolled.[11]

Whites similarly segregated themselves in church attendance and seating patterns, and in some cases kept separate Sunday Schools. Colour prejudice persisted well into the 1960s. The all-white congregation at the Spanish Wells Methodist Church violently protested in 1954 the idea of a black minister preaching to them. When the black Barbadian minister, Edwin Taylor, arrived at the invitation of Harold Ward, the English minister there, half of the congregation refused to attend. They withdrew from the Methodist Church and built one of their own, severing connections completely.[12]

The perpetuation of the rigid colour bar in the Bahamas was upheld by the most influential churches, the Anglican and Methodist, which claimed to accept the status quo for economic reasons. Their main benefactors were white. While poverty remained the norm for the majority of the population, the predominantly white merchant class, well established during slavery by means of oppressive labour systems, including the credit and truck and the share systems,[13] was able to consolidate its position and its control of the economy and the Bahamas' House of Assembly. It profited from any bonanza in the economy.

Nassau, because of its strategic position and fine harbour, became a transhipment area during the American Civil War. The increase in trade mainly benefited the Nassau mercantile class, and not the Bahamas generally. The Blockade-Running era brought brief prosperity to Nassau, and strengthened the position of the merchant class. It also helped to underline social divisions in Nassau society which were based mainly on race. Governor Bayley admitted in 1860 that 'colour separates the people'. He added that whites did not mix well with coloureds or blacks.[14]

Ties with the United States strengthened during the latter part of the nineteenth century. Besides remaining trading partners, American investment further developed the colony's small tourism industry. The purchase of the Royal Victoria Hotel in 1898 and the construction of the Colonial by H.M. Flagler established it as a part of the hotel system he had built up on the eastern coast of Florida. At the beginning of the First World War, Nassau was recognized as a winter health and pleasure resort, attracting many American and Canadian visitors. The American influence served to reinforce existing racial divisions. Bahamian migration, (permanent and short term) to the United States also influenced race relations in the Bahamas. Labour migration to Key West and Miami in the late nineteenth and early twentieth centuries had some impact. More important perhaps were the temporary migrations of

Bahamian labourers to Charleston during the First World War and contract workers to Florida and other parts of the United States between 1943 and 1966. Despite the customary and accepted colour line drawn in the Bahamas, most Bahamians, from all black communities, were shocked at the legally enforced 'Jim Crow' standards then common throughout the south.[15]

Prohibition in the United States profoundly affected Bahamian society. The unprecedented boom in the colony's economy after the passage of the Volstead Act in 1919, while creating many material improvements in Nassau, widened the gap between the classes and races. Before the 1920s, an entrenched mercantile elite had little real capital. Their colour more than wealth separated them from the coloureds and blacks. Bootlegging profits, augmented by those from the land boom, brought quick money into Nassau, consolidating the wealth and power of the established elite and creating a new monied class which was mostly white. The *nouveaux riches* soon consolidated their wealth in successful businesses, safeguarded themselves against immigrant competition and, to ensure political and social power, sought seats in the legislature.[16]

As Colin Hughes asserts, 'wealth has had a pre-eminent place' in determining social relations in the Bahamas. The wealthy, who were usually white, attracted power and authority, while blacks were usually poor and underprivileged.[17] As a Methodist Minister so succinctly put it, in the mid-1920s:

> The race question is far keener here than elsewhere in the West Indies. The feeling is growing harder. I raised this matter with one of the sanest of our coloured people, and he is emphatic in saying that it is far worse now than formerly.[18]

American investment, following in the wake of bootlegging and the Florida land boom, brought investors, including Frank Munson. With them came the Jim Crow attitudes and hardening of racial attitudes. More rigid segregation, although not legislated, was practised in hotels, exclusive clubs, movie theatres, some restaurants and barber shops.

As the Wesleyan Methodist Missionary Society acknowledged: 'As to the colour question you will have to keep very quiet and be very silent. Things have gone on for generations and the new invasion by America has no doubt accentuated the difficulty.'[19]

By the mid 1930s Nassau had gained international recognition not only as a tourist destination but also as a seasonal resort for the wealthy and, owing to its loose tax structure, a pioneer tax haven. Increased foreign investment stimulated activity in real estate and land values rose. In post-war years tourism experienced phenomenal growth, bringing unprecedented prosperity to Nassau. Under the able chairmanship of the powerful, brilliant but reactionary Stafford Sands, the acknowledged leader of Bay Street, the

Development Board, through planned publicity and aggressive advertising campaigns, especially in the United States and Canada, attracted ever increasing numbers of visitors to the colony. Numbers of tourists increased from 37,856 in 1947 to 132,434 in 1955, ushering in a new era in the Bahamas' tourist industry. The former seasonal elite tourism gave way to all-year-round mass tourism.[20]

Benefiting most from the economic expansion was the white mercantile elite. It controlled not only the House of Assembly, but also the strategic business enterprises, including law, real estate, liquor and the major wholesale and retail businesses. Through its control of the small but active Immigration Department it safeguarded its own interests by limiting the numbers of foreigners.[21]

By upholding an archaic constitutional framework and perpetuating corrupt election practices, Bay Street merchants consolidated their legislative strength. Political representation had not dramatically changed in ethnic terms since the turn of the century. Whereas in 1890, six non-whites sat in the Lower House, in 1956, in spite of the introduction of the secret ballot, there were only eight. Still elected as independents, white members, although at times highly individualistic, generally united on major policy issues.[22]

The Colonial Office, while keenly aware of the inequalities in Bahamian society, the existing racial tensions and the potential of the three-year-old political party, the Progressive Liberal Party (PLP), was not prepared to risk financial collapse for constitutional reform.[23]

The influence of the British official class in the Bahamas lessened as the white mercantile class increased its power. While demonstratively loyal to Britain, the white elite purposely kept the salaries of the higher posts in the civil service low. This discouraged 'good and experienced officers from other colonies' from applying for vacancies. Even the governor, who often clashed with the members of the House of Assembly, but who was financially dependent on them, therefore walked a fine line, trying to introduce long-needed reforms, while attempting to maintain the cooperation and good will of the sensitive and intransigent white clique in the Assembly. The wrath of the Nassau white elite, once aroused, could be devastating. For example, in 1952, a petition was sent by white members of the House of Assembly asking the Colonial Office to remove Governor Neville when he, by personal example, such as attending black and coloured functions, tried to break down colour barriers in Nassau.[24]

Moreover, the white elite made their feelings for Neville known. According to Hilary St. George Saunders, former Librarian of the House of Commons, who had been commissioned by the House of Assembly in 1950 to write a history of the Bahamas, the Bay Street 'tycoons' condemned Neville in public in language of 'great violence' for 'consorting too much with the coloured people'.[25]

The coloured and black middle class also benefited to a limited degree from the prosperity that tourism brought. However, as Nassau's reputation grew internationally, the influence and wealth of the white mercantile elite increased while that of the coloured and black middle class relatively diminished. Increasingly, non-white businessmen, pitted against wealthy white competition, were being pushed off Bay Street. The dominance of the white merchant class and its control of the legislature allowed for the underdevelopment of education, resulting in a shortage of non-white professionals and potential leaders. There was a general lack of political sophistication among coloureds and blacks. The power and paternalistic policies of the Bay Street clique created a syndrome of dependency and a lack of self confidence on the part of the middle stratum and the black majority.[26]

Proximity to the United States and the development of tourism, and exposure to so many whites, tended to emphasize the already innate feelings of inferiority among blacks. Among the coloured middle class the absorption of white values through travel and mass media local experiences caused racial divisiveness (as they did in many Caribbean societies) and class hierarchy within the black community. This resulted in an obsession with skin colour, 'good' (European type) features and hair. Many light-skinned people of the middle stratum, in fact, 'passed' into the white society.[27]

The 'trickle down effect' of economic prosperity brought better job opportunities for the middle stratum, in the civil service, improved chances in the menial jobs in business, greater availability of borrowed money and more educational opportunities. However, non-white qualified professionals on returning to the Bahamas often found themselves obstructed by the Bay Street clique. Kendal Isaacs, a product of the brown middle class, after obtaining a law degree at Cambridge and being called to the Bar in 1950, found on his return to Nassau that there was no business available. He was forced to accept the post of Stipendiary and Circuit Magistrate – the first non-white to be appointed to that position.[28]

In the Caribbean generally, nationalist movements developed after the protests of the 1930s led mainly by members of the middle stratum. Political change was delayed in the Bahamas and even after the 1942 Riot no such leadership emerged. Several reasons contributed towards the slowness in political organization and constitutional advance in the Bahamas. Although there was a growth of racial consciousness during the 1930s and 1940s there was no sustained unity among the black majority.

Several attempts were made in the 1940s and 1950s by the coloured and black middle class to unite against social injustices and the blatant discrimination upheld by the white elite. In 1944, it united over the permanency of the secret ballot in New Providence and its extension to the Out Islands. On the passage of the Ballot Act in July of that year, making the secret ballot permanent in New Providence, the pact between the various groups and individuals dissolved.

Similarly, the Citizens' Committee, a black middle class organization headed by Maxwell Thompson and Cleveland Eneas, among others, had little success. It was most concerned with the extreme discrimination practised by the elite, and particularly with its banning of several films that explored the 'negro problem'. Discriminated against themselves, the Citizens' Committee suffered from conservatism and the ruthless and narrow policies of the Bay Street elite. Young non-white middle class professionals, as already noted, found it difficult to make a decent living in Nassau.[29]

Non-white middle class leadership failed to espouse the fledgling trade union movement and did not unite to back the labourers during the disturbances of 1942. Neither did it embrace the Progressive Liberal Party. Established in October 1953 by a group of light-skinned Bahamians, the majority with roots in the Out Islands, including Henry M. Taylor, Cyril Stevenson and William Cartwright, the PLP's platform extended an invitation to all Bahamians, calling for political and social changes. The *Herald*, the official propaganda organ of the PLP, was more critical of the Establishment than Dupuch's *Tribune* which was cautious and expressed reformist views.

The PLP made slow progress at first, suffering from Bay Street obstructionism which discouraged membership by more moderate middle class non-whites. Despite its leadership, the PLP, through its branches in New Providence and the Out Islands and public meetings educated the black masses in party organization, political issues, current affairs and labour matters. By 1953 over half the population lived on New Providence, whereas at the turn of the century 77 per cent resided in the Out Islands. Many members of the Citizens' Committee and other moderate non-whites felt uncomfortable with the black adherents of the party. The latter distrusted coloureds, who dominated the leadership of the PLP. Influenced by the Civil Rights Movement in the United States and the nationalist movements in the West Indies, some of the leaders, including Milo Butler and Lynden Pindling, used racial issues in appealing to the black majority. Politics in the Bahamas was becoming polarized on colour rather than purely class lines.[30]

Etienne Dupuch, coloured editor of the evening daily *Nassau Tribune*, member of the House of Assembly for the Eastern District and leader of the Bahamas Democratic League (BDL) was also concerned over the formation of the PLP and its 'hate propaganda'. While Dupuch himself criticized racial injustices and was personally affected by the colour bar, his views had clearly changed since 1918 when he had returned from World War I an embittered man, caused by the treatment he had received in the Army. While he deplored the treatment of blacks in Bahamian society, he favoured middle class leadership, a view shared by educated coloureds and blacks of the day.[31]

Dupuch was also embarrassed when foreign blacks, especially West Indians, were affected by racial discrimination. He became personally involved in the incident when Hugh Springer, eminent Barbadian barrister and Registrar of the University College of the West Indies, was victim of the Bahamas' colour bar.[32] On an unscheduled stop at Nassau, Springer was unable to dine at the Prince George Hotel on Bay Street. While other passengers were taken to the hotel, Springer was invited to have dinner at the airport cafeteria. To avoid further humiliation, Springer contacted Etienne Dupuch, whom he had met in London. Dupuch hosted him to dinner and put him up for the night.[33]

The incident, widely publicized in the British press[34] also brought protest from the West Indies, including a sharp letter to the Colonial Office from Sir Hugh Foot, governor of Jamaica.[35] The leading newspapers also highlighted it but were not as severe in their criticism. While the pro-Bay Street *Nassau Guardian* regretted the incident, its chief concern was how it affected Nassau's reputation as a tourist resort. Etienne Dupuch in the *Tribune* cautiously commented that it was 'just another one of those unpleasant incidents that should give thoughtful people in this community cause for serious pause'.[36]

Three years later, Dupuch, more widely travelled and aware of the Civil Rights Movement in the United States, was more outspoken. Having attended meetings of the Commonwealth Press Union in New Zealand, he met 'Jerry' Fletcher, a Jamaican of English parentage and managing editor of the Jamaican newspaper, the *Gleaner*. Fletcher taunted him about the blatant discrimination practised in Nassau. Apparently, a prominent Jamaican doctor (Lenworth Jacobs) and his wife, forced to overnight in Nassau in late 1955, were refused accommodation at the Montagu Beach Hotel because they were black. This story had made the front page of the *Gleaner*.

Etienne Dupuch, humiliated, was stirred into action. He realized then that discrimination in public places had to be stopped and promised Jerry Fletcher that he was going 'to bust this business wide open'.[37] Dupuch was also encouraged by Norman Manley's strong protest to the governor of the Bahamas and by questions that had been asked in the House of Commons. In Nassau, the governor appointed a Committee of the Executive Council to consult with the Bahamas Hotel Association which in 1953 had agreed, under pressure, that provision should be made at first class hotels for coloured passengers who were stranded in Nassau.[38]

Upon his return to Nassau, he began writing articles about the discrimination in Nassau hotels and alluded to the Springer and Jacobs incidents. Criticizing the government for merely exploring the problem as it related to travellers passing through Nassau, he warned that the people's patience was now at breaking point.[39]

During the first two weeks in January 1956, numerous letters on racial discrimination appeared in the *Tribune*. A. Leon McKinney, black businessman and a founder of the Penny Savings Bank, questioned whether it was right for the Bahamas Hotel Association to offer accommodation to coloured travellers and not Bahamians. He suggested that the government appoint a commission to study and report on the whole problem of segregation and discrimination and make recommendations to the legislature.[40] This letter probably inspired Dupuch.

Henry Taylor, Chairman of the PLP, was also moved by the Jacobs incident. The PLP had vowed in its platform to eliminate racial segregation in the colony. Taylor took immediate action and tabled a number of questions to the leader of the government on the subject.[41] The Speaker of the House of Assembly, Asa Pritchard, delayed putting the questions on the agenda for several meetings and when he did they were not answered immediately.[42]

In the interim, Taylor stated that he discussed his plan of action with several of his friends including McKinney who was also a friend of Etienne Dupuch. According to Taylor, Dupuch who faced stiff competition from the PLP, was worried about his chances of being re-elected in the Eastern District, which he had represented since 1949. He also felt that he needed to impress voters in his nine-month-old party, the BDL, which had made little progress.[43]

Etienne Dupuch also discussed his chances with friends, including McKinney who, Taylor states, advised him to do something 'spectacular' like bringing the question of discrimination to the floor of the House to gain support. McKinney warned Dupuch of Taylor's intention to do likewise and advised him to move swiftly.[44] Dupuch gave notice on January 17 that he would move an Anti-Discrimination Resolution in the House at its next meeting.

The resolution asked for a Commission of Inquiry to investigate all matters relating to discrimination in the colony:

> Resolved that this House is of the opinion that discrimination in hotels, theatres and other places in the Colony against persons on account of their race or colour is not in the public interest.

> Resolved further that this House is of the opinion that a Commission of Enquiry should be appointed under the Commissions of Enquiry Act to investigate all matters relating to such discrimination in the Colony with power to make recommendations for eliminating this evil by legislation or otherwise.[45]

The PLP made it known at public meetings that the resolution would be moved and debated on the floor of the House on January 23. Hundreds of persons, many of them supporters of the PLP, descended on the House. As Dupuch recalls: 'Every seat in the gallery was occupied by coloured men and women, halls and passage ways were crowded, and hundreds of coloured people milled around in the public square and streets outside' on the night he moved his resolution.[46]

Etienne Dupuch made an impassioned and lengthy speech. He asked for a public declaration whether Bahamians were one or two groups of people. He recalled meeting a young Bahamian in London recently who was ashamed to admit he was from the Bahamas because of its blatant colour-bar discrimination. Comparing the Bahamas with other West Indian tourist resorts and the United States, he deplored the Bahamas' notorious reputation for its callous treatment of coloured visitors and the humiliation suffered by Bahamians, and dared the House to discuss a subject which it always had avoided.[47]

Bert Cambridge, who himself had presented a similar petition in 1951, acknowledged that he was himself a victim of discrimination: 'I have worked in hotels in this island and I know that common prostitutes are admitted to places on Bay Street because they are white and decent coloured people are refused admission.'[48] Other coloured members who endorsed the motion included Gerald Cash, Henry M. Taylor, Marcus Bethel, Eugene Dupuch and C.R. Walker. Cash and Taylor recounted embarrassing incidents of discrimination which had recently occurred in Nassau. Cash, noting that people were reluctant to talk about racial issues, called for an open discussion of the issue.

The majority of whites maintained an 'eloquent silence' but, surprisingly, two supported Dupuch. Donald McKinney admitted that the racial problem was the biggest question facing the colony, but queried whether the effect of discrimination on tourism might not be exaggerated.[49] Dr Raymond Sawyer saw no harm in appointing a commission to consider the matter. Frank Christie moved, and it was carried by 11-9, that the resolution be referred to a Select Committee. This was the usual way of killing a motion.

When the Speaker appointed Frank Christie as the chairman of the Committee, Etienne Dupuch sprang to his feet and protested. The Speaker ordered Dupuch to sit down. He refused and the Speaker threatened to have a police sergeant remove him. Dupuch continued his protest but the Speaker repeated his threat. Dupuch, who was pounding on the table, replied defiantly: 'you may call the whole Police Force, you may call the whole British Army.... I will go to gaol tonight, but I refuse to sit down, and I am ready to resign and go back to the people.'[50]

The crowd, including many PLPs, suddenly rose in loud protest, declaring that Mr Dupuch 'would not be touched by anyone'. A roar went up from those gathered outside in the square and the House of Assembly was in turmoil. Mr McKinney moved quickly for an adjournment. The Speaker's procession from the chair was interrupted by the crowd which surged protectively around Dupuch, their hero. In fact, although he denied it, according to eye witnesses, the crowd lifted Dupuch on their shoulders and carried him around the square. The PLP leaders took advantage of the moment and spoke to the crowds rallying outside in the square.[51]

It was ironic, as H.M. Taylor and the leaders of the PLP recognized that Dupuch, a strong critic of the PLP, gained mileage by supporting a plank in that party's platform. Public opinion, due mainly to the PLP's efforts had changed. While Dupuch was being lauded, members of the Bay Street clique were booed and heckled by a large crowd as they emerged from the House that night and on the following evening when the House met briefly.[52]

There was almost immediate reaction from the majority of the Nassau hotels. They issued statements informing the public that their doors were open to all, regardless of race. Most denied that there had ever been discrimination and said, as did Charles Wong, proprietor of the Golden Dragon, that anyone, regardless of colour, who was well behaved, properly dressed and able to pay would be welcome.[53]

The Bahamas Hotel Association, in early February, after discussion with a sub-committee of the Executive Council, had acknowledged that the Jacobs incident was 'regrettable' and was due to a misunderstanding over the reservations made by BOAC for its passengers. At that time, all members of the Association had agreed to accommodate in-transit airline passengers.[54]

The Anti-discrimination Committee met several times. Etienne Dupuch assured the public that considerable progress was being made and to 'be patient ... but vigilant'[55] and that legislation from other countries and colonies was being obtained by the committee, which had given an interim report to the House of Assembly on February 20, 1956.[56] It returned a resolution on February 29 which was practically the same as the first part of Dupuch's and which condemned discrimination in 'public' places on grounds of race and colour. This was unanimously passed by the House. However, it rejected Dupuch's original request for a Commission of Inquiry and Gerald C. Cash's argument that legislation was necessary. Committee chairman, Frank H. Christie felt that the age-old problem had been adequately addressed by the House.

Etienne Dupuch, disagreeing with Cash (who brought a minority report), abandoned the second half of his resolution. At the time he admitted that legislation might be needed later. In retrospect, he declared that the resolution almost overnight changed the whole social structure of the colony without a single disturbance or drop of blood.[57]

Why did Dupuch compromise? He was severely criticized by the PLP. H.M. Taylor, its Chairman, who said that the resolution meant nothing. Gerald Cash argued that the resolution did not go far enough. It was a step forward but no solution.[58] A Commission of Inquiry would have exposed the severe racism which existed and those who perpetuated it, namely the majority of the House. While it was understandable that the Bay Street clique feared the repercussions of opening up the racial issue, Etienne Dupuch could only have gained political mileage among blacks, judging by the numerous letters, telephone calls and personal communications which he received after tabling the resolution.[59]

However, aware of changing public opinion, he feared violence and as a 'man of moderation' he urged restraint. Not entirely altruistic, Dupuch faced economic and political realities. He needed to make a decent living to support his large family and did not wish to upset his few white liberal benefactors who had kept him afloat financially in 1956 when he suffered a serious loss of business. Politically, he knew he had lost a lot of black support because of his moderation and wished to regain his seat and continue to lead the fledgling 'middle of the road' and racially mixed party, the Bahamas Democratic League.

The 1956 Resolution, as Hughes and Doris Johnson argued, demonstrated a new determination by blacks. They had made their presence felt around the House of Assembly and showed that they could force Bay Street to back down. 'The barriers had begun to fall.' Doris Johnson attributed this new confidence felt by black Bahamians to the PLP.[60] The aftermath of the successful passage of half of the Resolution also exploded the myth that desegregation would turn tourists away and destroy the economy. Tourism in fact increased dramatically after 1956. The incident also demonstrated the intransigent attitude of the mercantile elite, its unwillingness to yield an inch and to do all in its power to secure its own ends. The Select Committee refused to consider the second half of the Resolution, which would have allowed for a Commission of Enquiry to air the whole issue and possibly recommend the passage of legislation.[61]

According to Dupuch and Doris Johnson, immediately after the passing of the Resolution, coloureds and blacks flocked to the hotels, restaurants and the Savoy Theatre. However, this trend did not continue because most blacks could not afford to frequent such establishments and were not comfortable in all-white establishments.[62]

Despite Dupuch's claim that there was revolutionary change in the social structure [63] after the passing of the Resolution, discrimination in public places took some time to be completely broken down. The hotels claimed that they did not discriminate because of colour, but certain establishments did not welcome blacks. They subtly practised segregation by making excuses. For example, white scantily clad tourists would be served in some establishments but blacks would be turned away because 'they were improperly dressed' or 'it was a membership club'. Sir Clifford Darling, a PLP Senator at the time, said that as late as 1964, he was refused service in a downtown restaurant.[64]

Real estate in certain areas, such as The Grove off West Bay and Westward Villas, was governed by restrictive covenants. Realtors, who were predominantly white, did not even show certain properties to blacks. As late as the early 1970s, a black couple answering an advertisement for the sale of apartments in the exclusive Cable Beach area visited the complex and was told that none was available. The next day a young English lawyer who was a friend inquired and was given red carpet treatment. Not only were several apartments available, but financing as well.[65]

Banks and other financial institutions, excluding the Penny Savings Bank, with few exceptions did not employ non-whites as tellers or executives. In 1958, the only blacks hired were cleaners and messengers. St Andrew's School's colour bar was not broken until 1967 when, with urging from the Progressive Liberal Party, Milo Butler's grandchildren were admitted.[66]

The Colonial Office, while noting that discrimination in hotels and public places had ceased, acknowledged that private clubs were another matter. It seemed satisfied with this position, accepting that 'it was up to the membership'. Membership clubs such as the Nassau Yacht Club did not admit blacks or coloureds until the late 1960s, while the Royal Nassau Sailing Club maintains a white membership even to this day. In the Out Islands, the Peace and Plenty Hotel discriminated on the basis of colour and had to be advised by Governor Arthur in 1959 of the passage of the 1956 Resolution.[67]

Racial discrimination generally persisted in the Bahamas well into the 1970s; some would argue it still exists. Although there were few race-related incidents after the Resolution, tension in fact increased especially during pre-election periods. Ranfurly was concerned that the 1956 election campaign, the first one contested by the PLP, was fought mainly on 'a racial basis' and that 'much bitter feeling was aroused'.[68] This trend continued as the PLP gained in popularity among the masses and racial polarization resulted with the hardening of social divisions.

The dependence on the tourism industry had a profound effect on the Bahamian way of life as it did on Bermuda. It brought great wealth to the Nassau white mercantile elite and created a cleavage which reinforced social and racial divisions.[69] White, coloured and black Bahamians, seldom socialized together. A struggle resulted between the 'haves' who tended to be mostly white and the 'have nots' who were mainly black.[70]

Even after the 'Quiet Revolution', the coming of majority rule in 1967 and Independence six years later, the Bahamian economy, like those of Barbados and Bermuda, was controlled by whites. Karch's observation on Barbados is equally true of the Bahamas: that despite the modification of class and race after blacks gained political control, the 'basic divisions within the society continues to be a dichotomy between black and white'. In the post-independence tourist economy, she argued, where 'control is local, it is white'.[71]

The Nassau mercantile elite continued its narrow-minded policies and was determined to maintain its grip over the Bahamas' political system, even though it feared the rising political power of the black population. Tourism profits stimulated the growth of the coloured and black middle class but real wealth remained in the hands of a white minority. Wealth and power came to be equated with colour. The economic and political dominance and wealth of the Nassau merchant elite in the late 1950s made social integration unlikely. As the Colonial Office noted:

> There remains, however, a fairly rigid colour bar in the Colony's social life. As it happens there are few, if any coloured Bahamians, who have the financial means to keep up with those who constitute the Colony's 'upper set' and they are not likely to achieve the necessary riches if the ruling class has anything to do with it.[72]

Notes

1. Bridget Brereton, 'Society and Culture in the Caribbean. The British and French West Indies, 1870-1980', in *The Modern Caribbean*, ed. by Franklin W. Knight and Colin A. Palmer (Chapel Hill and London: 1989), 88; 'Social Organization and Class, Racial and Cultural Conflict in 19th Century Trinidad', in *Trinidad Ethnicity*, ed. by Kevin Yelvington (London: Macmillan Caribbean, 1993), 43. See also M.G. Smith, *The Plural Society in the British West Indies* (Berkeley: University of California Press, 1965), 162-175 and *Culture, Race and Class in the Commonwealth Caribbean* (University of the West Indies, 1990), 17-35; David Lowenthal, *West Indian Societies* (Oxford University Press, 1972), 91-100; Kelvin Singh, *Race and Class Struggles in a Colonial State, Trinidad 1917-1945* (University of Calgary Press and University of The West Indies: 1994), XIX-13.
2. Gordon K. Lewis, *The Growth of The Modern West Indies* (New York and London: 1968), 308. See also Barry Higman, *Slave Populations of the British Caribbean 1807-1834* (Baltimore and London: Johns Hopkins University Press, 1984), 395-398.
3. Gordon K. Lewis, *Growth of the Modern West Indies*, 227; 253; 308-318; Colin Hughes, *Race and Politics in The Bahamas* (St Lucia, London: University of Queensland Press, 1981), 224-225; Bridget Brereton, 'Society and Culture in the Caribbean', 92-93; Ralph M. Henry, 'Notes on the Evolution of Inequity in Trinidad and Tobago' in *Trinidad Ethnicity*, Ralph K. Premdas, 'Ethnic Conflict in The Caribbean: The Case of Guyana' in *The Enigma of Ethnicity: An Analysis of Race in the Caribbean and the World* (St Augustine, University of The West Indies: 1993), 160; Hilary Beckles, 'Independence and the Social Crisis of Nationalism in Barbados', in Hilary Beckles and Verene Shepherd, eds., *Caribbean Freedom and Society from Emancipation to the Present* (Kingston: Ian Randle Publishers and London: James Curry Publishers,1993), 529.
4. See Hughes, *Race and Politics*, 44-46; Doris Johnson, *The Quiet Revolution in the Bahamas* (Nassau: 1972), 34; Henry M. Taylor, *My Political Memoirs: A Political History of The Bahamas in the 20th Century* (Nassau: 1972), 202-208; Paul Albury, *The Story of The Bahamas* (London: 1975), 275; Etienne Dupuch, *The Tribune Story* (London: 1967), 146-52.
5. Gordon Lewis, *Growth of the Modern West Indies*, 310.

6. Michael Craton and Gail Saunders, *Islanders in The Stream. A History of the Bahamian People*, 2 vols. (Athens Georgia: University of Georgia Press, 1992-98), 177, 188-190, 195.
7. Ibid., 187-188.
8. Hughes, *Race and Politics*, 24.
9. Harry Hoetink, *The Two Variants in Caribbean Race Relations*, (Oxford: 1967), 161.
10. Dyer to Noble Nov. 7, 1945. Nassau, WMMS. See also Minutes of the Queens College School Committee, May 7, 1948.
11. Memorandum of Association of St Andrew's School, Nov. 11, 1948. Registrar General's Department. See also Gail Saunders, 'The Social History of The Bahamas 1890-1953' (Unpublished PhD thesis, University of Waterloo, 1985), 466.
12. Taped Interview with the Rev. Edwin Taylor, Oct. 15, 1993. After the service a number of coloured men and women from the mainland walked behind the Taylors and the Rev. Ward saying nothing but supplying protection.
13. See Howard Johnson, *The Bahamas in Slavery and Freedom* (Kingston: 1991), 55-109.
14. Bayley to Newcastle, Aug. 15, 1860, CO23/163/69-71.
15. Saunders, 'Social History', 450 and Tracey Thompson, 'Remembering The Contract. Insights Towards a Thesis' (presented at the 25th Conference of Caribbean Historians, Mona, Jamaica, 1993). For labour migration in nineteenth and early twentieth centuries see Howard Johnson, *The Bahamas*, 163-80.
16. Gail Saunders, 'Social History', 288.
17. Hughes, *Race and Politics*, 22.
18. Philip Cash, Shirley Gordon and Gail Saunders, *Sources of Bahamian History* (London and Basingstoke: 1991), 278.
19. Ibid.
20. Polly Patullo, *Last Resorts. The Cost of Tourism in The Caribbean*, (Kingston: Ian Randle Publishers, 1996), 7-12; See also chapter 9 of this book; Tom Barry, Beth Wood and Deb Preusch, *The Other Side of Paradise. Foreign Control in the Caribbean* (New York: 1984), 260. See also CO23/861, Murphy to Creech Jones, July 20, 1949.
21. Howard Johnson, '"Safeguarding Our Traders": The Beginnings of Immigration Restrictions 1925-33' in *The Bahamas*, 125-48.
22. Saunders, 'Social History', 522.
23. CO1031/1348/21, Colonial Office File Note. Edith Mercer. August 25,1955.
24. CO23/889, Minute S.E.V. Luke to Lloyd, May 2, 1952. See also Saunders, 'Social History', 523, and Etienne Dupuch, *Tribune Story* (London: 1967), 31.
25. CO23/889, Hilary St George, Saunders to Brigadier Head, Nov. 11, 1951.
26. For an extended discussion see chapter 1 of this book.
27. Bridget Brereton, 'Society and Culture, in *The Modern Caribbean*, 92; See also chapter 1 in this book; David Lowenthal, *West Indian Societies*, 93-100.
28. Interview with E. Basil North and Audrey V. North, Aug. 10, 1984. See also Saunders, 'Social History', 468.

29. Saunders, 'Social History', 467-468. For the 1942 riot, see chapter 11 of this book.
30. See Hughes, *Race and Politics in The Bahamas*, 46-47.
31. Ibid., 40; *Tribune* June 13, 1931 and Jan. 27, 1956.
32. Saunders, 'Social History', 530. See also *Tribune* Dec. 3, 1953 and CO1031/ 1041, 'Policy Regarding Racial Discrimination in the Bahamas.'
33. Saunders, 'Social History', 530. See also *Evening Standard*, Dec. 5, 1953 and Dupuch, *Tribune Story*, 146.
34. See *Daily Herald, Daily Telegraph, Manchester Guardian, Daily Sketch, Daily Express, Birmingham Post*, Dec. 7, 1953 and the *Evening Standard*, Dec. 5, 1953.
35. CO1031/1041, Hugh Foot to Lyttleton, Dec. 14, 1953.
36. *Tribune*, Dec. 3, 1953 and *Nassau Guardian*, Dec. 6, 1953.
37. *Tribune*, Jan. 3, 1956, and Dupuch, *Tribune Story*, 147.
38. Minutes of the Executive Council, Jan. 4 and 18, 1956 and *Tribune*, Jan. 3, 1956.
39. Ibid.
40. Ibid., Jan. 6, 1956.
41. Taylor, *My Political Memoirs*, 200.
42. *Tribune*, Feb. 10, 1956.
43. Taylor, *My Political Memoirs*, 201.
44. Ibid., 202; *Tribune*, Jan. 17, 1956.
45. Hughes, *Race and Politics*, 44; *Tribune*, Jan. 24, 1956; Votes of The House of Assembly, Nov. 17, 1955-May 17, 1956 (Nassau: 1956), 163-64; 217-18; 286, 381.
46. CO1031/1532, Dupuch, *Tribune Story*, 148; Office Note. Colonial Office, July 30, 1956.
47. *Tribune*, Jan. 24, 1956.
48. Ibid.
49. Ibid. See also Hughes, *Race and Politics*, 45.
50. *Tribune*, Jan. 24, 1956; See also Dupuch, *Tribune Story*, 149.
51. Hughes, *Race and Politics*, 451; Dupuch, *Tribune Story*, 149; Interview with Arthur D. Hanna, Jan. 1 , 1994.
52. *Tribune*, January 24, 1956; Dupuch, *Tribune Story*, 149; Taylor, *My Political Memoirs*, 205.
53. *Tribune*, Jan. 26 and 28, 1956.
54. Wesley T. Keenan to Ranfurly, Feb. 1, 1956. File. Colour Bar. Unofficial. Sept. 25, 1943- July 4, 1959.
55. *Tribune*, Feb. 2 and 8, 1956.
56. Ibid., Feb. 21, 1956; *Nassau Guardian*, Feb. 22, 1956; Votes of The House of Assembly, 1955-1956, 217-218.
57. Dupuch, *Tribune Story*, 152.
58. *Tribune*, March 1, 1956.
59. Ibid., Jan. 26 and 27, 1956.
60. Johnson, *Quiet Revolution*, 34; Hughes, *Race and Politics*, 214.
61. Hughes, *Race and Politics*, 214.
62. Dupuch, *Tribune Story*, 152; Johnson, *Quiet Revolution*, 34.
63. Dupuch, Ibid.
64. Interview with Sir Clifford Darling Oct.18, 1991.

65. Interview with Winston Saunders, Dec. 10, 1993, and personal recollection.
66. Interview with A.D. Hanna, Jan. 1, 1994.
67. Arthur to Etheridge, July 4, 1959. File. Colour Bar Unofficial, Sept. 25, 1943-July 4, 1959.
68. CO1031/1294/77, Extract from Bahamas Political Report. June 1956.
69. Gordon K. Lewis, *Growth of the Modern West Indies*, 327-329; See also chapter 9 in this book.
70. CO1031/2416, 'Policy Regarding Racial Discrimination in the Bahamas', 1957-1959.
71. Cecilia Karch, 'The Growth of the Corporate Economy in Barbados: Class/Race Factors 1890-1977' in Susan Craig, ed., *Contemporary Caribbean: A Sociological Reader*, Vol. I. (Port of Spain: The College Press), 213-241; Hilary Beckles, 'Independence and the Social Crisis of Nationalism in Barbados', 538, in *Caribbean Freedom*, eds. Hilary Beckles and Verene Shepherd (Kingston: 1993).
72. CO1031/2416 'Policy Regarding Racial Discrimination in the Bahamas'.

13

The 1958 General Strike in Nassau:

A Landmark in Bahamian Society

The wave of riots and strikes which swept through the British West Indies during the 1930s resulting in social and political change, including the rapid growth of labour unions and political parties, did not occur in the Bahamas. Its capital city, Nassau, experienced a riot in 1942 but it was characterized as a 'short-lived spontaneous outburst by a group of disgruntled labourers'. It highlighted the hostility of black labour against the white establishment and also the prevailing narrow socioeconomic and political policies, but it did not result in a political movement or a dramatic increase in activity among labour organizations.[1]

The masses remained largely unpoliticized and united black leadership took a long time to emerge. Trade union legislation which was passed as a result of the riot was defective and severely restricted membership in a union. Until the 1950s, trade unions, the first of which was established in 1936, were few and largely ineffective. The Progressive Liberal Party (PLP), the first successful political party established in the Bahamas, was organized in 1953. It was in the vanguard of political and social change and challenged the ruling white clique. In 1958, there was an impasse in a dispute between the Taxi-Cab Union and the hotel and tour cab operators. The PLP and the Bahamas Federation of Labour (BFL), having gained in strength and membership under effective leaders, supported the Taxi Cab Union in the first general strike in the Bahamas.

Until recently there was a dearth of literature on the 1958 strike. General historians such as Craton and Albury[2] briefly described the event. Recently, however, several authors have examined it in more detail. Included among them are Randol Fawkes, Colin Hughes, Hartley Saunders and Scott Moncrieff, all of whom recognized it as a turning point in the political history of the Bahamas. Two other writers, the late Dame Doris Johnson and Sir Henry Taylor, while stressing its far-reaching significance, only described it briefly.[3]

Only Moncrieff, in his as yet unpublished study, had access to the Colonial Office papers, which have only recently become available. This article, which takes into account the official documents, newspaper reports and oral history interviews, will examine and analyse the underlying causes of the strike and attempt to determine its social and political significance for the Bahamas.

Unlike the riot of 1942, which was spontaneous, the general strike was planned and well organized. Essentially a dispute between the Taxi-Cab Union and the Tour Companies, it won the support of the strengthened Labour Movement, headed by the BFL, and the PLP, the opposition party which had been affiliated with the Taxi-Cab Union since 1954. The strike occurred because of demands made for labour, constitutional, electoral and social reforms. The increasing political awareness ignited by the PLP, along with the new democratic ideas brought by returning students, professionals and contract workers,[4] coincided with the phenomenal growth in tourism and heightened expectations. Additionally, the changing worldwide mood prompted the Colonial Office to finally press for constitutional and electoral change in the Bahamas.

Fundamentally, the social structure of the Bahamas, its constitutional machinery and the electoral process remained unchanged between 1942 and 1958. The essentially mercantile based economy, dependent primarily on trade and commerce and not agriculture, and on indirect taxation, mainly custom duties, for its revenue, remained intact, greatly enhanced by the successful tourist industry.

The 'three-tier class racial structure', present in the Caribbean generally, at least until the 1940s,[5] survived in the Bahamas until the early 1960s, maybe even later. As Colin Hughes argued,[6] the racial situation there departed from the Caribbean norm creating a peculiar variant to the three-tier structure. In West Indian societies, colour was an important criterion of class and created a cleavage between whites, blacks and browns. In the late nineteenth century, the growth of the intermediate coloured class gained it a place in economic, social and political development.

In the Bahamas, an intermediate coloured class developed in Nassau and expanded by the late 1950s but it was weaker than its West Indian counterparts.[7] Hughes posits that certain factors such as the relatively high percentage of whites, the proximity of the Southern United States with its segregation practices, and the close cultural ties between white and black Bahamians and the United States, made for more antagonistic race relations in the Bahamas.[8] Moreover, 'wealth had a pre-eminent place in the Bahamas. Wealth attracted power and authority and therefore in the Bahamas, racial difference was linked to economic relationships'.[9]

Constitutionally, the Bahamas like Barbados and Bermuda retained the Old Representative System. Although in theory the colonial governors wielded much power, the Bahamian House of Assembly controlled the purse; it raised revenue and authorized expenditure. The outmoded Board system which directed departments of government was controlled by the members of the House of Assembly, the majority of whom represented 'Bay Street'. The reactionary Assembly used its traditional obstructionist tactics to delay social, constitutional and political change.[10]

The Bay Street clique retained power and delayed the expansion of the democratic process by maintaining a limited and restricted franchise. Whereas universal adult suffrage was being introduced in Jamaica, Barbados, and Trinidad during the mid 1940s and early 1950s,[11] voting in the Bahamas was reserved for male property owners over 21. Women were denied the vote completely. Plural and company voting endured and elections were held for a number of days, sometimes weeks, over the widely scattered archipelago. As a result, the Bay Street political machinery could be concentrated on each isolated community which usually looked forward to the excitement, payoffs, food and rum given out at election time.[12] After the 1956 election women on at least one Out Island could be seen wearing £5 notes on their dresses.[13]

Internally, significant developments were converging to create an atmosphere which would result in organized protest. The expansion of tourism in post-war years with its ancillary spin-offs in construction, finance, real estate and foreign investment generated many jobs, especially in Nassau, and contributed greatly to a high level of prosperity and optimism. Generally, wages paid in the Bahamas were considerably higher than those paid in the British West Indies. In addition, a greater proportion of the Bahamian population was employed including a large number of women in Nassau who worked in the tourist industry, the civil service and domestic services.[14]

While the national income per head was higher than in the British West Indian colonies, the cost of living in the Bahamas was the highest in the Caribbean.[15] This did not significantly affect the top income group – the 'Bay Street Boys' – who absorbed a large proportion of the total profits. Devoting much time and energy to public affairs, they ensured that the benefits largely accrued to themselves, their relatives and friends and created 'private wealthy empires'.[16]

The small black intermediate class and a growing white middle class,[17] both of which comprised professionals, civil servants, small business persons and shop clerks, also benefited, but to a lesser degree. The middle class whites did not belong to the older elite many of whom were members of the legislature and who owned lucrative businesses, mainly on Bay Street. The majority of the working population, mainly blacks, profited least and poverty persisted. Urban blacks and Out Islanders suffered, receiving much less than the average income. The majority of people lived in poverty while a small percentage, mainly whites, had enormous wealth. As Gordon Lewis succinctly stated: 'In effect, the Bahamas government was deliberately kept a poor government in a rich economy.'[18]

This uneven distribution of wealth was reflected in the rapid development of downtown Nassau and the neglect of the black urban section of Over-the-Hill (Nassau) and the Out Islands. In Nassau, especially its black section, numbers were pressing on limited resources partly due to an increasing birthrate, but mainly to accelerated migration from the Out Islands. By the mid-1950s, over half the Bahamas' population lived in Nassau. While the downtown or white section of Nassau could be described as 'quaint and bustling', its seaside suburbs to the east and west as attractive, the Over-the-Hill area, largely ignored, was deteriorating into a slum. There was also an increasing division between the colony's cultivated capital and the neglected Out Islands.[19]

Significant but guarded progress was also made on the race issue. As noted above, racial prejudice permeated Bahamian society even in the 1950s. In Nassau and the Out Islands, white communities sought to preserve their racial integrity by isolating themselves from coloureds and blacks as much as possible. Racial tension had been an underlying cause of the 1942 Riot as the Duke of Windsor and the American Vice-Consul admitted privately.[20] Coloured and black leaders felt indignant about the severe discriminatory practices in Nassau which barred non-whites from all hotels, some restaurants, movie houses and certain schools. Indeed, some had tried to stop such practices through various organizations such as the Citizens' Committee and the House of Assembly.[21] However, it was not until after two embarrassing incidents involving prominent black West Indians stranded in Nassau, that the issue of discrimination was brought to a head.[22]

Progress was made in 1956 when Etienne Dupuch, editor of the *Tribune* and representative for the Eastern District, brought a Resolution condemning discrimination in public places and asking for a Commission of Inquiry to be appointed to investigate all matters pertaining to discrimination.[23] It was significant that the first part of the resolution was accepted, but also that crowds gathered inside and outside of the House of Assembly on the night that it was brought, noisily supporting Dupuch and heckling the Bay Street politicians.[24] Their behaviour demonstrated that public opinion was changing.

At the time of the strike discrimination was 'for all intents and purposes' abolished in hotels and public places, but social inequalities remained and 'a fairly rigid colour bar existed in the Colony's social life'. Colour and class were linked to economics as noted in a special Colonial Office report:

> As it happens there are very few, if any coloured Bahamians who have the financial means to keep up with those who constitute the Colony's 'upper set', and they are not likely to achieve the necessary riches if the ruling class has anything to do with it.[25]

Discrimination was represented by residential segregation (which was informal and not legislated) and physically by Collins Wall which separated a predominantly white residential area (near to a shopping area) from a densely black section immediately west and south of the wall. Demands by Etienne Dupuch and petitions from the middle class party, the Bahamas Democratic

League, to open the wall to accommodate blacks working in the east, fell on deaf ears. The wall was not 'breached' until 1959.[26]

While 'overt acts of social discrimination (in the late '50s) had become rare', subtle discriminatory practices persisted. Private clubs, elite societies, charitable organizations, some business houses including banks and certain schools, especially the racially exclusive St Andrews and to a lesser extent Queen's College, still practised segregation. Blacks were never promoted to certain top posts in the Civil Service. Racial tension was real during the strike and before the 1962 election. This issue was used successfully by the PLP in successive election campaigns.[27]

As colour consciousness grew among Bahamian coloureds and blacks, they turned increasingly to education for salvation. The Bahamas' educational system compared poorly with those of the major British West Indian colonies. For the majority of Bahamians education facilities left much to be desired. Board of Education schools suffered from inadequate and overcrowded buildings, short supplies of textbooks and most importantly from the lack of trained teachers.[28]

While most blacks were debarred from obtaining a secondary education, a small number did, and greatly benefited from the improved standards of the Government High School established in 1925. Others attended the more recently opened Roman Catholic St Augustine's College, Fox Hill, or the Anglican St John's College on Market Street, founded in 1947.

Secondary education became the crucial factor in the growth of the black middle class, a means of mobility for the coloured middle class and also increased opportunities for some blacks from traditionally poor Over-the Hill districts. By the 1940s and 1950s, substantial numbers of coloureds and blacks, men and women, who had studied abroad in areas such as medicine, dentistry, law, engineering, nursing and education, were returning to Nassau.[29]

The graduates, especially those who had studied in London, brought home their skills as well as new nationalistic ideas about decolonization and constitutional changes taking place in the British Caribbean and elsewhere. Among those returning was Lynden O. Pindling a young, black and dynamic lawyer with roots in Over-the-Hill in New Providence and Jamaica. He joined the PLP in October 1953 as its legal advisor.[30] From that moment, as would become evident in later years, the 'Quiet Revolution' – which had deep social and political underpinnings – began.

Bahamian labourers returning from the 'Project' or 'Contract' in the United States also had a significant impact on Bahamian society especially during the late 1950s. While the 'Project' helped to rid Nassau temporarily of the potentially explosive elements of unemployed labour, it had a longer term effect. The workers gained experiences which were important in shaping their views and were able to easily identify with the racial issues being raised in the 1950s. Despite the customary colour line drawn in the Bahamas, most

Bahamian labourers, especially Out Islanders from black communities, were shocked at the legally enforced 'Jim Crow' standards common throughout the Southern United States. For the first time many Bahamians were called 'nigger' by whites[31] and were humiliated by them. The harsh discriminatory practices deeply affected the labourers and a sizeable proportion of the Bahamian population.[32]

Many were now independent, having accumulated a substantial amount of cash, therefore they were no longer prepared to accept the *status quo*. Some set up their own businesses, bought real estate and cars, while others became taxi drivers and participated in the burgeoning tourist industry, independent of the white minority.[33] As Randol Fawkes demonstrated, they also identified with the labour movement, 'democracy and the right to vote...To them the British monarchy and the white colonial administration were no longer sacred cows. It was time for the black man's voice to be heard in the halls of justice and in Parliament.'[34]

To achieve this, blacks needed a strong united voice. Until 1956 parliamentarians in the Bahamas were elected as independents. The formation of political parties came generally later than those in the British West Indies. The first successful political party[35] to be formed in the Bahamas was the Progressive Liberal Party in September 1953. Established by a group of light-skinned Bahamians, mosty notably Henry M. Taylor, William Cartwright and Cyril Stevenson (all with Out Island roots), the PLP's formation was a significant milestone. It was important in arousing public opinion and supported the Taxi-Cab Union and the Labour movement generally.

During its early years it grew 'slowly but steadily.'[36] Initially, it did not attract the traditional coloured and black middle class which was suspicious and distrustful of the party. Additionally, well established business, professional and employed blacks, who were benefiting from the profits of tourism and its spin-offs, feared, and justifiably so, reprisals from the Bay Street politicians and merchants.[37]

Under the chairmanship of Taylor, the PLP drew up and published a Constitution and Platform which enunciated its aims and policy. While demanding political and social change, it pledged itself as a party for all men whether rich or poor, black, brown or white and of whatever religious creed. It called for wider representation in the House of Assembly, the enfranchisement of women and the reduction of the life of the House from seven to five years. Addressing the issue of labour, it promised protection of labourers, decent wages for all and the introduction of more enlightened labour legislation.[38]

Through its branches in New Providence and the Out Islands, its public meetings and conventions, it educated the black masses in party organization, political issues, current affairs and labour matters. It also reached the people through the traditionally anti-Establishment newspaper, the *Nassau Herald*, edited by the Party's Secretary-General, Cyril Stevenson.[39] The *Herald* became the mouth piece and the 'beacon of freedom ... a guiding light'. As Hartley Saunders stated, 'Without this paper the success of the PLP would not have been as great'.[40] It succeeded in spreading news and also racial propaganda, which was to be used successfully in elections from 1962, a development which the party's Chairman regretted and Etienne Dupuch condemned.[41]

In 1956, the PLP, fighting its first election as a party, won six of the twenty-nine seats in the House of Assembly. Although the racial composition of the House was not changed, the election was very significant. The PLP had won a third of the votes and three-quarters of the votes cast were for candidates who identified either with the 'Bay Street Boys' or with the PLP. 'Party politics had definitely arrived in the Bahamas.'[42] The recently formed moderate, middle class party, the Bahamas Democratic League led by Etienne Dupuch, was rejected and collapsed shortly after the elections. In less than two years the 'Bay Street Boys', in reaction to the growing strength of the PLP and probably with some encouragement from the Colonial Office,[43] formed themselves into a party. Officially established in March 1958, the United Bahamian Party (UBP), comprised the twenty-one white members of the House of Assembly elected in 1956.[44]

More importantly, after the 1956 election, Lynden O. Pindling, a natural leader, lawyer and orator, emerged as Parliamentary Leader of the PLP, Taylor having lost his seat. Realizing the significance of the PLP's election performance, Pindling presented a communication to the obdurate Speaker, Asa Pritchard, requesting recognition of the PLP.

The PLP members in the House of Assembly were not discouraged when this request was rejected. Known as the 'Magnificent Six', they challenged the Bay Street clique on nearly every issue. The party also informed the Colonial Office of their grievances regarding electoral and constitutional issues. As early as October 1956, a delegation comprising Taylor, Milo Butler and Lynden Pindling visited London and met with officials of the Colonial Office.[45] During the latter part of the following year, the PLP requested urgent constitutional reforms including the introduction of ministerial government. Although British officials made no firm decision, they were made aware of viable opposition leadership and took note of its demands for political and constitutional change.[46]

Many of the PLP demands coincided with those of the labour unions. In fact, as Ann Spackman demonstrated, during the 1930s and 1940s an important development in the British Caribbean was the linking of trade unions with political parties. In most British West Indian colonies a merger between parties and trade unions resulted.[47] In the Bahamas during the 1950s, unions and the PLP were separate organizations but were intrinsically linked in aims and philosophy, and gave mutual support. Following the 1956 elections, the PLP and the BFL were 'to be the eyes, the ears and the voices for the poor and disinherited masses'.[48] However, it was the Taxi-Cab Union and the trade movement headed by Fawkes and the BFL which brought matters to a climax. The PLP, despite its initial caution in support of the strike, took advantage of the unrest and widened the demands made by the Taxi-Cab Union and the BFL at the time.

The unrest in the British West Indies during the 1930s generally led to the strengthening and consolidation of the trade union movement. As Bridget Brereton has stated, the British labour movement and the Colonial Office assisted West Indian labourers in organizing trade union movements along 'sound' constitutional and British lines. 'The "responsible" type of union leadership ... and trade union movement could be consolidated and institutionalized in the years after 1940.'[49]

In the Bahamas, which was by-passed by the Moyne Commission, the 1942 Riot resulted in limited labour reforms. The trade union movement, universally and traditionally rejected by the Bahamian middle class, was not very popular with the poorly educated black majority. Unions remained weak and mainly ineffective. While the Trade Union and Workmen's Compensations Acts (1943) and the Labour Board Act (1946) made provisions for the registration of trade unions, the legality of strikes, compensation for injuries inflicted during employment and an arbitration body, they fell short of acceptable 'modern standards'. The Trade Union Act, for example, barred civil servants, domestics, hotel and agricultural workers from union privileges. Attempts to amend the legislation were blocked by the Legislature controlled by the inflexible Bay Street politicians, many of them employers who disliked unions, seeing them as 'a threat to the system of business control'.[50]

It was not until the 1950s that the unions became more militant and numerous. At the time of the Riot there were only two, the Labour Union and the Federation of Labour established in 1936 and 1942 respectively.[51] The enactment of the new labour laws in the early 1940s led to the growth, albeit slow, of the labour movement. In 1950 there were five trade unions registered in the colony with a membership of 333; one dispute was dealt with during that period. Four years later, thirteen unions with a membership of 820 were registered and ten disputes were arbitrated. At the time of the strike, twelve unions existed, and demands were becoming more vocal.[52]

The catalyst for the Bahamian labour movement during the mid 1950s was its leader Randol Fawkes, a graduate of the Government High School, who trained locally as a lawyer under Thaddeus A. Toote, one of the early Bahamian black lawyers.[53] Fawkes, like Tubal Uriah Butler in Trinidad, was obsessed with a sense of mission, seeking to bring more dignity to the black masses. He saw himself as a 'fearless fighter for social justice' and the 'deliverer of the Bahamian people'.[54] Audley Green, a Bahamian 'Project' labourer, who migrated to the United States, admitted that at the time, workers felt that

Randol Fawkes could 'move heaven and Earth'. They considered him to be their 'Moses'.[55]

Born in the Over-the-Hill section of Nassau, Randol Fawkes, proud of his achievements, valued higher education, seeing it as a key to progress for oppressed blacks. He fought in vain during the early 1950s for the Bahamas to become affiliated with the University College of the West Indies. However, at that time, in the minds of most Bahamians, particularly the governing elite, the College and the West Indies generally stood for something 'dangerous and subversive'.[56] Recognizing the importance of financial independence, Fawkes, along with several other black professionals from various callings, founded the Penny Savings Bank, an institution which represented the value of 'thrift' and catered to 'the little people', – that is, poor blacks.[57]

Suspended from the Bahamas Bar for two years, Fawkes went to New York where he spent a year eking out 'a meagre living' performing menial tasks. During that year he broadened his education for the task which he was convinced lay ahead of him, seeing his exile in a Biblical context, as Moses did. He also experienced the beginning of the Civil Rights Movement and was inspired by a speech by Emperor Hailie Selassie when he visited Harlem in July 1954 and the singing of the powerful black entertainer, Paul Robeson. He returned to Nassau 'to overthrow the white oligarchy' and, like Moses, deliver his people.[58]

Fawkes sought to do this through the mobilization of the trade union movement. He established an employment agency, the first of its kind. Attracting workers from all fields he 'organized them into craft unions and successfully negotiated on their behalf for better working conditions'. Finally, under pressure from the Bay Street merchants and the government, which tried to 'suppress the movement', Fawkes established the BFL which was an organization of unions and members of individual trade unions divided into branches according to their trades. The Taxi-Cab Union although self-governing was affiliated with and paid dues to the BFL.[59]

The labour movement was very active during the mid-1950s. Public meetings were held condemning colonialism and elucidating the aims of the unions. Fawkes won the support of hotel workers who were not able to form independent trade unions. He led several strikes demanding higher wages and shorter hours. He soon joined the PLP and along with Pindling was chosen to contest one of the two seats for the Southern District in the 1956 General Election. He also wrote a weekly column on 'bread and butter issues' in the party's paper, the *Nassau Herald*.[60]

On June 1, 1956, Fawkes and William Mallory, leader of the BFL, organized the first Labour Day Parade. All important unions including the Taxi-Cab Union and the BFL participated. A crowd of about 20,000 marched from Windsor Park to the Southern Recreation Grounds where both the governor and the president of the BFL addressed them. A week later, Fawkes was elected to the House of Assembly. This placed him in a position to continue to push for political and social changes.

He worked tirelessly to change the antiquated labour laws and according to Henry Taylor 'tried to implement his labour policy without reference to the Party's council'.[61] The causes of the PLP and BFL were closely linked. While sharing a common membership for the most part, Fawkes, as leader of the BFL was often at odds with the PLP and his own membership.[62] His dedication to the cause of labour reform, despite his differences with the PLP, helped to precipitate the general strike, as there were no apparent grievances relating to wages or conditions of work. Felix Bethel and Michael Stevenson argue that the 1958 strike marked Fawkes' last attempt to regain control of the labour movement, the members of which also supported the PLP and Pindling, and seemed poised to gain power.[63]

While Henry Taylor argued that Fawkes' image 'was enhanced by this strike' and that 'never before had labour been so successfully organized in the colony', Governor Sir Raynor Arthur thought differently. He was critical of Fawkes' behaviour and stated that opposition to him grew stronger after the strike because of his inconsistent behaviour and the way he conducted the BFL elections.[64]

A variety of external forces combined with the local progressive movements in Nassau to ignite political consciousness. The Civil Rights Movement in the United States was mobilized by 1958 and its leader, Martin Luther King, was known to some labour and political leaders. Incidents such as Rosa Park's defiance in 1955, the boycott of the Montgomery Bus Company and the integration of Little Rock Central High were all reported in the local press (at least in the *Tribune* and the *Herald*).[65]

The movement also deeply influenced labour and political leaders such as Fawkes and Pindling, who actually met with King. They both followed King's philosophy of non-violence. In December 1958 Fawkes invited him, while on a private visit, to speak to a capacity audience of BFL members.

There was also a change in the 'gradualist' Imperial policy in post-war years. The constitutional advances which took place in the British West Indian colonies in the 1940s and 1950s were accelerated not only by the unrest of the mid and late 1930s, but also by the Second World War. Returning West Indian professionals and veterans brought home democratic ideas and knowledge about the nationalistic struggles for independence in places like India, Burma and the Gold Coast.[66]

Britain, weakened materially and morally, found it difficult to maintain its possessions abroad and to stop the nationalistic movements. The Labour Government elected in 1945, more than its Conservative successor, was committed to granting greater self-government to black colonies. Changes in Imperial policy were also affected by the outcome of World War II and America's commitment to decolonization. The Cold War and the development of international organizations which encouraged Britain to ensure that colonies would develop in a democratic fashion and be insulated against the growing threat of Communism, also influenced British administrators.

The independent House of Assembly, controlled by a mercantile elite, prided itself that during the 1940s and 1950s it did not need grants from the British Government to balance its budget. As Hughes stated: 'At Whitehall and Westminister no news from the colonies has generally been good news.' The Colonial Office had always been reluctant to interfere in the local affairs of the Bahamas. It avoided upsetting the Bay Street clique, which through its development of tourism, had brought sustained prosperity to the colony. However, the 1958 strike shocked the Colonial Office and 'shook it off the fence it had straddled for so long'.[67] Fear of black anger and the growing militancy of unions and the PLP, whose leaders were then considered left wing extremists, coupled with intense international pressure, forced Britain to re-examine its position on political developments in the Bahamas.

The original dispute which led to the strike in January of 1958 occurred on November 2, 1957. For some years there had been tension between the Taxi-Cab Union (comprising independent taxi-drivers and owners) and the operators of hotel and tour bus companies. The Taxi-Cab Union complained that the tour companies were competing with them for tourist traffic. The official opening of the new airport at Windsor Field, over 11 miles west of Nassau, was scheduled for November 16, 1957. The longer journey meant larger fares for taxi cab drivers. However, the tour companies started providing their own transport for passengers coming to Nassau under the auspices of the Hotel Association headed by John L. Cota.

The Taxi-Cab Union learnt that the Nassau hotel operators were negotiating an agreement with a local bus company operated by Dan Knowles and a large, white-owned company, which had started providing its own transport for passengers coming to Bahamas under its auspices. The intention was that the local bus company and meter taxi-cab firm would be given 'franchises' to convey passengers between the airport and the hotels. Such a scheme would have led to a 'considerable increase of the seating capacity of hotel vehicles' and probably would have ended in a monopoly which excluded the Taxi-Cab Union entirely.[68]

Government became involved in the dispute because the Airports Board controlled parking regulations at the airport. For the hotels to succeed in this 'franchise' project, the Airports Board had to allocate large areas of parking space for the 'franchise' operators. It realized that such a move would be unpopular with the Taxi-Cab Union and that 'a large body of opinion in Nassau resented what was alleged to be another move by wealthy Bay Street merchants to squeeze out the small operator'.[69] On the other hand, the Airports Board could not agree that the Taxi-Cab Union should have the monopoly on collecting passengers from the airport. It decided that the system whereby the hotel buses, and tour company cars were allowed to transport passengers from the Oakes Field airport should continue.

By October 26, 1957, the government learned that the Taxi-Cab Union intended to make trouble on the day of the unofficial opening of Windsor Field (November 2). As a result, a transport sub-committee of the Executive Council, under the Chairmanship of Attorney General L.A.W. Orr, was convened to try to settle the dispute. The Taxi-Cab Union was represented by Pindling and Clifford Darling, its president. The tour operators were represented by Knowles and Edward Leggatt, president of the Meter Taxi-Cab firm. The Attorney General persuaded the Hotel Association to agree that the hotel and tour drivers should not increase total seating capacity of their vehicles beyond the level that had been established at Oakes Field. However, since no accurate statistics of established share of traffic were available, the union was not satisfied.[70]

On the morning of November 2 when the new airport was opened for traffic, the Taxi-Cab Union led by Darling, Nick Musgrove, Lochivar Lockhart, Jimmy Shepherd and Wilbert Moss decided to show its dissatisfaction. Nearly all of the 193 union drivers arrived at the airport determined to force the withdrawal of hotel transportation. When the first batch of visitors arrived and tried to enter hotel transportation, the Union drivers approached the vehicles and persuaded the passengers to travel by taxi. Darling stated 'We are here ... to protect our interest - the small man's interest against big monopolies and a few individuals who wish to destroy us'.[71]

The 'attitude of the drivers was surly and uncompromising' and the chairman of the Airports Board temporarily refused to allow hotel transportation. After checking with government officials, hotel vehicles were allowed. As a result, Union drivers blockaded all roads to and from the airport. Encouraged by government workers, including those from Customs, Immigration and Civil Aviation, they defied police orders to move their vehicles. Junior police officers obviously sympathized with the demonstrators who were also encouraged by PLP supporters.[72]

The road blocks ended after twenty-four hours when the chairman of the Airports Board agreed to enter into discussion with the Union. A temporary settlement was agreed upon. During an eight week period the hotels would not send transport to the airport. Meanwhile the transport committee, under the Attorney General, would attempt to obtain a permanent settlement.[73]

Approximately thirty Union drivers were charged in the Magistrate's Court with obstruction and three with assault.[74] This action did not have the desired effect and served only to anger the taxi drivers.[75]

Meetings were held and it seemed that an agreement had been reached in December. Nineteen points of the twenty put forward had been agreed upon. Tour companies were allowed to supply three vehicles each in transporting passengers from the airport and hotels. However, point twenty, the original bone of contention, still gave tour companies the exclusive rights of transporting passengers from Nassau to the airport in cars of their own choice. The union refused to accept this and demanded a 'first come, first serve' system whereby the first drivers on the line would be assured of a fare. This agreement caused a breakdown in negotiations.

On January 8, 1958, Darling demanded and got the appointment of a three-man tribunal to break the deadlock. However, the Union objected to all three and sought to have Fawkes as an arbitrator. The Tour companies objected to Fawkes and negotiations reached a standstill. Fawkes and Pindling subsequently met with the governor, but he did not immediately agree to appoint an impartial Commission of Enquiry to investigate the causes of the dispute.[76] Darling then appealed to the BFL for 'active assistance'. He stated that 'the situation is very grave indeed, as negotiations have completely broken down'.[77]

The BFL responded positively. At a well-attended meeting on January 11, 1958, the BFL, after hearing from speakers representing the PLP, BFL and Taxi-Cab Union, voted in favour of calling a general strike to support the Union and to protest long- standing injustices.[78]

At 8:30 a.m. on Sunday January 12, Pindling and Fawkes entered the Emerald Beach Hotel. Resting their right hands on the right shoulder of Saul Campbell, president of the Hotel Workers' Branch Union, they whispered 'Now!' This was repeated throughout New Providence at other hotels. By that evening, all major hotels were virtually closed[79] and the Taxi-Cab Union had withdrawn all of its taxis. On Monday, January 13 hotels gave notice of their closure. Meanwhile many construction workers, bakers, garbage collectors, airport porters, employees of the Electricity Corporation, a number from the Public Works Department and some private employees had already stopped work. The general strike had begun.[80]

When Governor Arthur opened the Legislature on January 14 he and the Bay Street politicians were booed while Fawkes and the PLP leaders, whom he described as 'extremist left wing political leaders', were applauded.[81]

There was no violence by the striking workers. For the duration of the strike, both men and women picketed and boycotted leading Bay Street businesses. Darling admitted that workers were angry and wished to burn down Bay Street but he and other leaders urged them to be calm.[82] However, Arthur had alerted the Commander of the Caribbean Area about the incident and asked for a company of troops to be sent from Jamaica. He initially feared that the tense racial situation might result in disorder. The arrival of the Worcestershire Regiment on January 15 had 'a sobering effect' and 'public confidence' was 'much improved'. A frigate, *HMS ULSTER*, arrived a few days later with technicians to maintain essential services and public utilities.[83]

The governor's reluctance to have the white troops withdrawn was more to placate the nervousness of the white population than in anticipation of serious violence. He admitted that 'The Bay Street group feels safe as long as the troops are here, but would feel very insecure if they were to be withdrawn'.[84]

The strike continued until January 29. On January 25, just before it was called off, employees from the Electrical Corporation resumed work and by Tuesday January 28, all public health workers and two-thirds of the striking Public Works Department employees had returned to work. By January 30 there was a general resumption of work and a return to normal, although major hotels remained closed for a few days until tourist traffic resumed. While all government employees were accepted, not all hotel employees were re-employed immediately.[85]

News of the strike was reported in the British, Canadian and American press. The latter suggested that political issues were the real cause of the strike. The *New York Times* reported that 'negroes have been demanding welfare legislation and modern laws. Efforts of the Governor and the British Colonial Office to obtain reforms have been blocked by a Legislature dominated by a small group of wealthy whites'.[86]

Press reaction embarrassed the British Embassy in Washington which feared that support for the Bahamas' Assembly would bring international ridicule. One of its officers stated that there was 'interest in the events in Nassau throughout the Carolinas, Georgia and Florida' where the 'Bay Street Boys' were 'regarded as the biggest gang of pirates yet unhung'.[87] The Embassy's official line was that while it had little sympathy with the 'Bay Street Boys' it was difficult to intervene in their affairs. From the media's point of view 'this issue seems to be the hottest thing since Mau Mau'.[88]

Pressure also came from American and international labour leaders including those in other British West Indian colonies, even though the Bahamas was not a part of the West Indies Federation. Fawkes spoke to labour organizations in New York and was supported by American labour leaders who telegraphed the Secretary of State pledging support and urging the British government to establish democracy in the Bahamas.[89] Several foreign labour officials, such as Mr Ken Sterling, representing the International Confederation of Free Trade Unions, Mr Wesley Wainwright of the National Workers' Union of Jamaica, and Martin Pounder, Trade Union Congress representative for the Caribbean, actually visited to offer advice and assistance. Pounder and Sterling were shocked to discover that the dispute which had given rise to the strike was not a trade dispute but a disagreement between two conflicting commercial interests. Despite this however they, particularly Pounder, assisted in settling the strike.[90]

Support for the unions and the PLP also came from other British Caribbean colonies. The Jamaican House of Representatives unanimously passed a resolution condemning the 'disgraceful and outmoded system and attitudes' in the Bahamas and calling for the establishment of a Royal

Commission of Enquiry.[91] As Hughes stated, the strike cemented 'relations between the PLP leaders and their West Indian counter-parts'.[92]

Due to internal events, strong local public opinion and sustained international criticism, Arthur pressed the Colonial Office to take urgent action in instituting reforms in the Bahamas.[93] Arthur personally deplored the colony's constitution, seeing it as 'morally indefensible' and a 'hopeless anachronism.' He did not agree with Bay Street's request to keep the troops in the Bahamas indefinitely and was afraid that if it pressed for constitutional change before any labour and political reforms were made it might turn the Bahamas into 'a little South Africa.'[94] Arthur was convinced that the Bay Street politicians should 'start getting their house in order in the eyes of the world' and wondered 'how long should we back up Bay Street with British bayonets?'[95]

Arthur's appeal to the Colonial Office finally brought results. In March 1958, it announced that the Secretary of State for the Colonies would visit the Bahamas in early April to investigate the underlying causes of the strike and to make recommendations for change.[96]

It is perhaps surprising that Lennox Boyd personally visited the Bahamas after the strike. No explicit reasons can be found in the documents, but from an examination of the Colonial Office papers for this period, it can be conjectured that the Office was embarrassed not only by the archaic constitution, but also by international reaction to the strike, especially that of the United States. The British government had to be seen to promote democracy, and Arthur persuaded his colleagues in London that something must be done to liberalize the Bahamian constitution. He recognized the reactionary mood of the Bay Street politicians, especially Stafford Sands whom he described as 'obdurate'. While he felt he might successfully sway Roland Symonette he was less confident about Sands, whom he recognized as the dominant leader. In fact, younger Bay Street politicians felt that change was needed.[97] Additionally, some at the Colonial Office had met PLP leaders Taylor and Pindling who had made sound suggestions for constitutional advance. A viable opposition to Bay Street was emerging. Recognizing the existing racial antagonism and acknowledging the successful tourist industry, the Colonial Office wished Bay Street to make the necessary reforms to avoid trouble and possible bloodshed in the future.

By the time of the visit, Arthur had brought together the Taxi-Cab Union and the tour companies to sign an agreement providing more equitable transportation to and from Nassau's International Airport.[98] He also promised that legislation would be passed allowing hotel and agricultural workers to unionize and that a Labour Department and a Bahamas Transport Authority would be established.[99] The governor's well-received speech over the local radio station, after his announcements, urged all parties to work together, forget the past and look to the future. However, the following week, his attempt to introduce an Emergency Powers Act, giving him overriding powers, was opposed by the Bay Street politicians who cherished their power and independence. After the debate in the Assembly it was referred to a Select Committee where it died.[100] The Bay Street politicians in the Assembly, by March, had formed the UBP and refused to rush any reforms.

The 1958 strike stirred the usually complacent Colonial Office into action. It was Lennox Boyd's visit to the Bahamas which accelerated change and had a significant impact on Bahamian constitutional and political development. The recommended reforms eased much of the tension, which might have led to violence, and ultimately resulted in the 'Quiet Revolution' – the peaceful transition to majority rule. His presence was also significant in that no British representative of his stature had ever visited the Bahamas in a working capacity. During a week's stay, Lennox Boyd met with the UBP, the PLP and representatives from the BFL. He also visited several Out Islands including Eleuthera, Crooked Island, Acklins and Exuma.

After listening to all groups he informed the UBP that the British government was serious about reform and issued a warning that it was determined to support a majority opinion regardless of the House of Assembly's makeup. If the Bahamian government failed to implement the proposed reforms, 'no one is in doubt as to the ultimate authority of the Imperial Parliament'.[101] Lennox Boyd reiterated the Colonial Office's view that if Bay Street did not reform its constitution, it might end up with one it did not like. A year earlier in London, Arthur had discussed the matter of constitutional change with Symonette and Sands. The subject of British honours arose and might have served as an incentive for the two most powerful men in the Assembly, who were later knighted. They were able to coerce the Assembly into supporting the suggested electoral changes.

Lennox Boyd's intervention was an important milestone. The Colonial Office, besides demanding electoral changes, examined labour matters, and also investigated educational and medical conditions. Two important reports, the Houghton Report on Education and the Hughes Report on Medical Services were produced[102] and eventually led to social changes including reorganization of the educational system and improvement in medical services especially on the Out Islands. With the help of Pounder and others, a Labour Department and Board were established almost immediately. The Trade Union and Industrial Conciliation Act, which enabled every Bahamian worker to form independent unions, came into effect on October 1, 1958.[103]

Significant electoral reforms were incorporated in the General Assembly Election Act of 1959.[104] Male suffrage was introduced giving all males over 21 years of age the right to vote; the company vote was abolished and the plural vote, which allowed one person to vote in every constituency, was limited to two. In order to bring the constituencies into line with the movement of population, four additional seats in New Providence (two in the South and two in the East) were created with provision to be made for by-elections as soon as possible. Lennox Boyd, strongly influenced by his discussion with the PLP, made these latter recommendations in an attempt to redress the imbalance of representation between Nassau and the Out Islands. Although Lennox Boyd saw no need, or evidence of widespread demand, for granting women the vote, his visit highlighted the woman's suffrage movement which had existed since the mid-1950s.[105] The movement was mobilized and after some agitation women were enfranchised in 1961. They voted for the first time in the 1962 general elections.

The origin of the dispute which precipitated the strike was economic and the demands narrow in scope. It was the labour movement and the PLP which, in support of the protest, widened the demands, calling for labour, constitutional and electoral reforms. Agitation from both movements and the 1958 strike accelerated change. Labour grievances were largely satisfied by the Trade Union and Industrial Conciliation Act which gave all Bahamian workers the right to form independent unions. It also provided for adequate machinery including a Labour Department to deal with grievances. The labour movement was organized and for a short time Fawkes' leadership was enhanced.[106]

As Gordon Lewis argued, there were no structural changes in the constitution immediately following the strike. Bay Street politicians were firmly entrenched and in control of 'a gerrymandered electoral constituency system'[107] demonstrated by their resounding victory in the 1962 general elections. However, due to Colonial Office pressure some important electoral changes were instituted. The Colonial Office was determined to support reforms but was against radicalism and upsetting the prosperous tourist economy. Embarrassed by Bay Street's conservatism and obstinacy, it was wary of Fawkes and probably recognized Pindling's potential as representative of 'conservative middle class nationalism'.[108] The widening of the franchise, abolition of the company vote and reduction of the plural vote helped to democratize the election process. These reforms encouraged the PLP which from this time, with Pindling as its Parliamentary leader, became the primary opponent of Bay Street. They also led to important political gains. All four newly created seats were won by the PLP in the 1960 by-election. In April 1960, the Assembly also agreed to reduce its term from seven to five years.

The PLP, with an expanded membership, though 'shocked and surprised' at its defeat in 1962, especially after its by-election windfall, was encouraged by the large numbers of votes and continued to mobilize its mass following and growing middle class support which it needed to gain respectability. The party's reputation as a viable political force was greatly strengthened. The racial factor, which was to be used repeatedly with much success, naturally became an important element in politics. A Colonial Office Report noted:

> Political life in the Bahamas is dividing itself into a struggle between the 'Haves' and 'Have Nots' and unfortunately the 'have nots' tend to be Black and the 'Haves' tend to be mainly whites.[109]

The gains made in 1958 created optimism and hope for the black majority. There was no turning back despite the power of Bay Street. As Michael Craton stated, 'a breeze of reform immediately appeared to waft through public affairs'.[110] A new constitution in 1964 introduced the ministerial system, granted internal self-government and led finally to independence in 1973. Six years earlier the PLP in a 'Quiet Revolution' and in an atmosphere of sustained prosperity, had defeated Bay Street: majority rule had begun. The PLP had eclipsed the BFL and Pindling had replaced Fawkes as the crowd's hero.[111]

An important catalyst in these developments was the transformation of Colonial Office policy evident from its more decisive actions towards the Bahamas. As Hughes noted, before the strike, Bahamian politics could be seen as a bilateral contest fought between white and black politicians. The 1958 strike 'was to bring the third party in at last in an open declaration of what should be done'.[112] Lennox Boyd's visit significantly changed the course of Bahamian history. His meeting with Bay Street, PLP politicians and labour leaders, who aired their views, grievances and demands, led to important electoral changes and ultimately to the ascendancy of the PLP and Pindling. Continued negotiations and pressure resulted eventually in dramatic constitutional, social and political changes. In the words of Randol Fawkes:

> The General strike marked the beginning of the end of British Colonialism [in The Bahamas] and all that it stood for; white supremacy and racial discrimination; economic exploitation and votelessness of the Bahamian mass; inequality before the bar of justice, illiteracy and all the sordid aspects of second class citizenship.[113]

Notes

1. Gail Saunders, 'The 1942 Riot in Nassau. A Demand for Change?' *The Journal of Caribbean History*, 20: 2, (1985-86), 117-146; See also chapter 11 in this book.
2. Michael Craton, *A History of The Bahamas*, 3rd ed. (Waterloo, Canada: 1986). First published in London by Collins in 1962, 273-274; Paul Albury, *Story of The Bahamas* (London: 1975), 227 and 275-276.
3. Sir Randol Fawkes, *The Faith That Moved The Mountain* (Nassau: 1979), 98-126; Colin Hughes, *Race and Politics in The Bahamas* (St Lucia, Australia: University of Queensland Press, 1981), 62-67; Hartley Saunders, *The Other Bahamas* (Nassau: 1991), 310-321; Dame Doris Johnson, *The Quiet Revolution in The Bahamas* (Nassau: 1972), 35-37; Sir Henry Taylor, *My Political Memoirs. A Political History of The Bahamas in the 20th Century* (Nassau: 1987), 239-240 and Scott Moncrieff, 'Study of the Decolonization of the Bahamas with particular reference to the 1958 General Strike and the Sequential Reforms'. (Unpublished BA dissertation, University of Stirling, April, 1990).
4. After the 1942 Riot, the Duke of Windsor, then governor of the Bahamas, negotiated an agreement with the American Government

for the recruitment of Bahamian labourers to Florida to relieve American manpower shortages created by the war. The programme, known as The Project or The Contract, continued until the mid-1960s absorbing up to 5,000 Bahamian workers at a time. See Windsor to Stanley, Aug. 10, 1943, Secret, CO23/760/51; Albury, *The Story of The Bahamas* (London: 1975), 218; Gail Saunders, 'The Social History of The Bahamas,' (Unpublished PhD thesis, University of Waterloo, 1985), 445-451 and Tracey L. Thompson, 'Remembering the Contract. Insights Towards a Thesis', Paper presented at the 25th Conference of Caribbean Historians, Mona, Jamaica 1993.

5. Bridget Brereton, 'Society and Culture in the Caribbean. The British and French West Indies, 1870-1980', in *The Modern Caribbean*, ed. by Franklin W. Knight and Colin A. Palmer (Chapel Hill and London: 1989), 88.
6. Hughes, 224.
7. Gail Saunders, 'Role of The Coloured Middle Class in Nassau 1890-1942', *Ethnic and Racial Studies*, 10, no. 4 (Oct., 1987), 448-465; See also chapter 1 of this book.
8. Hughes, 20-31.
9. Ibid., 22.
10. Gordon Lewis, *The Growth of The Modern West Indies* (New York and London: 1968), 320-321; Hughes, 36; Ann Spackman, *Constitutional Development of the West Indies 1922-1968*. A Selection from the Major Documents (Barbados: Caribbean University Press, 1975), 52-53 and chapter 11 in this book.
11. See Morley Ayearst, *The British West Indies. The Search for Self-Government* (London: 1960), 70-84. The first election in Jamaica to be held under universal suffrage was in 1944, in Trinidad in 1946, in Barbados in 1950.
12. Plural voting allowed Bahamians (mainly white) with just enough land in each of 29 constituencies (including the Out Islands) to be able to vote 29 times, that is once in each constituency. The Company vote allowed Bay Street lawyers (for example, Stafford Sands) to abuse the system. Lawyers could draft numerous nominal companies so that the white elite could vote many times over. See 'Legal Report on General Assembly Amendments'. CO1031/2136. See Taylor, 1-3 and 145.
13. Personal communication with the Rev. Edwin Taylor, March 3, 1992.
14. The Economist Intelligence Unit, 'A Comparison of the Level of Living in The Bahamas and Other Caribbean Islands. Preliminary Report. Dec. 1958'. CO1031/2467. The national income per head in the Bahamas in 1958 was £352 compared to £139 in Trinidad. The Bahamas' national income was double that for Jamaica and over six times that for Antigua. Wages in the Bahamas were considerably higher than those in most British Caribbean Colonies.
15. *Colonial Office Report on The Bahamas 1958 and 1959* (London: HMSO, 1961), 7.
16. Lewis, 320 and Pridie to Luke, Nov.12, 1950 CO23/888.
17. See Saunders, 'Social History', 353-355 and 529.
18. Lewis, 320.
19. Saunders, 'Social History', 501.
20. Saunders, 'The 1942 riot in Nassau', 21.

21. The Citizens' Committee established in December 1950 to address the injustices in the society was a coloured and black middle class organization headed by Maxwell J. Thompson. Its formation was triggered by government's refusal to let Bahamians see several films which explored the Negro problem. Saunders, 'Social History', 467-469.
22. Ibid., 530-531; Hughes, 43; Taylor, 199-200.
23. *Bahamas Votes of The House of Assembly 17 Nov.-17 May, 1956* (Nassau: Nassau Guardian, 1956), 286.
24. Etienne Dupuch, *The Tribune Story* (London: 1967), 149-150.
25. 'Policy Regarding Racial Discrimination in the Bahamas, 1957-1959', CO1031/2416.
26. Hughes, 41-42.
27. Ibid., 210. Hughes states that 'The political myths that have shaped Bahamian political disputation have been framed in racial terms: the enemy has been the *other* race.'
28. A Comparison of the Level of Living in The Bahamas and Other Caribbean Islands, Cited n. 14; see also H. Houghton, *Report on Education in The Bahamas* (Colonial Office, 1958), 24.
29. H. Saunders, *The Other Bahamas*, 241-243.
30. Saunders, 'Social History', 473 and Hughes, 38. Lynden O. Pindling was the son of Arnold and Viola (Bain) Pindling. His father, who was a Jamaican, came to Nassau in the early 1920s.
31. Saunders, 'Social History' 450. See also David Greenberg, 'The Contract, "The Project" and Work Experiences' in *Strangers No More. Anthropological Studies of Cat Island Bahamas*, ed. by Joel S. Savishinsky (Ithaca, New York: 1978), 204.
32. Murphy to Hall, Jan. 23, 1946, CO23/814.
33. H. Saunders, *The Other Bahamas*, 225.
34. Fawkes, 104.
35. Attempts had been made to form other parties, for example, the 'Christian Democratic Party' but each failed. See Hughes, 36-37.
36. Ibid., 46.
37. H.M. Taylor, Chairman of the PLP was fired from British South American Airways under pressure from Bay Street. See Taylor, 132 and H. Saunders, 281.
37. See *Nassau Herald* Aug. 21, 1954; *Tribune*, Oct. 26, 1953; Hughes, 38 and H. Saunders, 267-276. Labelled as a leftist party, the PLP vowed its opposition to Communism while promising a more equitable social system. It also promised a New Deal for the neglected Out Islands and to develop agriculture. *Herald* June 12, 1954.
39. Hughes, 35.
40. H. Saunders, 281.
41. Dupuch, 139.
42. Hughes, 52.
43. No reference could be found in the Colonial Office Papers in connection with this. Pindling stated that it was pressure from the Colonial Office which caused the establishment of the UBP while Robert Symonette also a member of Parliament at the time, recalled that the UBP was formed in reaction to the PLP. A cohesive group was needed to deal with the revisions which were recommended. Interview with Sir Lynden

O. Pindling, March 2, 1992 and telephone interview with Robert H. Symonette, May 4, 1993.
44. Hughes, 72. Also elected were independent Gerald C. Cash and Bahamas Democratic League candidate, Etienne A.P. Dupuch.
45. *Nassau Guardian*, Oct. 22 and 27, 1956.
46. Letter to Arthur from Taylor, Chairman, PLP and Pindling, Opposition Leader in the Assembly, Oct. 19, 1957, CO1031/2477.
47. Spackman, 33.
48. Fawkes, 85. Colin Hughes suggests that the PLP was hesitant and cautious in support of the strike. James Shepherd agrees but stated that individuals in the party spoke in support, not the party organization. Interview with James Shepherd (by Tracey L. Thompson) Nassau June 2, 1982. Shepherd said that the PLP took advantage of the strike for political purposes.
49. Bridget Brereton, *A History of Modern Trinidad, 1783-1962* (Kingston, Port of Spain, London: 1981), 189.
50. Cecil Thompson, 'History of Bahamas Union of Teachers 1956-1977', (undergraduate paper, University of The West Indies, Mona, 1979), 3.
51. The Labour Union was headed initially by a white Bahamian, Percy Christie but by the time of the riot the Union and the Federation of Labour were headed by Charles Rhodriquez, a black dry-goods merchant. See chapter 11 of this book.
52. *Colonial Office Reports on The Bahamas, 1950-1951*, 9, 1954-55, 9-10 and 1958-59, 9.
53. See chapter 11 in this book.
54. Fawkes, 62.
55. Interview with Audley Green, Nassau, Feb. 4, 1992.
56. Houghton, *Report on Education in The Bahamas*, 36.
57. Fawkes, 50-56.
58. Ibid. 68.
59. Interview with Sir Randol Fawkes, Nassau, Oct. 25, 1991.
60. Fawkes, 76. See for example the *Herald*, April 8 and 30 and May 7, 1955.
61. Taylor, 237.
62. Fawkes was in and out of the PLP. The PLP expelled him in 1956 accusing him of wanting to have his own way. He remained outside the PLP for several years. The BFL, which had also expelled him after a stormy meeting in June 1957, reinstated him. He was elected president, heading a new slate of officers. He founded the Labour Party in 1959. Hughes, 58-59. See also Arthur to Lennox Boyd, 24 June 1958, CO1031/2723.
63. Felix Bethel and Michael Stevenson, 'The State, The Crowd, and the Heroes: The Struggle for Control in The Bahamas: 1958-1968'. Paper delivered at the 24th Conference of Caribbean Historians, Nassau, 1992. Using Singham's *The Hero and the Crowd in a Colonial Polity* (New Haven and London, Yale University Press: 1968), these two authors saw the PLP as Fawkes' rivals. They 'steadily and stealthily' wooed the same 'crowd'.
64. Arthur to Lennox Boyd, June 24, 1958, CO1031/2723; Taylor, 240.
65. See *Tribune*, Feb. 2, 15, 19, 22, 28, 1957; Sept. 5, 9, 26, 27, 1957; Oct. 1, 3, 1957 and *Herald*, Jan. 12, 1957.

66. Selwyn Ryan, *Race and Nationalism in Trinidad and Tobago. A Study of Decolonization of a Multi-Racial Society* (Toronto: University of Toronto Press, 1972), 70-71.
67. Hughes, 32. The Bahamas chose to remain outside of the Colonial Development and Welfare Benefits rather than reform local legislation.
68. Acting governor to Lennox Boyd, Nov. 6, 1957, CO1031/2835. For earlier disputes see *Nassau Herald*, June 19 and 26, and July 31, 1954. The Taxi-Cab Union comprised self-employed men but had formed themselves into a group to bargain with tour operators and 'to talk to the police, who used to hassle us'. Interview with James Shepherd (by Tracey L. Thompson), Nassau, June 2, 1982. Dan Knowles, from Long Island in the 1930s established a Taxi and Livery Service. By the 1950s he had added buses to his fleet and his company became known as Dan Knowles Taxi, Livery and Bus Service.
69. Acting governor to Lennox Boyd, Nov. 6, 1957, CO1031/2835. The Meter Taxi Cab firm alone asked the Airport Board for a parking area at the airport for two large buses, four 8-door limousines and six other cars.
70. Ibid. The Meter Taxi Cab firm was owned by Edward Leggatt, a British resident who was president, Donald and Andrew McKinney and Robert Symonette who identified with Bay Street.
71. *The Tribune*, Nov. 2, 1957.
72. Acting governor to Lennox Boyd, Nov. 5, 1957, CO1031/2835.
73. Ibid., Nov. 6, 1957, CO1031/2835.
74. While charges against Darling and Wilbert Moss were dismissed, several of their colleagues, including Oswald Barnard, James Glinton and Leon Bowe were found guilty of obstruction and assault and were fined. In addition, James Shepherd was found guilty of refusing to move his vehicle; Jerome Hutcheson was found guilty of obstruction and refusing to move and James Pratt, a 74 year old, found guilty of assault. *Tribune* Nov. 29 and Dec. 4, 1957.
75. Fawkes, 98.
76. Arthur to Lennox Boyd, Jan. 28, 1958, CO1031/2835.
77. Fawkes, 100.
78. Ibid. 102.
79. Profumo to Roland Robinson, Jan. 30, 1958 CO1031/2835. The hotels tried to carry on with white staff and loyal black helpers but tourists soon left the colony. On Monday, Jan. 13, hotels gave notice that they would close unless staff returned to work. By 9 a.m. on Wednesday, workers had not returned and all hotels closed. According to the *Tribune*, Taxi-Cab Union cars ceased operations on Sunday, Jan. 12, 1958. *Tribune*, Jan. 13, 1958.
80. Ibid. See also Arthur to Lennox Boyd, Jan. 13, 1958, CO1031/2835.
81. Arthur to Commander of the Caribbean Area No.11 repeated to the Secretary of State Jan. 14, 1958, CO1031/2835.
82. Interview with Sir Clifford Darling, Nassau, Oct. 18, 1991.
83. Arthur to Lennox Boyd, Jan. 20, 1958, CO1031/2835.
84. Secret Despatch. Arthur to Philip Rogers, Feb. 10, 1958, CO1031/2950. The troops were kept in Nassau for over two years: *Colonial Office Report, 1958 and 1959* (London: HMSO, 1961). The 1958

strike created a security problem in the British Caribbean; the presence of the Worcestershire Regiment in Nassau (numbering about 150), left a shortage of troops in the southern Caribbean. However, Arthur was reluctant to part with the regiment because of the possibility of further violence and the nervousness of the white population.

85. The strike caused a severe set back in the tourist industry. At first recovery was slow. However, it accelerated and by the end of 1959, the industry could be described as being in a 'flourishing condition.'
86. *New York Times*, Jan. 14, 1958. Cited Douglas Williams, Colonial Attache to John Stacpoole, Colonial Office, London, Jan. 29, 1958, CO1031/2835.
87. *New York Times*, Jan. 14, 1958
88. Ibid.
89. Fawkes, 114.
90. Intelligence Report Jan. 1958, CO1031/2835. See also Macpherson to Tewson, Feb. 11, 1958, CO1031/2835. Pounder, according to Arthur, perhaps gave the greatest assistance in settling the strike. 'His weight of experience and sound common sense retained the wilder spirits, and his influence was all to turn away unionism from domination by opportunists and politicians.'
91. Fawkes, 114.
92. Hughes, 65.
93. Lennox Boyd to Arthur, Feb. 28, 1958, CO1031/2950. Arthur served as governor of the Bahamas between 1957 and 1960.
94. Arthur to Philip Rogers, Colonial Office, July 9, 1957, CO1031/2472. Arthur allied himself with R.T. Symonette whom he saw as more moderate in contrast to Sands who was, he thought, an extremist. See also Ibid, Conf., June 30, 1959, CO1031/2429.
95. Arthur to Rogers, Feb. 10, 1958, CO1031/2835.
96. Fawkes, 123.
97. Interview with Robert H. Symonette, (son of Roland Symonette) May 4, 1993. See also Moncrieff who argues that Arthur tried to 'eradicate social injustice, while not alienating the powerful and unpredictable Bay Street'.
98. Arthur to Lennox Boyd, Feb. 6, 1958 CO1031/2835.
99. This resulted in the Road Traffic Act 1958 which related to motor vehicles and public transportation and provided for the establishment of a Road Traffic Authority. 57 of 1958, *Statute Law of The Bahama Islands*, Vol. V1, London, 1965, 3069-3141.
100. Fawkes, 121-122. *Votes of the House of Assembly*, Jan. 14-Sept. 18, 1958 (Nassau: Nassau Guardian, 1958), 113-114.
101. *Tribune*, April 14, 1958 and Craton, 274.
102. Houghton, *Report on Education in The Bahamas, 1958*; H.L. Glyn Hughes, *A Survey of the Medical Services* (Nassau: 1960). The Houghton Report, critical of the inefficiency of the Board System and political influence wielded on it, recommended that new comprehensive education legislation be enacted, an Advisory Council on Education be appointed, a Sixth Form at Government High School and perhaps at Queen's College be developed, and the training of teachers and the supervision of schools be improved. The Hughes Report decried among other problems the lack of qualified doctors on most Out Islands. See

also M. Craton, 274 and Gordon Lewis, 319-320.
103. The Trade Union and Industrial Conciliation Act. 30 of 1958, *Statute Law of The Bahama Islands* Vol. 5,. 2757-2818.
104. The House of Assembly Elections Act. 39 of 1959. *Statute Law of The Bahama Islands*, Vol. 1, 157-271.
105. See Kim Outten, 'A Chronological History of Women's Suffrage in the Bahamas', in the series, 'Aspects of Bahamian History', Department of Archives, in the *Nassau Guardian*, Nov. 23, 1987.
106. *Colonial Office Report on The Bahamas 1958 and 1959*, 4. While the PLP grew in strength and numbers the trade union movement failed to develop stability and effective leadership. In the late 1960s and early '70s it was weak and divided and 'prone to squabbles'. Unions failed to formulate sound objectives except 'an instinctive pressure for wage increase'. See Hughes, 155-156.
107. Lewis, 321.
108. Spackman, 37.
109. 'Policy Regarding Racial Discrimination in the Bahamas', 1957-1959, CO1031/2416.
110. Craton, 274.
111. Bethel and Stevenson, 17.
112. Hughes, 214.
113. Fawkes, 127.

14

Race Relations and National Identity in the Formation of the Bahamian Society:

A Historical Perspective

As Professor Rex Nettleford has stated, the need for 'roots and the attendant quest for identity' are natural to 'people everywhere'.[1] Race and racial attitudes are important in mixed Caribbean societies which often suffered from a type of schizophrenia and self contempt because of race and racial mixtures.

One of the most important legacies of slavery was racism. The majority of Caribbean people were of African descent but were considered morally inferior to Europeans by the local and metropolitan whites.

This racist belief, one of the main pillars of slave society, persisted into post-emancipation years and dominated Caribbean societies. Racist attitudes 'were not only held by whites, but were also internalised by non-whites, i.e. blacks and browns'. Some browns and blacks believed themselves to be inferior to Europeans, and despised anything African.[2]

In the early years of settlement during the late seventeenth and early eighteenth centuries whites outnumbered blacks in the Bahamas. However, despite this, the laws and regulations made during those years showed that whites were concerned and sought strictly to coerce the slaves. Their movements were strictly controlled; their economic activities strictly limited; manumissions (i.e. the freeing of slaves) regulated and the holding of dangerous assemblies prevented. As the black population increased, so did the laws to control them as evidenced by the 1767 Act 'For the Governing of Negroes, Mulattoes and Indians'. It legislated against 'heinous and grievous' crimes, violence to white persons, carrying dangerous weapons or assembling together in a riotous or noisy manner.[3] Slaves could give evidence against one another but could not against white persons except in cases of debt. These laws which gave whites controlling powers, discriminated against blacks and helped to cement racial separation.

The coming of the Loyalists and their slaves between 1784-89 influenced the structure of society in the Bahamas. The white Loyalists introduced their own concept of plantation life and that of the relationship of master and slave. While the white ruling class headed the social pyramid, slaves occupied the lowest level with the free coloureds and free blacks in between. These racial and colour barriers were intensified after the coming of the Loyalists who introduced tighter social controls by the passing of harsh vagrancy laws and regulations to separate the races on New Providence and Out Islands. This resulted in residential separation. Before the advent of the Loyalists, housing for whites and blacks was intermixed throughout Nassau, some slaves living either within or behind the larger homes of their owners. Freed blacks resided in the town. But with a trebled black population after 1785, stricter control for segregating them from the whites in the town was enforced. An Act for Regulating the Police of the Town of Nassau and Suburbs passed between 1795 and 1798, demanded that all people of colour be off the streets of the town of Nassau after 9:00 p.m. when the Town Bell rang.[4]

Areas including Grant's Town, a wooded, swampy area surveyed in the 1820s, and Delancey Town, named after a slave owner and Chief Justice of the Bahamas Stephen Delancey, were set aside for blacks, that is, ex-slaves and Liberated Africans in New Providence during slavery. Bain Town, adjacent to Grant's Town, was developed in the 1840s.

While Nassau developed into a quaint and architecturally attractive colonial town, reserved for the white elite, the Over-the-Hill area had more humble African inspired dwellings and its settlers lacked the capital to develop it properly. In its early years it boasted a market and had many fruit and other trees. Vegetables were also grown there. As the Nassau market and the town grew, a slow decline began in the Over-the-Hill areas, exacerbated by the migration of some families abroad and others into the suburbs. Later, as the geographers Doran and Landis argued,[5] the Over-the-Hill area changed from owner occupied to tenant occupied. This had a profound effect on the area which came to be looked down upon as an enclave for social inferiors. Race obviously influenced the ruling oligarchy in its policy to ensure residential separation. On the other hand, it came to depend on the residents of Over-the-Hill to provide their services as domestics, labourers, gardeners, carpenters, masons and the like. Whites expected blacks to be docile, polite and to return to their area when work was over.[6] White Nassau discriminated against

A vendor from Grant's Town, early 1900s
(Courtesy of the Department of Archives, Nassau)

From a postcard entitled: 'Two Natives', Nassau, Bahamas
(Courtesy of the Department of Archives and the C. Thackray Charitable Trust)

blacks residentially, employment-wise (blacks could not work as clerks in shops) and in the places they could attend socially. Downtown Nassau was the preserve of the white elite while Over-The-Hill was set aside for blacks.[7]

In Nassau, as in most West Indian societies, social divisions developed by class and colour but in the Out Islands class lines were not as clearly demarcated. From the late eighteenth century, with the dismal outlook for a plantation economy, whites rapidly adapted to the lifestyle of the Old Inhabitants in Harbour Island and Eleuthera. In Abaco they established all white settlements, such as Cherokee Sound, Hope Town on Elbow Cay, Man-O-War Cay and Great Guana Cay on cays off the mainland. These endogamous isolated communities maintained closer social contact with the whites of northern Eleuthera than with the Abaco blacks who lived scattered along the mainland shore. Bi-racial settlements such as Marsh Harbour and Green Turtle Cay practised rigid social and racial separation.[8]

The substantial white population in the Bahamas, as Hughes has argued, made for significant differences with the West Indies. The white population in the Bahamas has always represented ten per cent or more of the population.[9] This 'poor white' element of which Hoetink writes of the United States, was present in the West Indies, notably Barbados, the Saintes (a group of small islands under the administration of Guadeloupe) and the Bahamas. Poor whites in the Out Islands shared the prejudices of those in Nassau and did not mix socially with coloureds or blacks. The socio-racial structure in the Out Islands more resembled the Deep South variant, (where no intermediate social position for the coloureds was accepted) than the North-West European Caribbean variant.[10]

In post-emancipation years in the Caribbean the traditional elite maintained its control over the society, its economic resources, especially land, and its 'manipulation of the political and legal systems'. Socially, too, it perpetuated, in Bridget Brereton's words, the 'racist conviction of the superiority of the European "race" and its civilization and the irremediable inferiority of Africans and their culture.'[11] The complex colour situation and self-contempt felt by non-whites enabled the elite to control the society. As in the Caribbean generally, the traditional elites were predominantly European, the middle strata of the European-African mixture and the masses were of African origin. 'Racism was directed against blacks and coloureds' and there developed a preoccupation with 'colour and shade'. As Brereton argued for Trinidad, post-emancipation Caribbean societies were 'based on racism and sensitivity to colour and shade, even though no formal apartheid system existed and in law all were equal'.[12]

In Nassau, a coloured and black middle class emerged after Emanicpation.[13] Through education, ownership of land, success in business and the civil service and occasionally in politics, the coloured intermediate class was recognized in Bahamian society. Some light-skinned coloureds, as elsewhere in the Caribbean, 'passed' for white and were accepted by the elite. There was an ambiguous colour line in Nassau with fair-skinned coloureds being accepted as white.[14] A person might not be pure white, but his associates would always be 'light' or lighter. Indeed, someone who was 'passing' would not 'associate with anyone a shade darker than themselves'.[15]

The definition of a coloured person in the Bahamas was still ambiguous in the 1950s, varying greatly according to a person's family or attitude, the texture of hair and facial structure. There were 'colour' divisions within families. The term 'Bahamian white' or 'Long Island white' described a person who 'is not really white but passes for white'.[16]

The racial situation in the Bahamas perhaps was not as harsh as in the Southern States of America with its inflexible colour line, but on the other hand it did not conform to the West Indian norm. As Northcroft observed: 'It lacks the exclusiveness of the former and the equality of the latter'.[17]

This was probably due to the Bahamas' relatively large white population as noted before, the dispersed nature of the Bahamian archipelago and its physical and economic separation from the British Caribbean which made for isolation and conservatism. Intense racial feeling and deep-set colour prejudice, especially where blacks and whites lived in the same community, seriously affected social life and all forms of associations, particularly marriage.

Bahamian society with long historical links with North America was also affected by the bias of social Darwinism and its offshoot 'anthropo-sociology' which claimed that its views (which ranked blacks at the bottom of the racial scale) were based on scientific data. These theories influenced European and

American ideas and caused the hardening of racist attitudes in the latter part of the nineteenth century.[18]

Bahamian society was segregated in almost every respect. Colour separated the races in housing, education, occupation and in social intercourse. Even certain mail boats, like the *Dart* which plied between Nassau and Harbour Island, had sections for whites only. No coloureds were allowed to enter the *Dart*'s cabin.

The nature of the Bahamian economy affected race relations. Poverty was the Bahamian norm. There was always a scarcity of money but the Bahamas benefited from various outside influences such as the American Civil War (1860-65) and Prohibition (1919-33) which created a 'boom and 'bust' characteristic in its economy with fishing and farming as the mainstay.

The longstanding industries in the nineteenth century Bahamas, such as sponging, pineapple, sisal, citrus and tomato, one by one failed for various reasons, and agriculture was never put on a sound economic basis. The 'bonanza' type profits experienced during the American Civil War and the Prohibition era, denuded the rural Out Island settlements of their population, boosted Nassau's economy and led eventually to the consolidation of capitalist business ethics. When the adventurers and foreign commercial agents left, the Bahamian merchant class (mainly whites) was provided with a foundation upon which to build fortunes.[19]

The blockade running era helped to underline the social divisions in Nassau society which were based mainly on race. Governor Bayley stated in 1860 that 'colour separates the people'. He added that whites did not mix well with coloureds or blacks and did not even exchange common courtesies.[20]

Prohibition in the United States also profoundly affected Bahamian society. The unprecedented boom in the colony's economy after the passage of the Volstead Act in 1919, while creating many material improvements in Nassau, widened the gap between the classes and races. Before the 1920s, an entrenched mercantile elite had little real capital. Their colour more than wealth separated them from the coloureds and blacks. Bootlegging profits, augmented by those from the land boom, brought quick money into Nassau, consolidating the wealth and power of the established elite and creating a new monied class which was mostly white. *Nouveaux riches* soon consolidated their wealth in successful businesses, safeguarded themselves against immigrant competition and, to ensure political and social power, sought seats in the legislature.[21]

As Colin Hughes asserts, M.G. Smith's distinction of five dimensions of colour concept, *Structural Colour* is the most important for political change in the Bahamas. Hughes' contention that in the categories which define and constitute the social framework, 'Wealth has had a pre-eminent place in the Bahamas' and can be accepted in examining social relations in the Bahamas. The wealthy, who were usually white, attracted power and authority. Blacks were usually the poorer class. Therefore racial differences were linked to economic relationships. Racial differences rather than class differences 'determined the predominant features of social, economic and political relationships'.[22]

The white mercantile elite profited most from the tourist and financial industries. It controlled not only the strategic business enterprises but also the political machinery. The cleavage between rich and poor and white and black widened. Coloured and black businessmen on or near Bay Street who had also benefited from Prohibition, pitted against wealthy competition, were pushed off Bay Street in the 1930s.

Racial discrimination worsened in the 1920s and 1930s and the white elite used tourism as an excuse for upholding racial discrimination. As Frank Taylor demonstrated, racism was 'historically a built in feature of West Indian tradition of hospitality'.[23]

The new wealth brought by Prohibition and tourism changed social values and widened the gap between races and classes. It exacerbated the already ingrained self-hatred and inferiority complex held by non-whites. Known for its divisive element, some coloured businesses also practised discrimination.

The black and coloured middle class were not the only people aware of the racial injustices in the society. The masses were also conscious of these issues. Race was in fact a strong factor in the cause of the 1942 riot.

The Citizens' Committee, a black middle class organization established in 1950, headed among others, by lawyer Maxwell J. Thompson, dentist Cleveland Eneas, Baptist Minister A.E. Hutcheson, businessman Leon McKinney and labour leader Charles Rhodriquez was also concerned with the extreme racial discrimination practised by the elite. The formation of the organization, although triggered by the government's refusal to let Bahamians see three films, *No Way Out*, *Lost Boundaries*, and *Pinky*, all of which explored the 'negro problem', aimed to also address itself generally to the injustices in the society. Its Constitution vowed to 'generally protect, improve, preserve and defend the economic, educational and political rights and liberties of all Bahamians'.[24]

Discriminated against the Citizens' Committee suffered from the ruthless and narrow policies of the Bay Street elite. Young coloured and black middle class professionals found it difficult to make a decent living in Nassau. Lawyers, for example, stood little chance of attracting wealthy clients and the lucrative corporate business was dominated by the elite.[25]

More vocal in its criticism of the Establishment was the Progressive Liberal Party (PLP), the first organized political party in the Bahamas. Its paper, the bi-weekly *Herald*, edited by Cyril Stevenson, became critical of racial injustices. Certain members of the PLP, including Milo Butler and Lynden Pindling in the early to mid-1950s used racial issues in appealing to the black majority.

Politics in the Bahamas was becoming polarized on colour rather than purely class lines.[26]

The PLP, although founded by idealistic light-skinned Bahamians, soon attracted working class blacks who had little to lose and saw the party as a means of liberation from discrimination and the iniquitous social structure. As more educated black men became members, their oratory at public meetings appealed mostly to the black masses. The 'racial character of its propaganda hardened' and its appeal to the masses was founded on racial discrimination.[27] Much to Taylor's (the Founding Chairman's) dismay, the PLP became a 'Negro Party' as no whites had the courage to support it. The PLP became a party of the black majority and aligned itself with the Civil Rights and later the Black Power Movements in the United States, adopting their rhetoric and more aggressive tactics.

Etienne Dupuch, coloured editor of the *Nassau Tribune*, deplored the treatment of blacks in Bahamian society, although he was critical of the PLP racial propaganda. Dupuch, however, was embarrassed when foreign blacks, especially West Indians, were affected by racial discrimination. He became personally involved in an incident when Hugh Springer, eminent Barbadian barrister and Registrar of the University College of the West Indies, was victim of the Bahamas' colour bar in December 1953.

Etienne Dupuch, humiliated, was stirred into action. In January 1956, he moved an Anti-Discrimination Resolution calling for the end of racial discrimination in public places and for a Commission of Enquiry on race. The Committee appointed by the House of Assembly accepted only the first part of the resolution condemning discrimination in public places on grounds of race and colour.[28]

Despite Dupuch's claim that there was revolutionary change in the social structure after the passing of the Resolution, discrimination in public places took some time to be completely broken down. The hotels claimed that they did not discriminate because of colour, but certain establishments did not welcome blacks.

Historically, the Bahamas can be described as a racist society. Racism was instituted during slavery and this trend continued in post-emancipation years. The bonanza type economy and later the development of tourism on a large scale, boosted revenues and benefited a small mercantile elite who were mainly white. The majority of Bahamians who were black, lived in poverty until the 1950s. Tourism underlined class and racial divisions and race relations worsened with discriminatory practices in public places continuing unabated until the Anti-Discriminatory Resolution in 1956. Even after the Resolution and the coming of majority rule (1967) and independence (1973), the white mercantile elite continued as the 'prominent beneficiaries' of tourism, while blacks still plagued with low self-esteem continued to occupy mainly servile positions catering to a mostly white clientele in an 'intrinsically...neo-plantation enterprise'.[29]

Racism played an important part in shaping political and social attitudes and the cultural identity of Bahamians. Racial antagonism was severe and pervasive. Bahamian society remained 'divided into two antagonistic groups by racial differences'[30] well into the 1960s. The coming of majority rule in 1967 transformed the socio-political structure in the Bahamas. It failed however to alter fundamentally the economic structure; while Bahamian whites were more or less marginalized, lowering their profiles, during the PLP's heyday, they still dominated Bahamian businesses and indeed expanded them. For many, the PLP's administration brought unprecedented economic prosperity.[31] The traditional elite maintained control over the economy for several decades after the 'Quiet Revolution.'

Notes

1. Rex Nettleford, *Mirror, Mirror. Identity, Race and Protest in Jamaica* (London: Collins and Kingston: Sangster, 1970), 9.
2. Bridget Brereton, *Social Life in the Caribbean 1838-1938*, Heinemann CXC History Series (Oxford: 1985); 'Society and Culture in the Caribbean. The British and French West Indies, 1870-1980' in *The Modern Caribbean*, ed. by Franklin W. Knight and Colin A. Palmer (Chapel Hill and London: 1989), 88; 'Social Organization and Class, Racial and Cultural Conflict in 19th Century Trinidad', in *Trinidad Ethnicity*, ed. by Kevin Yelvington (London: 1993), 43.
3. Gail Saunders, *Slavery in The Bahamas 1648-1838* (Nassau: 1995), 8.
4. Gail Saunders, *Bahamian Loyalists and Their Slaves* (London and Basingstoke: 1983), 44-45.
5. M.F. Doran and Renee A. Landis, 'Origins and Persistence of an Inner-City Slum in Nassau', *The Geographical Review*, 70, No. 2 (April 1980): 182-193.
6. See page 67 in this book.
7. Doran and Landis, 'Origins and Persistence of an Inner-City Slum in Nassau', 189.
8. Michael Craton and Gail Saunders, *Islanders in The Stream. A History of The Bahamian People*, 2 vols. (Athens and London: Georgia University Press, 1992 and 1998), 1: 187-188.
9. Colin Hughes, *Race and Politics in The Bahamas* (St Lucia, Australia: University of Queensland Press, 1981), 24.
10. Harry Hoetink, *The Two Variants in Caribbean Race Relations* (Oxford: 1967), 16.
11. Brereton, 'Social Organization and Class'in *Trinidad Ethnicity*, 43.
12. Ibid.
13. See Chapter 1 in this book.
14. L.D. Powles, *The Land of The Pink Pearl* (London: 1888), 120-121.
15. Powles, *Land of The Pink Pearl*, 120-121.

16. Daniel A. Segal, ' "Race" and "Colour" in Pre-independence Trinidad and Tobago', in *Trinidad Ethnicity*, 89-90.
17. G.J.H. Northcroft, *Sketches of Summerland, Giving Some Account of Nassau and The Bahama Islands* (Nassau: 1912), 61.
18. Gail Saunders, 'The Social History of The Bahamas 1890-1953' (PhD unpublished thesis, University of Waterloo, 1985), 75.
19. See pp. 96 and 134 in this book.
20. Bayley to Newcastle, Aug. 15, 1860, CO23/163/69, 71.
21. Howard Johnson, *The Bahamas in Slavery and Freedom* (Kingston: 1991), 125, 148; also see Saunders, 'Social History', 288.
22. Hughes, *Race and Politics*, 22.
23. Frank Taylor, 'Tourist Industry in Jamaica, 1919-1939', *Social and Economics Studies*, 22 (1973): 213.
24. Randol Fawkes, *The Faith That Moved The Mountain* (Nassau: Nassau Guardian, 1979), 45. *No Way Out* which starred Bahamian actor Sidney Poitier and portrayed the struggles of a young black doctor in a white community hospital, probably caused the greatest controversy. It was passed by the censors at the end of October, 1950 and later shown in Nassau.
25. Saunders, 'Social History', 468.
26. Hughes, *Race and Politics*, 46-47.
27. Extract from Bahamas Political Report for October 1954. Internal Political Matters. CO1031/1532/157.
28. See p. 157 in this book.
29. Frank F. Taylor, *To Hell With Paradise. A History of the Jamaica Tourist Industry*, (Pittsburgh and London: University of Pittsburgh Press, 1993), 175.
30. Hughes, *Race and Politics*, 30.
31. Michael Craton and Gail Saunders, *Islanders in The Stream: A History of The Bahamian People*, 2 Vols (Athens, Georgia and London: University of Georgia Press, 1998) 2: 440.

Index

Aaron Dixon Fund, 5, 15 n.28
Adderley, Alfred F., 8; as conservative, 13
Adderley, Alliday, 4
Adderley, Ethel, 13, 35
Adderley, Joseph, 4
Adderley, William P., 4, 8
African-Bahamians: folkways of, ii, 82; music among, 87; work and leisure of, 82
African retentions: in Over-the-Hill, 79; in religion, 85
Africans, liberated: settlements of, 91
Agriculture: decline of, in the 1920s, 51, 111
Albury, John, 67
Americanization, 126-218; fear of, 108,
Anderson, C.O., 4
Anderson, May, 5, 30
Anglican church: aspirations of blacks and coloureds to, 84
Anti-Discrimination Resolution, 172, 179-182, 219; effects of, 183-184; reactions to, 182
'Asue', iv, 27; explained, 82-83
'Atlantic Outposts', 171

B'Anansi, 89
Bahamas, the: in Caribbean context, i; changing atmosphere in, 191-192; class and race in, iv; colour bar in, 192; cost of living in, 157; dependency syndrome of, 177; distribution of wealth in, 191; electoral reforms in, 204; Garveyism and, 6; growth of middle class, vi; as health resort, 96; isolation of, 164; lack of labour organization in, 146; link between USA and, 172-173, 174; miscegenation in, 45, 67; monogamy in, 46; Old Representative System in, 190; pace of change in, 163-164; political reforms in, 163; Prohibition and, 113; public holidays in, 93 n.42; racism and, 192-193, 221 n.16; social divisions in, 173-174, 187; social structure of, 213; as tax haven, 124; in West Indian historiography, iv
Bahamas Democratic League, 178
Bahamas Federation of Labour (BFL): establishment of, 152; and support of general strike, 189
Bahamas from Slavery to Servitude, Howard Johnson, iv
Bahamas Home Industries Association, 35
Bahamas Rejuvenation League, 6
Bahamas Timber Company, 69
Bain, Charles H., 78
Bain Town, 77-78, 96
'Band of Inagua Terrors', 142, 143
Baptist Church: among Bahamian blacks, 84
'Bay Street Boys', 167 n.34
Bethel, Cecil, 12
Black, Harry S., 4
Black family: in post-emancipation Bahamas, 46
Black's Candy Kitchen, 3; discrimination at, 11, 132, 218
Blacks: in the Baptist Church, 84; and dancing, 21-22, 88; in the House of Assembly, 79; lack of sustained unity among, in the Bahamas, 177; life and culture among, v; marriage pattern of, 49-50; monogamy among, 47; unions of, 47-48
Blockade, U.S.: effect of, on the Bahamas, vi

Index

Blockade-running: the Bahamas and, 95, 217; beneficiaries of, 97-98, 99-100; end of, 99; negative effects of, 98-99; and trade, 96-100; employment during, 98
Bowen, Hilda, 28
Boyce, Enid, 29
Boyd, Lennox: visit to the Bahamas, 206
Boys Central School, 4
Brown, Holly: and support for underprivileged, 12
'Bunce', 73 n.63, 91
Burnside, Sybil, 31
Bush doctors, 66, 68; survival of, 87
Butler, Frances, 35
Butler, Isabel, 31
Butler, Milo, 13, 160, 168 n.47, 178, 218

Callender, Walter E.S., 8
Cambridge, Bert, 131, 160; on racial discrimination, 181
Cartwright, William, 194
Cash, Miriam, 32
Change: in the Bahamas, 164-165
Children: view of, 24
Christmas Day: celebration of, in the Bahamas, 90-91; in the Out Islands, 68
Christie, Harold G., 130
Christie, Percy: and the Labour Union, 152
Church: and education, 22-23; influence of, on family life in the Out Islands, 50. *See also* Religion
Citizens' Committee: establishment of, 208 n.21, 218
Civic League Working Women's Club, 35
Class: in Bahamian society, iv; in the Out Islands, 2
Clifford, Sir Bede, 131; and encouragement of tourism, 121
Cockburn, Joshua, 6
Colonial Hotel, 120

Colour: in the Bahamas, 1-2; definition of, 192, 216; growth of consciousness of, 172, 193
Coloureds: definition of, 13-14; hierarchy of, 14; as landowners, 4; middle class, in post-emancipation Bahamas, 1-14; and politics, 5; professionals, 8; racial consciousness of, 7-8; and secondary education, 4-5
Commission of Enquiry: into 1942 Nassau riot, 156
'Commonages', 61, 95
Communication system: development of, in Nassau, 107; improvements in, 124
'Conchie Joe', 160
Cotton plantations, 76
Craton, Michael: *Islanders in the Stream: A History of the Bahamian People*, iv
Culture, popular: survival of, in the Bahamas, 91
Cumberbatch, Roland, 8

Dancing: blacks and, 21, 88; in church, 85; fire dance, 21, 68; jumping dance, 21, 68; ring dance, 21, 68
Davis Cumberbatch, Meta, 36
Death rituals: among African-Bahamians, 87
DeGregory, Carmita, 31
Delancey, Stephen, 78
Delancey Town, 78, 96
Dependency syndrome: of the Bahamas, 177
Destroyer-Bases deal, 166 n.6
Dillett, Anne, 22
Divorce: increase in, in the 1970s and 1980s, 54; in the Out Islands, 49
Drums, goatskin, 88
Duke of Windsor: on Nassau riot, 161
Duncombe, Cynthia, 31
Dundas, Governor Charles, 34
Dundas Civic Centre, 34, 126
Dupuch, Etienne, 7-8, and Anti-Discrimination Resolution, 172, 179, 219; compromise on the resolution, 182-183

Dupuch, J.E., 99
Dupuch, Naomi, 30

Education: higher, among blacks and coloureds, 11-12; reorganization of, 204
Education, secondary: for black and coloured girls, 22-23; for black and coloured boys, 22-23; established churches and, 22-23; segregation in, 23; for whites, 22; for women, 32
Eldon, Rowena, 5, 11, 30, 35
Electoral reforms: in the Bahamas, 204-205
Electricity: introduction of, in Nassau, 28
Emancipation: celebration of, 21, 89-90; Day, 75; in Out Islands, 69; and Over-the-Hill residents, 77
Empire: idea of, 164
English settlers: family life among, 44
Erickson, Josiah, 141
Ex-slaves: condition of, in post-emancipation period, 77

Family, Bahamian: explained, 54
Family life: in the Bahamas, v; the church and, 50; factors affecting, in the 1920s-1960s, 51-53; among the early English settlers, 44; among the Lucayans, 44; matrifocality and, in the Bahamas, 53; migration and, 51; in the Out Islands, 47-48; Prohibition and, 51
Farm work. *See* Overseas Project
Farquharson, Theodore, 141
Fawkes, Randol: in the labour movement, 196-198, 205, 206, 209 n.62
Fire dance, 3, 21, 88
Flagler, Henry M.: and Bahamian tourism development, 120
Florida: migration of men to, 29
Fox Hill Day: celebration of, 21, 90
Freedom: meaning of, for ex-slaves, 75
Friendly societies: blacks and coloureds in, 20; establishment of, vi, 83; in Grant's Town, 80; and marking of Emancipation Day, 83; women in, 83

Garvey, Marcus, 158
Garveyism: and Bahamian society, 6-7, 158; black women and, 36
'Generation land', 61, 76, 95
Government High School: establishment of, 11-12, 32, 109
Grant's Town, 77, 96; friendly societies in, 83; riots in, in the 19th century, 79; straw vendors in, 80
Guy Fawkes Night: celebration of, 21, 90
Gym Tennis Club: establishment of, 21

Health and hygiene, 109-110
Herald, 194-195; establishment of, 12
Hill, Alice, 31
Hotel and Steamship Act (1898), 120
Hotels: expansion of, 120
Houghton Report: on Education, 204
House of Assembly: blacks in the, 79; financial qualification for, 167 n.37
Hughes Report: on Medical Services, 204

Illegitimacy: in Nassau, 33; in the Out Islands, 58; rise in, in the 1970s and 1980s, 54; stigma of, 24, 47
Immigrants, 129
Inagua: development of, 138-139; labour union in, 141; population of, 140; press reports on the riot, 144; racial tension, and riot in, 144-145; reasons for riot in, 147; report on riot, 145; riot in, in 1937, vi, 138, 141-144; salt production in, 139; strike in, 141
Inagua Record, 70, 140
Infant Welfare Centre: organization of, 35
Infrastructure: improvements in, in Nassau, 122-123
Isaacs, Edward, 9

Index

Islanders in the Stream: A History of the Bahamian People, Michael Craton and Gail Saunders, iv
Isolation: and cultural preservation in the Out Islands, 67-69; of the Out Islands, 57, 70

Jacobs, Lenworth: discrimination against, in the Bahamas, 179
Jim Crow, 11, 131, 175
Johnson, Howard: *Bahamas from Slavery to Servitude*, iv
Jumper Church, 85
Jumping dance, 21, 88
Junkanoo festival, 3, 15 n.18, 91, 134

King, Martin Luther, 198
Kinship system: in Bain Town, 24; in Over-the-Hill, 24
Knight, C.H., 7

Labour: control of, by merchants, vi, 53; system of, in the Out Islands, 61-62
Labour Day Parade, 197
Labour Department: establishment of, 204
Labour Union: establishment of, 152, 209 n.51
Land tenure: in the Out Islands, 61, 70
Lightbourn, Mrs Percy, 29
Lodges: blacks and coloureds in, 20; and poor Bahamians, 83; women's, 20
Lowe, Jack Stanley: and support for underprivileged, 12
Lucayans: family life among, 44

Maellet, Noel, 131
Mallory, William, 197
Malone family, 67
Malone, Wyannie, 67
Marketing: among black women, 26
Marriage: in Bahamian society, 23-24; among white elite, 46; intermarriage among white elite, 47; pattern of, among blacks, 49; and status, 49

Matthew Town, Inagua, 70, 140; newspaper of, 140
McCoy, William, 105
McPhee, Napoleon, 158
Medical Department Act (1911), 28
Medical services: improvements in, 204
Menendez Johnson, Ellen, 31
Middle class: growth of Bahamian, vii
Middle class, coloured, 1-15; expansion of, 9; racial consciousness of, 7-8; women, 29
Middle class, white: emergence of, 30
Midwives, 66; black women as, 27
Migration: and family life, 51; internal, to Nassau, 12, 33, 50; of men, to Florida, 29, 50, 69, 111; of Out Islanders, 111
Miscegenation: in the Bahamas, 45; and the Out Islands, 67
Monogamy: in the Bahamas, 46
Moseley, Mary, 29; and *Nassau Guardian*, 29
Motorcars: in Nassau, 107
Munson, Frank: and Jim Crowism, 11, 131,175
Music: among African-Bahamians, 87-88; in the life of Out Islanders, 68

Nassau, 96; advantages of, 57; and benefits of blockade-running, 98; celebration of holidays in, 91; coloured middle class in, 1-4; cost of living in, 112, 126; during Prohibition, 102-105; economy of, iv, ; impact of Prohibition on, 107-108; internal migration to, 12, 30, 50; prostitution in, 33; public health situation in, 127; race discrimination in, 11; riot in, in 1942, vi, 127, 138, 151-165; segregation in, 2; social problems in, 35, 51, 52; strike in, in 1958, vii; as tax haven, 175; wages in, 126
Nassau Collegiate School. *See* Queen's College
Nassau Grammar School, 5
Nassau Herald. See Herald
Nassau Lawn Tennis Club, 20

225

Nassau market, 26, 77
Nassau Riot: causes of, 155-162; course of, 154-155; political background to, 157; racial tension and, 159-161; Russell Commission on, 162; women in, 155
New Providence: advantages of, 57; and Operational Training Unit, 152; population increase in, 33, 111, 125
New Year's Day: celebration of, in New Plymouth, 73 n.63
Newspapers: *Herald*, 12, 194-195; *Inagua Record*, 70, 140
North, James A., 4
North, William B., 4, 9
North, Yvonne, 31
Nottage, Daisy, 87
Nursing: in the Bahamas in the 1920s, 31

Obeah: among black Bahamians, 86
Old Representative System, 190
'Old Skin', 73 n.63, 91
Oleander Club: founding of, 36
Operational Training Unit, 152
Out Islands: agriculture in, 61; all-black settlements in, 65-66; bi-racial communities in, 64, 65; class in, 2, 215; conditions in, 59; courtship in, 49; cultural preservation in, 67-69; culture of, v; divorce in, 49; economic opportunities for women in, 27-28; employment opportunities, 69-70; explained, 166 n.8; family life in, 48-50; herbal medicine in, 86; individuality of, 57; intermarriage in, 49, 67; isolation of, v, 57; labour conditions in, 61-62; land tenure in, 61; marriage in, 49-50; marriage among blacks in, 49; migration from, 69, 125; miscegenation and, 67; music in, 68; neglect of, in education, 33; outside children in, 49; public health conditions in, 110; recreational activities of, 68-69; residential segregation in, 64; salt industry in, 57, 59; share system in, 27; smuggling from Ragged Island, 59; social life in, 27; social status in, 66; sponge fishing in, 62; squatting in, 61; straw work in, 57; women farmers in, 27
'Outside children', 24; maintenance of, 33
Over-the-Hill, vi; African retentions in, 79; coloureds and blacks in business in, 10; community spirit in, 81; emancipation, and residents of, 77-81; explained, 77; friendly societies in, 80; isolation of residents of, 79; occupation of residents, 78; political status of, 79; and the 'Quiet Revolution', 81; social status of residents, 78-79, 214
Overseas Project: impact of, 52-53

Panama Canal: employment opportunities in, 70
Peasantry: development of, in the Bahamas, 76-77
Pindling, Lynden, 178, 195, 218; as parliamentary leader of the PLP, 195
Pineapples: in Bahamas' economy, 95
Pitt, Dr William, 8, 23
Political consciousness: of coloured middle class, 5; lack of, 13
Prices: 1938 and 1942, compared, 156-157
Progressive Liberal Party (PLP), 14, 36, 165, 176, 218; in first election, 195; establishment of, 178, 189, 194-195; in general strike, 189; strengthening of, 205-206
Prohibition: and Bahamian social structure, 9, 30, 113; and Bahamian society, vi, 100, 102, 113, 175, 217; and educational development, 109; effect of, on women in the workplace, 27, 31; and family life, 51; and health and hygiene, 109-110; impact of, on infrastructure of Nassau, 107-108
Project, the: wages on, 152
Prostitution: in Nassau, 33
Public holidays: in the Bahamas, 93 n.42

Index

Queen's College, 5, elite girls at, 23; segregation at, 173
'Quiet Revolution', 81, 193

Racial discrimination: Anti-Discrimination Resolution, 180-182; awareness of, in black and coloured women, 36; protests against, 180; in public places, 183-184, 192; resolution against, vii, 172, 180-182; tolerance of, in the Bahamas, 172; tourism and, 37, 131, 218
Race: in the Bahamas, ii, vii, 2, 192-193, 219; growth of consciousness in, 158; and national identity, vii, 213-220; and social status, 129
Real estate: investment and development, 108-109
Red Cross Society: establishment of, 35
Reeves, Anatol, 11, 32
Registration of Midwives Act, 28
Religion: African retentions in, 86; in Bahamian social life, 83-86
Rhodriquez, Charles, 153
Ring dance, 3, 21, 88
Riots: in 1937 and 1942, vi; in the nineteenth century, 79; in Inagua, vi-vii, 138, 141-144; in Nassau, 155-162; in the West Indies, in the 1930s, 146
Royal Victoria Hotel: building of, 119
Rum running: Bahamians and, 105, 106. *See also* Prohibition
'Rushin'': described, 85
Russell Commission, 169; on the Nassau riot, 162; recommendations of, 162

Salt: in Bahamas' economy, 97; in Inagua, 139; in the Out Islands, 57, 59
Sands, Stafford L., 130
Saunders, Gail: *Islanders in the Stream: A History of the Bahamian People*, iv
Segregation: in the Bahamas, 23, 173, 217; in churches, 65; in Nassau, 2; residential, in the Out Islands, 64; tourism and, 131; of women, 37
Settin' up, 68, 87

Sex ratio: in 1920s in the Bahamas, 50
Share-crop system, iv, vi, 3, 27, 61
Shouter Chapel, 22, 88
Sigrist, Frederick, 125, 136 n.29
Sisal industry: encouragement of, in the Bahamas, 63
Slave family: influence of American slaves on, 45
Smith, James C., 5; and the *Freeman*, 5
Social status: race and, 66, 78-79, 129, 214-215
Social structure: of the Bahamas, 213
Social values: tourism and changes in, 132
Solomon, A.K., 130
Spanish Wells: intermarriage in, 67; racism in, 64
Spirit possession, 84
Sponge fishing: in the Bahamas, 62, 102, 156; in the Out Islands, 62
Springer, Hugh: discrimination against, in the Bahamas, 179
Squatting: in the Out Islands, 61, 95
St Francis Xavier's Academy, 23
St Hilda's Anglican High School, 5, 23
Star of Hope No. 3 Daughters of Samaria Lodge, 20
Stevenson, Cyril, 178; and support for underprivileged, 12
Storytelling: among black Bahamians, 89; among Out Island blacks, 68; women and, 21
Straw craft industry, 49; development of, 34; in Grant's Town, 80; tourism and, 132
Strikes: general strike of 1958, vii, 189, 199-202; in Inagua, 141; reactions to the general strike, 202-204
Sturrup, Ruth E., 20
Symonette, Arthur L., 140
Symonette, Roland, 10
Symonette, Captain R.T., 105, 130

Tax haven: Nassau as, 175
Taxi-Cab Union: and general strike, 189, 199-202

Taylor, Henry M., 194; and support for underprivileged, 12
Telephones: installation of, in Nassau, 28
Tinker, Lettie, 36
Toote, Clarita, 11, 35
Toote, Frederick, 6
Toote, Thaddeus A., 6, 8
Tourism: American investment in, 174; and Americanization, 126-128, 133-134; attractions, 121-132; and Bahamian society, vi, 118; and Bahamian way of life, 184; and black entertainment, 132; and Caribbean indigenous culture, 133-134; and dependency syndrome, 134; and development of straw craft, 132; effects of, 124-134; and job creation, 126; and land values, 125; promotion of, in the 1920s and 1930s, 108, 119-124; and racism, 37, 131; and social problems, 128-129
Tourists: increase in, 124
Trade Union and Industrial Conciliation Act, 204
Trade unions: establishment of, in the Bahamas, 152, 189, 196; growth of, 196
Tribune, 7
Truck system, iv, vi, 3, 5, 61, 62, 77, 96, 140; explained, 15 n.21
Tucker Sands, Ella, 29

Unemployment: in Nassau, 126-127
Union Mercantile Association: proposed by Garveyites, 6
United Negro Improvement Association (UNIA), 6-7
United States of America (USA): links between the Bahamas and, 172-173, 174

Violence: against women, 24
Vote of Ballot Act, 160

Wages: in Nassau, 126; on the Project, 152; in tourism sector, 126
Wakes, 21, 68, 87
Walker, Claudius: and Bahamas Rejuvenation League, 6
Weatherspoon, Susannah, 78
West India Chemical Company, 141
White, Leonard, 131
Whites: in the Bahamas, 215; elites in Nassau, 3; elite, and political control, 129, 190; emergence of middle class, 9; intermarriage among, in Nassau, 24
Whitfield, Joseph, 9
Women: and charitable work, 35; in church activities, 22; and double standard in society, 24; economic opportunities for, 27-28; historical research on Bahamian, 18; occupations of, 50-51; opportunities for, in urban areas, 33-34; organization of, 35-36; race, colour, class and, 19, 37; violence against, 24
Women, black: and Garveyism, 36; marketing among, 26; Prohibition, 31; recreational activities of, 20-21; religion among, 22-23; in storytelling, 21; at wakes, 21; employment opportunities for, 26, 30; organization of, 36
Women, coloured middle class: Prohibition and, 31; social life of, 20-21; in temperance movement, 22; job opportunities for, 26, 30
Women, elite: in church activities, 22; Prohibition and, 31; racist attitudes of, 20; social life of, 19-20; in temperance movement, 22; job opportunities for, 25, 28
Women's Suffrage Movement: founding of, 36
World War II: effects of, on the Bahamas, 151-152
Worrell, E.S., 8
Worrell, Mamie, 35

www.ingramcontent.com/pod-product-compliance
Lightning Source LLC
Chambersburg PA
CBHW071154160426
43196CB00011B/2081